- THE LAST GRANDMASTER -

THE LEGEND OF HUA

BOOK ONE

BY

GRANDMASTER SIN KWANG THÉ

The text for this book is set in Baskerville.

Edited by Julia Pierrepont III
www.pierrepontproductions.com | Pierrepont Literary Group | Pierrepont
Productions | (818) 836-1315 | jp@pierrepontproduction.com

Book cover illustration by Sean Ghobad | www.seanghobad.com
Book design by Vivian Shih | www.vivianshih.com

Recommended books:
CHIN CHING
ISBN 978-0-9914355-0-0
10,000 STEPS STRAIGHT UP
ISBN 978-0-9968705-1-1
Both Books available through Barns and Noble and Amazon.com.

SHAOLINDO: Secret to the Temple
ISBN 078 721 2423
Available through Amazon.com or by phone, 1-800-228-0810.

SPECIAL THANKS

To Julia Pierrepont III - I have never seen anyone as gifted as Julia who can take someone else's written sentence, add a word here, take a word out there, and Voila! the whole sentence suddenly dances with life. I have never yet encountered anyone as talented as her, who can rearrange the configuration of several stories into a new sequence that will suddenly absorb and mesmerize you by its MAGIC. I feel extremely fortunate to have her bring her magic to my book. A MILLION THANKS TO YOU, JULIA.

I would like to thank Vivian Shih for designing my book, Sean Ghobad for a wonderful book cover illustration, and Christian Kephart for conceptualizing the art for the book cover.

I'd also like to express my sincere gratitude for Elder Master Bill Leonard and his wife, Dale, for running my Lexington Karate school so that I can spend the time to write my story. Senior Master John Price, his wife Cindy, and a group of their family members run my Yearly Tournament in Lexington, Kentucky.

A big thanks to Lexington Catholic for providing us the use of their gym for these events, and to Senior Master Joe Schaefer and his wife Master Sheryl for running " The Shaolinway " Newsletter and for developing a Strong Shaolindo Schools all over Texas.

Many thanks to all my Shaolindo Instructors for spreading the Shaolin Arts in ALL your regions.

THE THREE MAIN REASONS
I WROTE THIS BOOK

1. Shaolin Training Has Made Me Smarter and I Want To Share This Astonishing Ability With You

Science has finally proven that if you exercise your mind while you exercise your body, your mind will develop two to three times more rapidly than if you work your mind while sedentary.

This condition was first demonstrated through an experiment involving a group of mice learning to go through a series of mazes to locate their cheese. For this particular maze, it took ten tries for an average mice to locate the cheese. Yet when the mice were put in the maze with a moving treadmill floor, it took only two and a half tries to find the cheese!

Their short term memory was also sharper, it took three tries for the mouse on the stationary floor to find the cheese for the second time, whereas the ones on the treadmill found it on the first try every time.

It was only now that Western Science is coming to the realization of how valuable it is to train one's mind while exercising, whereas the ancient Shaolin Monks of China have known this for over two thousands years. The monks designed a series of complicated moves called *"forms"* for the students to study and train their minds, while their bodies are in a constant state of movement.

The intense Shaolin training I underwent in early childhood (and all the way through to my university days), caused my mental abilities to leapfrog far beyond my normal capacity when I was in the 6th grade. Suddenly from an average student, I became the best in class!

I want to *share* this unique and life-enhancing opportunity with you, my honorable readers. I encourage you to open your life to Shaolin training and let it benefit you as it did me.

Why not become the better, smarter, healthier, fitter version of yourself, so you and your chances of success in your chosen field in this increasingly competitive world will soar?

2. You Are Never Alone In Life

As you study a variety of Shaolin *forms* (similar to dance routines) that are rooted in ancient traditions and stories that have been passed down from generation to generation for thousands of years, you become powerfully linked with the spirits of the *Past*. You acquire a deeper sense of *belonging* to something greater than yourself. It opens your mind to miraculous mysteries and an awareness of the underlying order of life around you, making you *One* with the Universe.

This feeling gives you a tremendous sense of security and confidence about life and helps pave the way for your success.

When my father told me to go to a university in the United States to study, instead of West Germany as I had intended, I had no problem with the sudden switch, in spite of the fact I had been studying German, not English, so my English skills were rudimentary at best and this tended to isolate me from my fellow university students.

Plus, when I got to the States, I was so preoccupied with my studies, I hardly had any time to socialize with other students.

Yet, I never felt alone.

I could always feel the presence of a spiritual being that accompanied me throughout my life, Hua. So, when things didn't go well, Hua was there to lend me her support and when things went well, she was there to cheer me on. In my darkest hour, when death itself seemed inescapable, it was she who coached me to fight back, rekindle the spark of life and thus, saved my life.

I would love to see everyone of you find a spiritual friend or guardian like her through Shaolin training, plus the many, many exciting real life friends you will find in your fellow students and teachers!

3. Life Begins At 70! (or Whatever Age You Are!)

Three years ago I turned 70. Yet, instead of feeling old and worn out, I was amazed at how great and how full of life I felt! I had an abundance of *energy* to accomplish new things that I had never even imagined I could do when I was younger!

That is when it hit me: Life *begins* at 70!

All of the intense exercises I had done over my years of *Kung Fu* and *Nei Kung* Shaolin training, plus the super healthy diet I followed, were finally paying off!

Here I was at 70: writing my memoirs; teaching master-classes as the head of Shaolin Dao, the organization I had founded and the largest Chinese martial arts organization outside of China; traveling the world; taking voice lessons; spending precious time with my children and grandchildren; and making a Hollywood movie based on my stories! Wow!

You, too, can build a rich and fruitful life at any age!

The stories in my three books will chronicle my life experiences and collected wisdom passed down to me through two thousand years of Shaolin Masters, which I welcome you to learn from.

And, at the end of this Book 1, I will share with you the rare and secret *Nei Kung* techniques called *The Gift of Life* and *The Gift Of Health* that have also been handed down in secret for centuries, which will start you on your Journey to a wonderful, happy and healthy life.

For those interested in a more complete mastery of yourself and your life, please seek out one of our Shaolin Do martial arts schools near you where you can study under one of my personally-trained black-belt instructors, and reap further benefits from the Wisdom of The Ancient Shaolin Arts.

May the *Chi* be with you!

Grandmaster Sin Kwang Thé

1

-

THE BACKGROUND HISTORY
OF OUR STORY

THE UNIVERSE IS FULL OF MYSTERY. Many things that science and research have shown to be true today were impossible for ancient peoples to even conceive of.

And vice versa. Some things that ancient peoples instinctively knew to be true were proven right by scientists hundreds of years later.

For instance, since the dawn of Time, mankind has always been fascinated by the alignment and configurations of the stars and heavenly bodies. Ancient peoples all over the world have made up fables and tales and superstitions about these heavenly objects, starting with our own planet.

It is interesting to note that every nation and every culture in the world used to believe that the world is flat. They could only understand what they saw with their own eyes, and to the naked eye, the world looks flat. Sailors were afraid that if they sailed too far from the lands they knew, they might fall off the edge of the world into the terrifying 'Abyss'.

So, inadvertently, out of ignorance of the truth, humanity shared a mass disillusion that the world is flat. Even though Aristotle the great Greek philosopher and scientist gave a mathematical proof of the earth's spherical shape as early as 330 B.C., most of the world continued to believe the world was flat until well into the 14th Century!

The interesting question is of course, without the benefit of modern science or tools, how did Aristotle take his great leap forward to the truth? What made him, of all people in the history, the first to have the vision to see the truth and the courage to put his reputation on the line to share it with the rest of the world?

Sometimes, there is a force at work within us that pushes us to greatness…

Back then, before Sir Isaac Newton come up with the Theory of Gravity which explained the force that held everything in place on the globe, if one could have gone out into space and seen the world from that distance, how strange it would have been to see people apparently walking "upside down" on the planet. They would have thought it was magic.

Now we know and understand the forces of gravity that hold us to the earth – and there is no 'magic' about it - except the extraordinary mystical quality of existence itself.

And the further mysteries of the universe continued to unfold. As early as 1783, scientists hypothesized that a "super massive body" existed in the universe. This came to be known as a "Black Hole."

A Black Hole is a compact mass dense enough to deform space-time. Because of its super-high density, Black Holes also have super-high gravity – so high that even light cannot escape the event horizon of the Black Hole. It sucks everything in and nothing can escape, not even light, hence its name.

Back then, there was no way for scientists to confirm the existence of Black Holes. But in the 1960's and 1970's, many leading physicists, Stephen Hawking foremost amongst them, made huge discoveries that finally proved their existence. Recently, the Los Angeles Times actually reported the scientific observation of a distant star being swallowed up by a Black Hole!
Now science has confirmed that supermassive black holes form the center of most circular galaxies like our own.

Then there is the question of "Dark Matter," a form of matter that does not emit or absorb light and is invisible to the entire electromagnetic spectrum and to us.

The first formal exploration of dark matter was by the Swiss astrophysicist Fritz Zwicky, in 1933, who theorized that 'dark matter' was completely different than the regular matter that makes up all the stars, planets and life as we know it. He also calculated that there was more dark matter in our universe then regular matter!

Imagine what mysteries dark matter might explain in our world.

Both matter and dark matter are able to occupy the same space without interacting with each other, so on a humorous note, who knows if there are dark matter pink elephants dancing on our heads at this very moment?

But seriously, as a trained physicist myself, I would like to hypothesize that the mystery to the age-old question of the existence of spirits and ghosts may lie in dark matter. It may not be too much of a stretch to imagine that these entities originate in the dark matter realm, then are somehow able to manifest themselves into ours...

Since ordinary matter from our Universe and dark matter can co-exist in the same time, space and dimension, perhaps some type of portal opens up or a transformation occurs that allows dark matter to enter our world.

This is as good an explanation as any for the sighting of angels, ghosts, spirits of our departed loved ones, even visions of God.

Perhaps dark matter is an untapped channel to the Divine…

I believe that Galileo, Sir Isaac Newton, and all the ground-breaking scientists who have developed new theories on gravity, the solar system, black holes, etc., received help from Divine Inspiration.

A story on the great Dr. Jonas Salk, the discoverer of the vaccine for the dreaded polio disease is a case in point.

A group of nurses who were friends of one of my top students, Master Jeff Rose, worked for the Salk Institute in La Jolla, California. One of the nurses told me the wonderful story she had been told of how Dr. Salk came to discover the Polio vaccine.

Until his discovery of an effective vaccine in the 1950's, Polio was feared by the general public as much as an atomic holocaust. There was no known cure and it struck by the millions.

Salk was determined to defeat Polio, but had been working for years to discover an effective treatment, with no success.

He would extract samples of blood from horses carrying the live

Polio virus, then dilute their blood and inject it into volunteers, in the hopes of inciting a mild Polio condition that would make them immune to the more severe and debilitating form.

But, no matter how much he diluted the infected blood, full-blown Polio occurred, never a milder form. He had begun to despair that he would never find an effective vaccine.

But one night, after a particularly grueling day in the laboratory, he threw himself into bed, exhausted and immediately fell into a deep sleep.

In the middle of the night, he was awoken by someone shouting at him! Happily, he was in the habit of keeping a pad and pencil by the bed to write down his dreams, because he knew if he waited until the next morning, the dream would evaporate without a trace.

He quickly wrote down what was being shouted at him and promptly fell back asleep.

The next morning he was stunned to read a note in his own handwriting that said, "Use the *dead* virus, Dummy!"

Even though it didn't make sense to him, he tried using the dead virus in his vaccine and it worked! And the rest is history.

Dr. Salk went on to become the father of the modern Polio vaccine and saved millions that might otherwise have been struck down or killed.

That is what I call Divine Inspiration at the highest level.

So too, it was Divine Inspiration that enabled the ancient Chinese

Shaolin monks to discover over 720 'pressure points' located throughout the human body that dramatically impact our health, well-being and physical and mental abilities.

The Chinese believe that the human body is a micro-cosmos that mirrors the miracle of the entire Universe. They have studied these 720 pressure points for over 2000 years and discovered many miraculous effects they can cause.

By moving the *Chi*, or the life energy that constantly circulates throughout our bodies, through these pressure points in different patterns and sequences, you can influence your health, well being, vitality, your sense of self, even your luck and ability to prosper and become wealthy.

A good flow of Chi through the body makes us healthy and powerful. A poor flow of Chi can make us unhealthy and weak. It is for this reason that Chi is the most important underlying principle in martial arts and traditional Chinese medicine.

One scientific use of Chi, now widely adopted throughout the Western world as well, is the extraordinary science of Acupuncture. Acupuncture, or the practice of healing by inserting whisker-thin needles into specific pressure points or energy meridians, has been proven to heal a variety of sicknesses and diseases.

In many cases, certain ailments that Western doctors were unable to diagnose or cure can be successfully treated using Chinese acupuncture techniques.

This has led to a tremendous upsurge in support for acupuncture amongst the current global medical community and with patients seeking alternative approaches for their afflictions.

Professional athletes are especially open to using acupuncture techniques, and instead of spending the rest of the season sidelined on the bench for a serious injury, they get back in the game in a far shorter time using acupuncture treatments.

Of course the most famous example of the effects of acupuncture occurred when President Nixon visited China and witnessed a fascinating surgical procedure.

Archival footage shows him watching a woman undergoing open-heart surgery, anesthetized only with acupuncture needles! While the Doctor sawed open her chest, she was wide-awake, felt no pain, and sat sipping lemon juice!

THE 720 PRESSURE POINTS

The Shaolin Temple was founded in 495 AD, in Song Mountain, Henan Province in ancient China. This was the world-renowned birthplace of martial arts as we know it. The Temple is revered for refining and developing this extraordinary art form for the next 1500 years.

Kung Fu, Karate, Tae Kwan Do, Jujitsu, Judo, Pencha Silat, etc. all derived from the work of the dedicated monks of the Shaolin Temple.

Bodhidarma, the great Indian mystic, called Damo by the Chinese, founded Dhyana Bhuddism at the Shaolin Temple in 527AD, which later spread throughout all of China.

Legend has it that pressure points and the consequences of hitting them was discovered by accident:
One day, centuries ago, a Shaolin Master was teaching his students some new sparring techniques. While demonstrating, he accidentally

struck one of his students just under his nose.

The unlucky student began to quiver uncontrollably, spouting gibberish that no one could understand. What in the world was happening...?

The master pondered this strange reaction. Calling on all his knowledge of the human body and the rudimentary science of acupuncture that the Shaolin monks were just beginning to explore, he began to prod, poke and massage the poor student in various places, trying to find a way to stop his bizarre reaction.

Through trial and error, the monk eventually found the right combination of pressure points to release the hapless student from his quivering state! The master was hailed as a hero and all the other monks were eager to learn this new technique.

At the height of the Shaolin Temple, it housed over two thousand monks, each one of them studing martial arts, the energy of Chi, and the science of human pressure points.

Imagine two thousand people fighting every day and collecting data on the undiscovered pressure points embedded in our bodies.

Over the centuries, the monastery built up a massive volume of knowledge, which was used to heal people, improve their wellbeing and of course, fight.

DIM MARK

But just as there are many good uses for the 720 pressure points, there are darker ones too...

The most dangerous of these is the science of *Dim Mark* or "Death

Touch." When an expert practitioner strikes specific combinations of pressure points, the *Death Touch* can have a devastating, even deadly affect on the human body. It can inflict excruciating pain, suffering, paralysis, malaise, disease and even death...

Many of the *Dim Mark* pressure points are 'Paralyzing Points'. When one hits one's opponent in these special points, it can cause that person to be paralyzed for a while.

The duration of the paralysis would depend on *which* points were hit, *how* they were hit, and how *hard* they were hit. But, typically, immobility could last from a few minutes to a several hours.

This technique has been popularized by the Star Trek television series and movies in which Dr. Spock renders his opponents unconscious by pinching a specific pressure point on their neck.

Over the years, the Shaolin monks concluded that there are 36 pressure points in the human body that could be classified as 'Death Points'. As their names imply, these are the points which, when struck with sufficient force, can cause the demise of the victim.

At some point along the way, understanding the danger this information posed, the elder monks become more restrictive of who was allowed to learn the entire set of pressure points - especially the deadly knowledge of *Dim Mark*. They began to keep these deadly secrets to themselves.

Further experiments by the Shaolin Temple and the wider martial arts world of China led to the discovery of the *"Delayed Death Touch,"* which could work unseen in the body for several days or even weeks, until the victim suddenly succumbed for no apparent reason.

This technique became very popular throughout China amongst dueling martial arts masters, because if any of them chose to kill someone instantaneously, they could be arrested for murder. But if the victim's death occurred long after their opponent had left, no one could hold them accountable.

The Art of *Dim Mark* was passed on for generations on the condition that for every point one learned that could cause someone to suffer or die, one must also learn the points that would reverse the effect. That way, a master could always nullify the negative effect he had just inflicted on someone. And, if the victim knew a martial arts master, then his/her teacher would also know the antidote point and could undo the damage.

However, like all weapons, *Dim Mark* never stopped evolving and some centuries ago, someone discovered an even more mysterious and deadly form of *Dim Mark* called, "*the Curve Shot.*"

The Curve Shot works much the same way as a curve ball in baseball. It comes at the victim straight, until the last moment, when it suddenly curves before it hits their body.

The angle it curves at before striking its victim was known only by the one who launched the strike – putting the victim entirely at their mercy.

So, when a death point is hit with a *Curved Shot* at a specific, secret angle, the attacker is the *only one* who knew the angle of attack and could nullify the effect. Without his or her mercy, the victim was doomed.

At the zenith of *Dim Mark*, there were many Kung Fu masters who had mastered the deadly *Curve Shot*, but as masters became more secretive of these deadly martial arts techniques, much of this arcane science was lost.

CHI KUNG

Parallel with the development of acupuncture and *Dim Mark*, was the exploration of *Chi Kung, the Science of Breath*. Every ancient civilization has developed some sort of breathing technique to be used in times of stress to help regulate the body, and was often coupled with meditation.

The ancient Egyptians, the Yogi of India, the Mayans etc., all had their own techniques, passed down over the centuries, some still in use today. The Yogi from India used 'Chakras', resonating points of spiritual energy within the body, as the foundation of their ideology, while the Chinese used the twelve "meridians", or lines of linked pressure points, and the 720 pressure points as their tools.

In *Nei Kung*, a special form of *Chi Kung*, one concentrates on the flow of his/her *Chi* (Ki in Japanese), or *Life Force*, throughout the whole body. The *Chi* must be trained to pass through specific pressure points in the body, depending on the specific effect desired. For instance, if one wanted to achieve better heath, higher energy, increase one's strength, power, or speed in athletic endeavors, increase one's sense of hearing or eyesight, have a more youthful appearance, etc. there are specific sequences of pressure points that can achieve those effects.

The process of discovering the powers of *Nei Kung* and *Chi Kung* was a long and fascinating one, stretching back over millennia.

In this book, we shall take you back to the Shaolin Temple where an unparalleled font of knowledge about the human body and its 720 pressure points was collected. In the early days, the monks knew only a few of the very basic pressure points that could produce a calming and soothing effect for health and longevity.

But that was soon to change.

Legend has it that the power to enhance ones physical performance by channeling ones *Chi* was first discovered by a humble Shaolin student, named Ah Song.

Picture a group of young, orange-robed monks sitting cross-legged on tightly woven straw mats, meditating. As initiates, they had only been introduced to the basic ways to manipulate the *Chi* in their bodies.

During their training, Ah Song and his fellow initiates were taught how to direct the *Chi* in their bodies through a specific series of pressure points that had been shown to produce a calming and soothing effect that would promote their overall health and longevity and improve their ability to meditate.

Their daily routine of martial arts training and mediation was strict, disciplined and grueling: ten hours or more every single day!

To top it off, at the end of the day, just before sunset, they would all have to run miles up a mountain behind the temple and back again before their evening meal.

Ah Song loved running. His duties and training were rigorous and all consuming, so running was one of the few times when he felt completely free. The day he made his historic discovery, he had been unable to concentrate properly on his standard *Chi* meditation, constantly daydreaming that he was already outside in the beautiful nature, running out of the gladness of his heart.

In his mind's eye, he could see himself running effortlessly up the mountain. His imagination was focused, powerful, he could actually feel the stones beneath his feet and the fresh breeze cooling his face as he ran.

Then a strange thing happened… the *Chi* that had been flowing through certain meridians in his body, as he had been instructed, suddenly switched to an entirely new set of pressure points! It made his body tingle in inexplicable ways as it responded to the energy coursing through these new meridians. Suddenly, he saw himself racing faster than a stallion - faster than any human had run before! He awoke from his daydream covered with sweat and charged with energy!

Later, that evening, unlike all his previous runs, this time when he raced up the mountain, it was the stuff of legend!

Normally an enthusiastic, but unexceptional runner, that fateful day he blazed by all the other monks, leaving them stunned and marveling at his sudden, superhuman speed. Before they knew it, he had crested the summit and was passing them on his way back while they were still struggling to reach the summit!

As he ran, a surge of energy overtook him, causing his heart to pound in his chest like a blacksmith's hammer and sending rivers of life-giving blood coursing through his veins. His leg muscles contracted like iron bands, yet felt strangely light, as if his body was as light as a feather or had no mass at all. His speed snapped his clothing against his skin like a windstorm, and he was so exhilarated, he burst into song as he ran! He felt one with the Earth, linked by a mysterious web of energy beyond his own body that seemed to be fueling his extraordinary feat.

Never had he felt so powerful. Never had he run so like a god!

When the story of Ah Song's extraordinary feat got back to the Headmaster, he summoned Ah Song to his room. How had this miraculous feat been possible, probed the Headmaster?

Ah Song described the strange sensations he had felt during meditation as his *Chi* had rerouted itself into entirely new channels while he had visualized himself running.

The Headmaster had an epiphany – the light dawned! By diverting your *Chi* into specific channels, you must be able to radically enhance your physical performance and attain superhuman strength and power! He quickly insisted that Ah Song identify and record the meridians his *Chi* had switched to and the sequence of flow.

So began the great fifteen hundred year study by the ancient Chinese Shaolin Masters to map and master the flow of *Chi* through our bodies to enable man to use it as a tool to run faster, jump higher, fight better, think smarter and live healthier and longer lives.

Ah Song and his Shaolin brethren are revered to this day for the invaluable science and art of the 720 pressure points of *Chi* that secretly rule our lives.

Throughout this book, I shall provide many more examples of the wonder and effects of *Chi* as it passes through the 720 pressure points around our human body.

It may be hard for many to believe the almost magical effects that these 720 pressure points can generate on our bodies. But, when in doubt, think back to the time when everyone believed the world was flat, and imagine how difficult it was for learned scholars to convince the general public that the Earth is actually round and you were really standing upside down, glued to the earth by Gravity!

So too, are meridians, *Chi* and pressure points real.

The ancient study of the extraordinary techniques used to channel one's *Chi* and manipulate the 720 pressure points of the human body has shaped my life in many powerful and mysterious ways.

This wisdom is part of what I wish to impart to you - today's seeker of knowledge and masters-in-training. Today, anyone who has the courage and determination to seek to attain lofty heights and enhanced abilities can do so, with the methods and knowledge contained in these pages.

I hope that you will be inspired, as I was, to master this great art, and by doing so, master yourself and attain your highest possible calling and achievement in life.

So open your mind up and enjoy my life's story and the mystical ride into ancient Chinese wisdom and techniques I experienced and share with you in these pages!

2

-

THE BEGINNING

FIRST, TO SET THE STAGE, A little Chinese history: In the mid-1600's, Emperor Chong Zhen, the Ming's Dynasty's final, ill-fated ruler, led a lavish and degenerate lifestyle in a court rampant with corruption and abuse of power. Wealthy and powerful subjects could bribe their way out of punishment for any crime, no matter how grievous, while the vast majority of the population suffered cruelty and injustice with no protection from the law.

So, when a peasant rebellion exploded in 1644, led by a forceful and charismatic rebel named Li Zicheng, the rebel mob was able to storm the Ming Palace and overthrow the corrupt rulers, forcing the debauched Emperor to commit suicide.

But leaders of the Emperor's scattered army were determined to regain control of the country and re-establish the Ming Dynasty. Since the Imperial army was in disarray, General Wu Sangui recruited the help of Dorgon and Hong Taiji, warrior sons of Nurhachi, the powerful Manchu ruler to the north. Foolishly, hoping to regain his own power, he let them and their armies across the border into Beijing and China.

Together, the Manchu and General Wu Sangui's forces crushed the peasant rebellion and drove Li Zicheng's forces into exile. But, no sooner had they claimed victory, when the Manchu turned on General Wu Sangui, betraying their short-lived alliance.

Using their superior might, the Manchu executed all the Ming heirs and seized power for themselves. They established the Qing Dynasty, which went on to rule China for the next three hundred years.
The majority of Chinese were Han Chinese, who resented being ruled by the minority Manchu-Qing race, who they considered foreigners. This resentment continued to boil beneath the surface, erupting from time to time in bloody rebellions against the Manchu. These rebellions ultimately cost an estimated twenty-five million lives during the course of the Qing reign.

But in the late 1800's, a new threat loomed: Western countries and Christian missionaries began to establish trade relations with China. Some were honorable and straight-dealing, but others used their growing influence in the final years of the waning Qing empire to seize a significant amount of power for themselves in certain regions and used that power to exploit the Chinese.

Portugal, Britain, France, Spain, and Holland, later joined by Germany, Japan, and the US, used their influence and military might to force the weak and outgunned Qing government to sign unequal and humiliating treaties that granted concessions to them that were bad for the Chinese economy and not in the best interest of the Chinese people.

These foreign powers carved out pieces of China for themselves. In Shanghai, long considered the Paris of the East and the Jewel in the Chinese Imperial Crown, they divided up the city into 'quarters' and each foreign country instituted their own rule of law in their quarter, setting themselves above Chinese law and making themselves untouchable.

Qing soldiers were afraid to arrest any foreigners who committed crimes in these districts, so corrupt foreigners would go scot free, without penalty or punishment. Justice was not served and inequality and corruption ran rampant, breeding fear and suspicion between foreigners and the local Chinese.

Because of these many injustices, the Chinese grew to despise the 'Foreign Devils' and this in turn fanned the hatred and discontent of the Han against their Manchu rulers who were too weak to curb the excesses of these loathed foreign invaders.

This uneasy discord may have continued for decades, had not a single commodity tipped relations out of balance to throw the entire country into chaos and war...Opium.

In 1832, William Jardine, a physician-turned merchant, and James Matheson, a sharp businessmen in the import-export trade, formed a partnership to exploit the China Market. They decided that their quickest path to wealth lay in helping to introduce the potent narcotic, opium, to China, where it was virtually unknown. Jardine and Matheson were skilled and savvy traders and well-connected in high society, so within three years they became the largest drug dealers in China.

English authorities supported opium trafficking as a way to correct the large imbalance of trade between Great Britain and China that heavily favored the Chinese. They succeeded beyond their wildest dreams.

Opium trading rapidly became the most profitable trading commodity for the British, eclipsing all others and swinging the trade imbalance well in Britain's favor.

Though reportedly considered good-hearted and charitable men with their friends and countrymen, Jardine and Matheson had no compunction about enslaving millions of Chinese peasants to opium addiction to line their own pockets.

In 1836, when the Qing Emperor Daoguang saw how badly opium was poisoning his subjects and draining China's wealth away to England, he finally took action. He issued an edict banning the importation and use of opium and appointed a Special Imperial Emissary, Lin Zexu, to root out the practice that was devastating his people.

By all accounts, Lin was a renowned scholar and an honorable, righteous man. He had witnessed the devastation that narcotic addiction was wreaking on his homeland and how it undermined the health and well-being of Chinese subjects from every walk of life – wealthy or poor, educated or ignorant. Opium dens abounded and an estimated twelve million Chinese were fully addicted to a drug that was sucking health and prosperity right out of them.
Moving quickly to follow his Emperor's orders, Lin demanded that all the foreign traders surrender their opium supplies to be destroyed. When the traders defied him - at Jardine's instigation - Lin's soldiers moved in and placed them under house arrest. Eventually, the foreign officers surrendered 2.6 million pounds of opium and Lin's soldiers burned it all in a huge pyre.

Outraged at having his drug sales curtailed, Jardine sailed for England to meet with the British Foreign Minister, Lord Palmerston, to urge him to wage war on China to protect Jardine's drugs. To promote his cause, Jardine provided the Foreign Minister with detailed plans for war he had drawn up himself, including battle strategies, maps, and suggestions for troop strength and disposition of warships that an armed conflict would likely require.

He also insisted that Britain demand compensation of the 2.6 million pounds of opium that Lin had confiscated, plus a viable commercial treaty that would prevent any further hostilities, and the opening of further ports of trade such as Nigbo, Fuzhou, and Keeson-chow.
Jardine also suggested that Britain would be wise to occupy a little-known island off the coast of China near Canton with a large, protected harbor, which could provide protected anchorage for British ships and a handy local home port.
That island was known as Hong Kong.

The British government followed his advice to the letter, creating a precedent now infamously known as 'Gunboat Diplomacy', where a weaker nation is forced at gunpoint to capitulate to the demands – no matter how unreasonable - of a better-armed and more powerful nation.
So it came to pass that in 1842, the Treaty of Nanking between Britain and China forced the Chinese to grant Britain an indemnity and extra-territoriality, to open five new treaty ports to them, and give them an exclusive, 99-year rule over the valuable island of Hong Kong.

Some defiant local and regional Chinese officials refused to submit to the unequal and humiliating treaty and refused British demands to reinstate and legalize opium dealing.
After a skirmish over an alleged pirate vessel, the British government renewed hostilities against the Chinese and called upon the French, Americans and Russians to join them. At that time, the American government ordered their forces to remain neutral and the Russians refused to join in too. At that time, only the French joined in the fighting with the British.
But this did not end hostilities. The Chinese retaliated, capturing and

imprisoning British nationals, including two British consuls and a reporter from The Times. Unfortunately, the prisoners were tortured and subsequently put to death by the angry Chinese mob.

British forces retaliated by attacking the Emperor's Summer Palace in Beijing, forcing the Emperor to flee. The British then burned the priceless historic palace to the ground as punishment.
In 1858, the British-French forces continued to fight against the regional governments and their Qing armies. The British, with help from French forces, crushed the Qing army with their superior weaponry and dictated a second, unequal settlement called the, "Tientsin Treaty."

The Tientsin Treaty forced the Qing government to make even more territorial and economic concessions. These concessions included legalizing opium, giving British drug-dealers unlimited trading rights - a death knell to the Chinese people.

The treaty also dictated what size tariff the Chinese government was allowed to levy on opium and all other foreign imports to China and gave foreigners the right to indenture Chinese citizens and transport them abroad to work as virtual slave laborers. It also gave foreigners the right to spread Christianity throughout China and ceded the valuable province of Kowloon, by Hong Kong, to the British as well. This conflict went down in history as the second Opium War and signaled the beginning of the downfall of the Qing dynasty.

Not all the British supported the opium drug trade, British intervention, and war against the Chinese. One British Prime Minister, William Ewart Gladstone, was violently opposed to British opium peddling and said in a famous speech in Parliament, that he was, "in dread of the judgments of God upon England for our national iniquity towards China. There never was a war more unjust in its origin, a war more calculated in its progress to cover this country with permanent disgrace."

Sadly, even a man in his exalted position of power was not able to prevail or prevent further British intervention and conflict in China. But in an astonishing move that demonstrated the power of the people, in 1900, Kung Fu changed Chinese history!

A group of ardent Kung Fu practitioners called the *Yi He Tuan* had finally had enough of foreign corruption, drug dealing and strident religious teachings, and they rose up against the foreign oppressors and took to the streets.

The foreign powers with the most power and influence in China at that time were: Britain, France, Russia, Austria-Hungry, Germany, Italy, the US, and Japan. Sensing their peril from these ardent rebels, these eight countries formed an alliance to fight back, and called it, predictably, the Eight Nation Alliance.

The *Yi He Tuan's* in Chinese meant "The Group of the Righteous and Harmonious", and they wanted to return China to health and prosperity. Because they were Kung Fu practitioners, Westerners mistakenly referred to them as 'boxers' – the only type of fist-fighting known in the West at that time.

So the rebellion started by the *Yi He Tuan* Kung Fu fighters came to be referred to as the "Boxer Rebellion", when it should rightly be known as the "Kung Fu Rebellion"!

This highly-skilled group of Kung Fu practitioners were experts in Nei Kung training. Many of them were said to have mastered the Nei Kung's secret *Time Slowing Method* that actually enabled highly advanced practitioners to *dodge* the foreigner's bullets while under heavy fire.

Word spread rapidly amongst the Chinese, that at last, a band of Chinese warriors had emerged that were immune to enemy weapons! This hope rallied a massive number of followers to their banner and the rebellion spread like wildfire.

In June of 1900, the Kung Fu Rebellion fighters, convinced they were *invulnerable* to foreign weapons, converged from all over China on Beijing, chanting, "Support the Qing government and exterminate the foreigners!"

Though the Empress Dowager Cixi was initially reluctant to encourage any kind of rebellion amongst her people, she quickly recognized the wisdom of supporting their cause to help her escape the tightening clutches of foreign control. She announced her support for the rebellion and China officially declared war on the Eight- Nation Alliance.

The Chinese, driven by hope and belief, came out strong and were initially able to inflict heavy casualties on the foreign powers and push them back out of occupied territories.

But, the foreigners had a wild card up their sleeve: they had soldiers and ships nearby in the Philippines and with them, managed to ship an extra 20,000 battle-hardened troops into China. This turned the tide on the Rebellion.

With so many reinforcements, the Eight-Nation Alliance was able to defeat the rebellion fighters and the Imperial army forces. Pushing the Chinese forces before them, the Eight Nation Alliance marched into Beijing, where they looted the Imperial Palace in the Forbidden City, and forced the Empress and her highest ranking government officials to flee to safety in Xi'an.

On September 7, 1901 the Qing government surrendered. Terrible atrocities were committed on both sides during the Rebellion which still reverberate through the region to this day.

After the Empress surrendered to the foreign powers, the Eight Nation Alliance demanded that the Qing government pay steep retribution for their losses during the war.

Chinese scholars and high-ranking officials saw the Chinese defeat by

Foreign Powers as a lesson to be learned. They saw how Britain and the US had become 'super powers' through the Industrial Revolution and rapid modernization. They realized they must learn from their success if there was ever to be a free China.

Experts at long-term planning, Chinese intellectuals and visionaries dreamt of building China into a super-power too one day. To do that, they knew that Chinese scholars would need to go abroad to study Western economics, finance, science, agriculture, medicine and any other subjects that could help their huge, old-fashioned country to modernize. Then, these bright, passionate students would return to China to implement the changes needed to reform and transform their great nation.

For this reason, shortly after the Boxer Rebellion, a mass exodus of students left China to study all over the world: they went to Japan, Europe and the United States.

Two of these students were to figure prominently in the tumultuous changes that would soon shape China's future.

One was the famed Doctor Sun Yet-sen, who would one day be called the "Father of the Chinese Nation." The other, lesser-known student, was Zheng Kai Chan, Sin's Great Grandfather. These two great men went to Japan as foreign exchange students to learn modernization techniques. They were fired up with a passion to transform China for the better. They met on campus in Tokyo and became fast friends and revolutionary colleagues who spent many long hours together, planning a transformative future for China.

In 1911, they returned to China and formed the first Republic of China - a move that was to shake the annals of History.
And ended almost three hundred years of Qing Imperial rule to make way for modern China...

3

—

SIN'S VENERABLE ANCESTOR

OUR STORY BEGINS WITH ZHENG KAI Chan, Master Sin The's great-grandfather, born in 1876 in Fu Ching City in China's Fukian province. From an early age, Zheng Kai's favorite subjects were reading and Kung Fu. He devoted himself to the study of *Nei Kung* Techniques, which seemed to him like drawing the 'Breath of the world' into his own body.

By combining his reading and *Nei Kung* skills, by the time he was twelve, he had mastered a technique that enabled him to read super-fast - twelve lines of text at a time!

Using this powerful technique, he began to read ten books a day, becoming exceptionally well-educated and learned at a very early age. Nei Kung also helped him with memory retention, so he was able to remember what he read.

Every year, following ancient Chinese traditions, a scholastic competition was held in Beijing. The top-ranked scholars from all over China came together to compete in poetry, literature, science, Chinese history and the arts. Each year, a million contestants participated. After days of stringent testing, one million contestants would be narrowed down to just twenty finalists who were tested by the Emperor himself in the Forbidden City. From these 20 Finalists, the Emperor would the select the ten winners, who were awarded the coveted title of *Zi Se*. This was a supreme honor and marked the winners as the best in all of China.

In 1895, when he was only nineteen, Zheng Kai Chan was chosen as one of the top ten ranking scholars in all of China by the Empress Dowager herself. He was awarded the honorable title of *Zi Se*, an unparalleled honor.

Most people who received this honorable title accepted prestigious and highly-paid government positions that enabled them to lead a prosperous and luxurious life ever after.

Zheng Kai Chan chose a different path. The path of Revolution and self-sacrifice.

Repulsed by the rampant corruption in the Imperial Government and determined to make his country a better place, Zheng Kai Chan decided to go abroad to study the teachings of the leading Western revolutionaries such as, Karl Marx, Vladimir Llyich Ulyanov (aka 'Lenin'), Engles, and others. Then he would return to China to use his new-found knowledge to serve the common good and perhaps even transform his own government.

His revolutionary ideas met with great resistance from the powerful traditionalist groups who lived off the patronage of the corrupt Manchu government. They demanded that if he knew what was good for him, he must give up his dangerous idea of studying abroad and stay and join them.

But, true to his own honor, Zheng Kai Chan refused to succumb to their pressure and left China to study in Tokyo.

There he met several Chinese foreign students who shared the same values and vision for the future that he did. When he first arrived, he met Chang Tai Yen and Lim Pai Sui.

Together, in 1903, they published a critical essay in their book, entitled "Let's Talk about Revolution". The book was extremely critical of the Manchu government.

The Chinese foreign students in Tokyo would congregate in the foreign student's office, because there they were able to read the Chinese newspapers provided by the university and keep abreast of the latest developments and news from their country. And, of course, there, they got to passionately argue their political ideas with other bright, passionate Chinese.

It was there that Zheng Kai Chan became famous. Initially it wasn't his political views that impressed the other students. It was his ability to read twelve lines of text in a single glance that took them by surprise. He would finish reading his newspaper while the others are still on the first page! Then, he would politely ask one of the other students if they would exchange papers with him. He would repeat this until he had read every paper in the room – Japanese, English, French, German, and Russian!

Thinking he might be faking to impress them, the other students would gather around him and bombard him questions. But, he made believers of them all when he could recite back to them the contents of every article he had read!

Then, they were curious to know how he did it. Kai Chan would explain about his early Nei Kung training that had enabled him to work up to his ability to read at such an astonishing speed and level of comprehension.

And, Nei Kung had also enabled him to acquire super memory ability as well, which he used to teach himself many foreign languages.

Several of the Chinese foreign students asked him to teach them these legendary *Nei Kung* techniques. Kai Chan agreed, but warned them that because they had started when they were far older, not to expect as much from the training.

Word travelled fast about his exceptional reading ability and prodigious memory, and soon he was drawing an audience of students from all over the university – from both the Chinese and international student communities.

To devote more of his time to teaching, he quit his dishwashing job at a local fish restaurant and began to charge a small fee for his classes, so he could pay for his tuition at the Tokyo University. Soon there were twenty to fifty students in each class, meeting twice a week for an hour or so each, and he was earning far more than he had working many more hours at the restaurant. This enabled him to spend more time for his engineering studies, which were very demanding as well.

But everything changed when, in 1905, Kai Chan met Dr. Sun Yat Sen.

Sun was from Kwang Tung province, neighboring Fu Kian province where Kai Chan came from. When they met at a lecture that Dr. Sun gave at the University in Tokyo, the two of them felt an instant kinship and quickly became good friends.

Dr. Sun was already well known for his "Three Principals" political philosophy: Nationalism, Democracy, and Welfare for the people. He called for the expulsion of the Ching (barbarian Tatar) from China and for rule to revert back to the Chinese. He also called for the equal distribution of land amongst the peasants in China. He had worked tirelessly in China to incite uprisings, and this had resulted in him being exiled from China.

During his exiled years he traveled extensively in Europe and America. On the spiritual side, he also converted to Christianity.

Dr. Sun's political leanings appealed to young Kai Chan's hot-blooded notions of heroism and nationalism. And, for his own part, Kai Chan had impressed Dr. Sun with sharp mind and thorough knowledge of global politics. Seeing that Kai Chan already had many students of his own, Dr. Sun invited him to form an organization with him in Tokyo to support revolution in China. Kai Chan thought it was a terrific idea and wholeheartedly agreed.

And so, on the 20th of August, 1905, Dr. Sun established an organization called *"Tung Men Hui"* or the United Union Group and Zheng Kai Chan became its first official member and co-leader. Kai Chan encouraged all his students to enlist and by 1906, membership in the United Union Group of Japan had grown in number to over one thousand members.

They all shared the same dream of expelling the Manchu and returning the country back to Han rule.

In 1906, Dr. Sun left Zheng Kai Chan in charge of the Japan chapter of the United Union Group to travel to Malaysia to spread their message. There, he founded the Malaysian chapter of the United Union Group and met with overseas Chinese businessmen to raise money for the revolutionary cause. In 1910, he hosted a Donation Conference in the city of Penang in Malaysia, which turned out to be a huge success, raising large sums of money for the revolution.

Back in Japan, the original United Union Group of Tokyo continued to flourish under the leadership of Zheng Kai Chan and he also succeeded in raising a lot of money to help fuel the uprisings in China.

In April, 1911, one of Dr. Sun's generals, named Huang Ching, led an uprising that became known as the *"Huang Hua Ti Ke Ming"* or *The Yellow Flower Earth Uprising*. Sadly, it failed miserably and some of his followers despaired. But, fortunately they persevered and on October 10, 1911, they staged another military uprising in Wuchang and this time they succeeded.

This finally put an end to the Ching Dynasty and gave birth to the first Republic of China.

Zheng Kai Chan was thrilled to hear the staggering news of the fall of the Manchu! He hurried back to China to help Dr. Sun to bring justice and order back to China through the founding of the Republic.

Unfortunately, as with any great endeavor, there were many obstacles along the way. Needing help to overcome some of them, Dr. Sun recruited one of the Ching generals, a Han Chinese named Yuan Se Kai.

Yuan took a large part of the Ching army that had been under his command with him when he agreed to join Dr. Sun's revolution and help defeat the Ching army. But, as soon as victory was at hand, he betrayed Dr. Sun and seized power for himself - declaring himself the new Emperor of China!

Dr. Sun Yat Sen's victory seemed destined to be a short-lived one.

But, Dr. Sun and Zheng Kai Chan and the Nationalist Party continued their revolution, fighting to wrestle power back from General Yuan Se Kai.

General Yuan had backed himself into a corner and had to fight not only Dr. Sun's revolutionary army, but also the diehard followers of the old Manchu regime that constantly threatened his life with assassination attempts.

In desperation, General Yuan made a deal with the devil. He sought out the help of the legions of the Japanese Army that were still stationed in China. The Japanese saw this as a perfect opportunity to further their invasion plans of China, and forced Yuan to sign many of the infamous treaties that effectively sold much of China out to the Japanese in order to keep himself in power.

It took Dr. Sun Yat San and his *Kuo Ming Tang*, Nationalist Party a long and brutal fight to finally bring Yuan Se Kai to his knees.

But, by then China was in a great political turmoil as opportunistic warlords sprang up all over the country and divided China into hundreds of corrupt, regional power bases. Every warlord claimed territory of their own, which they ruled with a cruel and iron fist.

It was one of the darkest eras in Chinese history.

On March 12, 1925, Dr. Su Yat San passed away at only 59. Sadly, he did not live to see his Nationalist Party finally unify China, but his dream and legacy was destined to live on far beyond his death.

In 1932, a vicious warlord named Lin Chin occupied the City of Fu Ching of Fu Kian province where Zheng Kai Chan lived. One day two hundred of Lin Chin's soldiers happened to pass by a local wedding ceremony. Noting how beautiful the bride was, the soldiers decided to have some "fun" with the locals.

The leader ordered his men to tie up the bridegroom, then, in front of him and all the wedding guests, raped his bride as the other soldiers cheered him on. When he was done, another soldier took his turn, and another, and another in a massive, brutal gang rape, leaving the poor bride near death.

Word spread like wildfire through the city and an enraged mob of villagers a thousand-people-strong rushed to the scene. Seeing the grisly truth of the hideous crime with their own eyes, nothing could stop the furious mob from exacting justice on the spot, and they stoned and beat to death all two hundred soldiers.

When Warlord Lin heard his soldiers had been massacred, he raced to the regional government in Fu Chou and lied to save his own skin. He reported that a local uprising had set upon and killed his soldiers in a vicious and unprovoked attack. He demanded that the authorities send government soldiers to arrest and hang the perpetrators!

Zheng Kai Chan got wind of Lin's lies and, determined to protect the people of his city, he took it upon himself to travel to Fu Chou and inform the authorities of the truth of what had actually happened.

Because he had been Dr. Sun Yat Sen's right hand man and had a sterling reputation as the President of United Union Group of Fu Jian province and Tokyo, the authorities accepted his version of the story and spared the brave men of Fu Ching.

This event was but one of many injustices and tragedies that occurred while the country was in chaos and disarray.

Zheng Kai Chan decided that he must take a new path to help shape China's future. Believing that China's future lay in its children, he sold all his property and belongings and used the proceeds to build an elementary and middle school in Fu Ching to teach future generations.

Zheng Kai Chan knew that only by educating the younger generations could China build a better tomorrow. He named his school "*Wen Kwang*" or Scholar's Light.

His school went on to receive high praise throughout China for the excellence of its education curriculum.

Zheng Kai Chan wanted to expand his school to include high shool students as well, so in 1937, he traveled to Malaysia and Indonesia to collect contributions from the overseas Chinese to help him build a high school. He took his nineteen year-old grandson, Zheng Sek Heng, with him.

Sek Heng fell in love with the beautiful culture of Indonesia and the country's lush and stunning landscapes. Sek Heng also noted the exceptional business opportunities that existed there and, when his grandfather was preparing to return to China, he asked if he could remain in Indonesia and try to make his living there.

Zheng Kai Chan had seen Sek Heng's love of Indonesia and how easily he had made many new friends during their short stay. He wanted to give his grandson the opportunity to make a name for himself in a new land. At the urging of the local Chinese community there, Zheng Kai Chan agreed to leave his grandson at their care.

Saddened that he would no longer have his beloved grandson at his side in China, but knowing it was the right thing to do for the boy, Zheng Kai Chan gave Sek Heng his consent and let him stay in Indonesia to build his own future, while he returned to China with a heavy heart.

4
-
SIN'S FATHER

LONG BEFORE HE SETTLED IN INDONESIA, Zheng Sek Heng, Sin's father, was born in Fuching, Fujian province of China on December 7th, 1918. His birth caused quite a commotion in the hospital amongst the doctors and nurses.

The doctor that delivered him discovered a strange membrane covering his entire body! They had to break through the membrane to enable the baby to breathe.

When the nurse told Heng's parents about it, Heng's grandfather, Zheng Kai Chan, told them that the same thing had happened to him and Heng's father when they had been born. It was a family genetic trait that affected all firstborns in their family. He also mentioned that each of these persons had been born with certain psychic abilities as well.

Heng was four years old when, out of the blue, he told his mother that his uncle Huang was going to die the following Saturday.

His mother quickly put her forefinger to her mouth and made a

"Sh...." sound and said, "Only you, your father, and Grandpa Kai Chan know this. Say nothing."

She warned Heng never to say anything to anyone about it, in case they thought he was crazy.

Heng was the first of seven grandchildren to Kai Chan, and he was very much attached to his grandfather. His grandfather loved him dearly, so much so, that he brought Heng with him everywhere he went. The two were inseparable.

When he was with his grandfather, Heng was privy to Kai Chan's meetings with businessmen and politicians who spoke with an extensive and erudite vocabulary. This helped Heng to learn to speak like an adult at a very early age. His language skills and vocabulary often amazed Kai Chan's associates and friends, which made Kai Chan proud of his grandson. Because of his political activities, Kai Chan spent a lot of time with foreign dignitaries and ambassadors to China. On many of these occasions, Kai Chan, being a multi-linguist, would speak to them in their native tongues.

Heng was like sponge. A gifted linguist himself, just by listening to his grandfather's conversations, Heng was able to pick up these languages as well. He asked Kai Chan to buy him foreign language books so he could study more formally. Kai Chan was impressed by Heng's keen interest in foreign languages and readily bought him books to foster his studies.

More importantly, Kai Chan also taught Heng his Nei Kung meditation techniques to enable him to read multiple lines at a glance and his Super Memory Training techniques.

So by the age of twelve, in addition to Fu Ching Hua (dialect of

Fu-Ching), these enhanced learning techniques had enabled Heng to learn to speak fluently in five other languages: Chinese, English, German, Japanese and Russian. He had also been able to jump to a higher grade in school several times, so he graduated from high school quite young, then graduated from Xia Men College, with majors in International Studies and a minor in Business, when he was only fifteen! His parents and grandfather were immensely proud of him.

Heng took a year off after university to travel with his Grandfather Kai Chan through several European countries, including England, France, Germany, Italy and Spain.

Kai Chan met with many Chinese businessmen and organizations overseas, helping to spread Dr. Sun Yet San's teaching and solicit donations for the Revolution.

Kai Chan was very glad to have his grandson with him when Heng turned out to be a very persuasive young man. Heng used his psychic abilities to sense people's minds. This enabled him to know what they were thinking, then he used a little bit of ingenuity to tell them what they needed to hear.

In no time, Heng had helped his grandfather raise a large sum of money for the Chinese national cause. Kai Chan beamed at his grandson with immense pride and affection.

After his European tour, Heng attended graduate school at Xia Men University, majoring in International Affairs and received his Master's degree in two years.

It was at that time that Kai Chan had liquidated all his holdings and wealth and used the proceeds to build an elementary and middle school in Fuching, in the Fujian province of China.

When Heng completed his Master's degree, Kai Chan decided to travel to Southeast Asia to help raise money for Dr. Sun Yet San's revolution and his high school projects in Fujian.

Again, Heng accompanied his grandfather on that fateful trip and ended up staying in Bandung, Indonesia to live and start a family.

When Heng settled in Bandung, many of the local Chinese were impressed by his scholastic achievement and encouraged him to become a teacher.

Because there were many Chinese immigrants residing in Bandung, the town had two Chinese elementary, middle, and high schools. One of them, Xiao Chung, was located in the middle of the town. The other, Xing Hua, was in a wealthy neighborhood on Chihamplas Street.

The Chinese schools were privately owned and operated, separate from the Indonesian government's official school system.

At that time, Indonesia had been ruled by the Dutch for over three hundred and fifty years and was still called the Dutch East Indies. Since the Dutch ruled the country, the official language in Indonesia back then was also Dutch.

All public school children were taught in the Dutch language. The curriculum of the Indonesian public school system strictly followed the demanding requirements of the Netherland's school system, which was an excellent, highly rated system. Amsterdam, Netherland's capital city, had been a famous gathering place for scholars and intellectuals to meet and debate their political and philosophical point of views since the Fourteenth Century.

Chinese private schools in Indonesia were also influenced by the Dutch educational system and required the students to follow a strict and demanding academic curriculum as well.

All the courses were taught in Chinese instead of Dutch. The Dutch language was always offered as an elective class at the Chinese school. But, since the majority of the Indonesian people spoke Indonesian as their mother tongue, Indonesian language was a requirement in all Chinese schools.

These schools also taught Chinese History, as well as Indonesian and World History. On the literary side, Chinese schools concentrated more on Chinese literature than European literature.

As any private school, tuition at Chinese schools was generally rather high. However, as most of the Chinese students were from families of relatively prosperous merchants and tradesmen, so they were able to afford the tuition for their children.

When Heng considered teaching as his new career, the local Chinese community agreed it would be a blessing for the top local Chinese school, Xing Hua, to have him as a teacher.

However, the teacher's salary at that time in Indonesia was very low, making Heng reluctant to commit to teaching for fear he would not be able to support the family he wanted to have one day.

The Chinese community went all out to induce him: they went to see the principal of the school and asked him to hire Sek Heng as a teacher and to agree to pay him three times the salary of a regular teacher. They would pick up the difference!

Of course the principal saw the wisdom of this deal and gladly hired the brilliant young scholar as their main teacher.

Having a gift for languages, Sek Heng had rapidly picked up Indonesian and Dutch. His other specialties were Mathematics, Physics, Chinese History and Literature. He looked forward to sharing these interesting subjects with his students, but was initially disappointed to find a general lack of interest and motivation in his students. He tried to motivate them by teaching his classes in a very upbeat and interesting way, using stories and puzzles to stimulate their interest.

This helped, but he also saw that his students lacked discipline and he was determined to instill it in them. He would get very upset if his students did not pay attention in class. Discipline was key back then and the parents encouraged teachers to smack a student's hand with their ruler if they were caught talking in class. Heng meant business and soon his students learned to pay attention and relish their studies.

5

-

SIN'S MOTHER

SIN'S MOTHER, SUI CHIN IE, WAS born on November 22, 1923 in Fuching, Fujian province of China. Her parents belonged to a minority Chinese group that had converted to Christianity.

As a child, she was very pretty and attracted a lot of attention. She was a cheerful, well-behaved child with a ready smile and a good demeanor. People would often stop and talk to her. She was never shy or afraid of people and got along with everyone. She was truly a happy child.

Her teachers adored her. Many of the other students were pesky or troublemakers, but Sui Ie was a good girl who followed the rules and was a model student. She was also a very lucky person. The other students and teachers found out that she was lucky when they played the 'scissor, paper, rock' game, and she always won! Pure Luck. She would also find four-leaf clovers all the time. And when some troublemakers threw things at her, strangely, they would miss her and hit someone else!

She was fifteen years old when her parents immigrated to Bandung,

Indonesia. Her father opened a jewelry shop shortly after they settled in.

In Indonesia, people loved to wear gold jewelry. Everyone wore a piece of 23 or 24 karat gold jewelry. Anything less than 23 karat was considered inferior.

Eighty percent of the Indonesian population were farmers. After a good harvest, the farmers would bring their wives and children to the city to celebrate by buying little gold trinkets and baubles. Unfortunately, they would often buy too much, and spend too much of their hard-earned money. So, when planting time came in the Spring, they would need money to buy seeds to plant crops. So, more often than not, they would return to the city to sell or pawn their jewelry. It was a tragic cycle that kept many of the Indonesians at a subsistence level. It also made owning a jewelry shop in Indonesia a profitable business.

In Bandung, Sui Chin attended Xing Hua Chinese High School. She found she was a bit isolated from the other students, since, unlike her, all the other Chinese students had been born and raised together in Indonesia and spoke Indonesian fluently. On top of that, since Bandung was situated in Western part of the island of Java, the local Javanese spoke a different dialect called *Sundanese*. The difference between the normal Indonesian language and Sundanese was as great as the difference between English and German!

Like all multilingual children, the other students tended to mingle these two languages with Mandarin Chinese when they spoke to each other. But, Sui Chin could only speak Mandarin and her local dialect in Fujian, *Fu Chiang Hua*. She felt at a total loss!

But not just the languages were different. The other students being born in Indonesia had a more European style of dressing and doing their hair and make up, compared to Sui Chin's.

But, cheerful and undaunted, she was quick and bright and determined to learn how to adapt her fashion sense and hairstyles to fit in. But the language problem would take longer to conquer!

Sek Heng had been teaching classes in Xing Hua for a year when Sui Chin's joined his class. He noticed her right away because she sat in the front row and conducted herself in a very serious way and was completely absorbed in the class material he taught. Also she wore her hair like the girls from his district in mainland China did. Right away, he knew she must have just immigrated. It was refreshing for him to have someone from his own province in class. He started to take an interest in her.

For Siu Chin, all the other teachers were predominately influenced by Western culture in their clothing styles and demeanor, so Sek Heng stuck out like a gem. Like her, this brilliant young teacher had also recently immigrated from China from her own province! All the students were talking about his brilliant academic achievements and him being the grandson of one of the Founding Fathers of Modern China, Zheng Kai Chan, the man who had helped Dr. Sun Yet San established The Republic of China.

Sui Chin couldn't help but develop a crush on her clever, good-looking teacher!

Sek Heng noticed right away that Sui Chin had not yet been fully accepted by the other students. He knew it was because of the language barrier and her more formal Chinese upbringing. Most of his students were second-generation Chinese who had been born in Indonesia. Hardly any of them communicated with each other in

Chinese. Since Sui Chin spoke only Mandarin, the other students were reluctant to socialize with her.

Heng felt bad that she seemed alone most of the time. So one day, he asked her to stay after class to have a talk with her. He asked her where she came from and was pleased to learn that she came from the same village he did! Right away they felt a strong kinship and got a chance to speak in their local Fu Chiang Hua dialect. They talked about places in the village where they had both loved to hang out after school and which vendors had the best foods and treats. They ended up laughing and having a great time together.

Heng pointed out to her in a sympathetic way that he had noticed the other students left her to herself a lot. He offered to teach her the Indonesian and Sundanese languages to help her overcome her language barrier.

Sui Chin was delighted and gladly accepted his offer. With his help, she knew she would soon be able to speak with the other students and have a chance to become popular again. And she loved the idea of being tutored privately by her heartthrob teacher! She left, thanking him profusely and was beaming when she came out of Heng's office and headed home.

Sui Chin was bright and contentious and threw herself into her language studies. She met with Sek Heng everyday after school and he gave her intensive training in both new languages for several hours each day.

She made great strides and within just a few short months, Sui Chin was able to converse with the other students in their own languages! She also updated her appearance by adopting the fashions her classmates favored. In the beginning she had worn her short, straight hair parted over her left ear and held in place with two bobby pins, one on each side, which was the prevalent style in mainland China at the time. Now, she curled her hair to make it wavy, let it grow past her shoulders and combed it straight back, just as her Indonesian friends did.

Her typical after-school outfit had been a buttoned-up, long-sleeve grey shirt with grey pants to match. Very conservative. Now she wore a colorful, short-sleeved shirt with a long-pleated skirt to match. She looked modern and stylish.

Once she had learned the language and looked so fashionable, her good nature and happy attitude enabled her to make new friends in no time.

Her rapid progress impressed all her teachers. Sek Heng in particular was pleased to witness such a drastic change in her. From a quiet and unknown girl, she became a popular, crowd-pleaser almost overnight.

Sek Heng had begun to feel a great affection for her – more than a teacher to a student. But, he kept that completely secret and waited until she graduated from her high school before asking her out.

Sui Chin was thrilled! She had had feelings for him for months and had had no idea if he had felt the same way! Ever since she'd became popular in school, many boys had asked her out, but she had turned them down, because her heart was secretly set on Sek Heng.

But when he had never asked her out, she began wondering if her affection for him was one-sided. Several of her close friends knew how she felt about him. So when they saw her looking depressed, they knew right away what is going on. One of them, Li Li, finally explained to Sui Chin that a teacher was not allowed to date a student.

But then Li Li said she could tell by the way Sek Heng looked at her that he must feel the same way! Sui Chin was relieved to hear this and looked forward to graduation, when she would no longer be a student. Then something might happen!

The night of their first date, Heng took Sui Chin to a popular oyster restaurant. Somehow he had found out that Sui Chin loved oysters, especially lightly battered and cooked in an onion and chive broth and served with egg noodle. He took her to a restaurant that specialized in this dish for their first date.

Needless to say she was delighted and they both enjoyed their meal tremendously. For desert, they ordered Indonesian fermented sweet rice with mango. They talked easily together, about how different the cultures and foods were in China and Indonesia.

The setting was ideal: the restaurant was beautifully landscaped and a gorgeous full moon hung over a cloudless night sky. A perfect romantic setting. They talked and talked till late that night. Neither of them wanted the evening to end.

Three months later, Sui Chin brought Heng home to meet her parents. Her family was Christian, while Heng, on the other hand, was a Buddhist. However, they got along very well as each respected the other's beliefs.

Sui Chin's father, Mui Mui, ran a jewelry shop that he had opened shortly after they moved to town. Now his shop was doing a tremendous business. He showed Heng his operation and Heng loved it! Ever since he had been a little boy, Heng had always had a fascination with gemstones. Jade, rubies, saffires, and emeralds were his favorites. He took pieces with those types of stones out and examined them under a magnifying glass, exclaiming over the gems' fine quality.

Mui Mui beamed, pleased that Heng showed such an interested in his business.

For the next six months, Heng spent his afterschool hours in Sui Chin's father's jewelry shop. He would venture into the jewelry- making workshop to watch how the pieces were made and see how the more valuable gemstones were mounted. Little-by-little, he picked up the craft of jewelry-making. Sometime he would stay in the front of the store and act as a salesperson to help Mui Mui sell his wares.

Mui Mui's shop was situated in a great location. Traffic was funneled to his store from several streets, so it was no surprise that his shop was always jammed with customers. Mui Mui needed three salespersons to handle the workload. Yet that was still not enough help in the late afternoons when the crowd surged after work. He was grateful when Heng was there to step in to help out.

Occasionally, foreigners would come into the shop, usually tourists from Europe or the U.S. They did not speak Indonesian or Chinese and none of the shopkeepers could speak to them. So, it was a blessing to have Heng there handle them.

Also, whenever high-ranking officials came to browse, the other employees always let Heng handle them. When Heng spoke to them in fluent Dutch, they felt they were being served by someone of their own educational and social level and grew more respectful of the shop. More often than not they chose to spend their money in Mui Mui's jewelry shop rather than go somewhere else. Word spread quickly and soon Mui Mui and Heng become well-known amongst the other jewelry shop owners. They were the envy of the town.

Heng and Sui Chin's friendship blossomed into love. One night, Heng decided he knew his heart and what he wanted and so he proposed to Sui Chin. She happily accepted! When they broke the news to Sui Chin parents, they were ecstatic! The Chinese community was also overjoyed at the news.

They set the wedding date and were married shortly thereafter. The two families hosted a large wedding reception in Bandung, and Heng's famous grandfather, Zheng Kai Chan, came all the way from China and brought many other high-ranking officials to commemorate the happy, auspicious event.

The reception was a lavish affair, with all sorts of Chinese delicacies served to guests at a big banquet room. After the reception, the honored guests formed a long line to personally congratulate the newlyweds, wish them good fortune, and shake their hands before taking their leave.

6

-

SIN KWANG THE'S BIRTH & CHILDHOOD YEARS

ALSO ACCORDING TO CHINESE TRADITION, GUESTS attending a wedding gave money to the bride and groom to help them start their new life together.

Since Sek Heng and Sui Chin's wedding was a large one attended by over 500 guests, the gifts of money they received amounted to a handsome sum and the whole family enjoyed counting it up and presenting it to the grateful newlyweds.

Sui Chin's father, Mui Mui, graciously funded all the wedding expenses and later rented a house for them to live in.

According to another old Chinese tradition, the bride's parents give the groom a dowry. This tradition has also been followed in other parts of the world at different times, such as England and Africa. The dowry from Sui Chin's parents and from Sek Heng's grandfather Kai Chan would be a tremendous help in their new life.

When Heng and Sui Chin totaled all their wedding gifts, dowry and savings, they realized it came to a substantial amount of money that would allow them to decide what direction they wanted their lives to take.

Sek Heng made a comfortable income as a teacher, but realized that his salary would not go far to cover the expenses of the growing family he hoped they would soon have. Raised by his grandfather, Kai Chan, in a comfortable life style, he dreamed of giving his own children the same lifestyle and comfort.

He shared his concerns with Sui Chin. She realized that ever since he had come to visit her parent's jewelry shop, he had really enjoyed dealing with jewelry. So they discussed their future and she suggested that he could quit his teaching job and open a jewelry shop. They could just afford a small shop with their combined wedding gifts and dowry. Then, when business got better, they could open a bigger one, like her parent's.

However Heng had a more innovative idea. He wanted to use their funding to buy a large quantity of jewelry from a local jewelry factory at a wholesale price through the discount his in-laws got on everything they bought. Then he would take the jewelry to the villages and sell it door-to-door. Traveling by train to the various villages was inexpensive, so he would only have to be mindful of keeping his wares secure.

That way he wouldn't have to pay any overhead for a rented store. Six months to a year later, if everything went the way he planned, he would have made enough profit to open the large jewelry shop they wanted.

Sui Chin worried about his safety travelling to such out-of-the-way places with such valuable merchandize, yet she knew Heng would do what he needed to do to achieve his dream. So she accepted his decision.

That night they had a wonderful night of lovemaking to celebrate their new future together.

But afterwards, Sui Chin tossed and turned, strangely restless. When she finally fell asleep, she had a strange dream.

She dreamt she was standing in a room full of fog. The fog slowly dissipated and she saw before her the Buddhist deity, Kwan Yin, the Goddess of Mercy!

Kwan Yin was holding a little bundle with her arms. She said gently to Sui Chin, "Come closer, My Child."

In awe, Sui Chin hesitantly approached the Goddess and took a peek inside the bundle.

It was a beautiful, newborn baby boy!

"Oh, it's a boy!" Sui Chin cried, ecstatic.

At that exact moment, Kwan Yin stretched out her hands and the dream baby entered her womb.

Sui Chin awoke, startled, with a warm sweat. The night was quiet and soundless. She looked down and touched her stomach in awe, certain that she was already carrying the quickening seed of their first-born son-to-be.

The next morning she fixed porridge, fried rice, and eggs for breakfast.

As they ate, Sui Chin smiled at her husband and said, "I'm pregnant with a boy."

Heng was a sensible man and regarded her in surprise. "We only made love for the first time last night. How could you be so sure? And you couldn't possibly know it's a boy."

Sui Chin went on, "You know I'm a Christian and don't believe in Buddhist deities, but last night I dreamt Kwan Yin came to me…"

She told Heng all about her dream, the baby boy in Kwan Yin's arms and her feeling it enter her womb.

Heng was amazed and excited by this, "What a blessing! Kwan Yin herself gave us our first-born son! He is going to be very special!"

He kissed Sui Chin and told her, "We will name our son '*Shen Kwang*' or Light of God. Sheng is the Mandarin pronunciation of the word Deity. Fujian Hua is Sin. Heng also said that they were going to celebrate the occasion by going to the best Chinese restaurant in town!

Heng quit his teaching position and bought a host of jewelry samples with their wedding money. Every day he would wake up early in the morning and take the train to the villages near Bandung. He would go door-to-door, selling his wares.

The villagers were pleased not to have to go to town and to buy jewelry in the comfort of their own house. It took some time to become accepted, but eventually, with Heng's sales skill and the good discounts he gave them, his business began to pay off. Without the overhead of a shop to support, Heng could give them a much better deal and still make a good profit. Word quickly spread amongst villagers and soon they all trusted him and would greet him with delight when he showed up at their door.

Meanwhile, Sui Chin also kept busy. Most Chinese would hire at least three servants to take care of the household chores: one servant to clean the house, one to cook and one to do the laundry. But, to do her part to save money, Sui Chin refused to hire servants in the beginning. She did all the household chores by herself and went to the market to shop for groceries.

In the evening, when Heng got home from his tiring day of work, she would do the accounts for him while he ate his supper. Heng would recount the day's events to amuse her while she went over the day's earnings and put them in the ledger.

She would tell him about her day too: what was happening at the market and how hard she had bargained with the vendors to get the best prices for the food she had bought. They would talk and laugh and enjoy the evening together.

Then early each morning, she would take his earnings to the bank and deposit them for safety.

By the time she was six months pregnant and could no longer move with ease, she finally consented to hire a servant to help with her the household chores.

On March 12, 1943, Sui Chin gave birth to a perfect, little baby boy. She was so pleased it was a boy, because now she knew that her dream of Kwan Yin was true.

Her friends had often asked her during her pregnancy if she wanted a boy or a girl? Her answer always took them by surprise.

"Oh, I already know it's a boy!"

Heng was delighted when she gave birth to a baby boy. He knew now that their son would be very special. To top it off, his birth set off a big commotion in the hospital because he too had been born completely wrapped in the same membrane as his father! The nurse had to break the membrane to take him out!

Culturally, the Chinese tended to favor boys over girls. But it didn't really make a difference to Heng if he had had a boy or a girl, because he was one of the few free thinkers that valued girls as much as boys. But he noticed his standing in the community was higher because he had had a boy.

Regardless of all that, now a doting dad, Heng was on cloud nine. He had a secret to share too. He had been waiting for the right moment to tell his wife that he had finally made enough money to open the largest jewelry store in Bandung!

Sui Chin was thrilled to hear it! She had never liked her husband traveling alone to remote villages carrying large sums of money and valuable jewelry. Now that they had a family to consider, it was just too risky.

Heng told Sui Chin about a perfect place he had found for the shop. Jalan Pasar Baru was one of the biggest commercial streets in Bandung and he had found a vacant shop for sale right in the heart of all the activity.

They made their move into their shop and things were going very well when WWII broke out!

During WWII, Japan allied with Germany, Italy, and Austria in an attempt to conquer the world. Under Hitler's regime, Germany conquered most of Europe and tried to conquer Russia, while Japan conquered China and much of Southeast Asia.

Fresh from conquering China, Japan moved on to Indochina, the Philippines, Malaysia, Singapore, and Indonesia. Malaysia and Singapore were under British rule and Britain had powerful fleets guarding them. The walls on these ships were made of thick steel plates that resisted Japanese shells. Japanese warplanes tried every which way to destroy these ships, but largely failed. Few of their bombs, except direct hits, could penetrate the ship's walls.

Finally one of the Japanese pilots had a horrific idea. With a shrieking cry of "Long live the Emperor!" he dove his plane right into the British warship!

The plane exploded and the bombs it was carrying detonated on impact, destroying the ship - and the Japanese pilot.

When other fanatical Japanese pilots saw that this suicidal maneuver had worked, they followed suit.

This horrific practice became known as a "Kamikazi Dive" done by fanatical Japanese pilots willing to sacrifice their lives to destroy the British fleet and enable Japan to conquer Malaysia and Singapore.

Japan then set its sights on Indonesia. They sent their warplanes ahead of their infantry. Batavia (the old name for Jakarta) was the capital city and their first target.

Indonesia had been ruled by the Dutch up until then. Zero's warplanes bombed Batavia to rubble and the Dutch soldiers deserted their posts in droves. By the time the Japanese soldiers landed, they met with next to no resistance and easily took control of the city.

Once in control of the capital city, they sent their warplanes to the second largest city in the country, Bandung, where Sin and his family lived.

The distance between Batavia to Bandung was only about 100 miles, but was separated by a mountain range, so it took the Japanese warplanes quite awhile to reach Bandung. That gave Bandung air raid stations some warning to sound the air raid sirens, giving the inhabitants more time to take cover.

But, it still wasn't enough. When the air-raid sirens went off, it sent the citizens into a blind panic. They grabbed a few essential items of food and valuables from their houses and stampeded toward the nearest air-raid shelter.

Heng and Sui Chin did the same, grabbing as much as they could carry in packs slung on their shoulders and had their servant, Nina, carry their 6 month-old baby, Sin, on her back.

Sui Chin kissed Sin on the head and instructed Nina to stay close to them as they headed out the door to the bomb shelter.

But, as soon as they left the house, they were bombarded by screaming and panicked crowds that nearly trampled them! They got pushed every which way in the frenzy. Many youngsters got pushed down and trampled to death by the hysterical masses!

It was horrifying!

Heng clung fiercely to Sui Chin with one hand and to Nina with the other, trying to make his way through the maddened crowd that was washing against them like a tidal wave. They couldn't see where they were going and surrendered to being driven along by the mob. It seemed like they been struggling for an eternity when suddenly they heard the Zero's warplanes coming up on them from behind!

RAT-TAT-TAT-TAT-TAT-TAT-TAT-TAT-TAT-TAT!!!

The planes swooped down on everyone, strafing deadly bullets into the unarmed crowd! Mass hysteria exploded! Screaming, dying people tumbled to the ground to be trampled underfoot, leaving the lucky ones scattering everywhere to stay alive.

Nina's hand was torn from Heng's iron grip and she and baby Sin were swallowed up and lost in the rushing mass of humanity!

Sui Chin saw her son sucked away and screamed in terror! Her lamentations were drowned out by the explosions and screaming frenzy of the panicked crowd.

She struggled to go after them, but Heng hung on to her hand with both of his for dear of life and pushed her through the crowd until they finally reached the bomb shelter. He hustled her inside to hide underground with a seething mass of hysterical people.

Sui Chin was sobbing about Sin, but Heng comforted and consoled her, saying that as soon as it was safe for them to go out, they would find Nina and Sin and bring him home safe.

"Our son is special. Remember his destiny. This war cannot take him from us," he told her confidently, holding her close. With a sob, she lay her head on his shoulder.

They couldn't leave the shelter for two days and two nights - as the bombs fell – and fighting raged outside. It was an eternity to Sui Chin who worried and cried the whole time. She would not eat any of the food they had brought with them and Heng started to despair for her health and sanity.

Finally the Japanese soldiers found the bomb shelter. They burst in and ordered everyone out. But, fortunately, intead of murdering them all, after checking everyone's ID, the soldiers let them go home.

After checking that Nina and Sin were not safe at home, Sui Chin immediately set out to look for them. Heng trailed behind her throughout the entire city, searching one street after another, but by nightfall they had failed to locate Nina and Sin and began to fear the worst.

They made it back to their house late that night and Sui Chin collapsed into a tortured, fitful sleep from nervous exhaustion. But, early the next morning before dawn had broken, she woke up her husband and they rushed back out to continue their desperate search.

They looked everywhere. But there was still no sign of them anywhere…

As the evening light began to slip from the sky, Sui Chin started to feel a heavy despair. Could her darling boy be gone forever?

They had reached the far outskirts of the city and were about to turn back when Sui Chin saw someone out of the corner of her eye hiding in a trench.

It was Nina!

Their nursemaid was squatting in a trench by the side of the road trying to feed their baby Sin a moist scrap of bread. The infant was crying pitifully from hunger and fatigue.

Sui Chin let out a scream of joy and raced to them. Nina's eyes lit up when she saw Sui Chin and they hugged overwhelmed with happiness as streams of tears ran down their cheeks.

Heng was beside himself with joy and relief to see his infant son again.

Sui Chin quickly took Sin out of Nina's hands and immediately breastfed the starving baby. Sin was so hungry, he sucked and sucked greedily until he finally fell asleep, gorged!

Heng patted his son's full belly with joyful relief, amazed they had all come through the brutal ordeal unscathed.

On their way home, they asked Nina why she had not come home.

Nina wrung her hands and nervously cried that she hadn't known the battle was over. She had stayed hiding in the trench from the Japanese army, fearing for their lives. But she had been terribly worried that the baby would starve to death with no milk to feed it. On the second day the baby was so hungry he began to suck on the moist pieces of bread she had had in her pocket, but soon the bread was almost gone and she had not known what to do!

She had been ecstatic when she saw them and they were amazed and grateful at her bravery and determination to save their beloved son.

Soon the Japanese controlled the entire country. The Indonesian resistance went underground and continued to work against the

Japanese in secret.

Japan ruled Indonesia with an iron fist from 1943 to 1945. Under Japan's stringent rule, they would exact onerous punishments, such as chopping off one's hand for stealing a loaf of bread or a cup of rice. And married folk who committed adultery were punished by forcing them to lie naked on a boiling hot tin roof under the scorching sun until their bodies slowly burned to death.

Fortunately, WWII ended with the defeat of Germany and Japan. When the United States dropped two atomic bombs at Hiroshima, the Emperor of Japan announced their surrender. Officials in the Japanese armies felt disgraced and performed a mass Harakiri – ritual suicide - by the thousands.

The Allies handed the Dutch East Indies - Indonesia - back to the Dutch, but the Indonesian Resistance, spearheaded by Bung Karno, refused to surrender their weapons to Dutch authorities. Instead, they continued to fight for their independence, this time against the Dutch army. Holland had exhausted their resources and will-for-war by fighting the Japanese army in Indonesia and Germans in their own country. They had nothing left to fight with.

So it was that on August 17, 1945, the Dutch agreed to withdraw and Indonesia declared independence with Bung Karno becoming its first President. He used his full name and became know as President Sukarno.

Like many vendors, Heng's jewelry shop had done poorly during the war. Few people in the city had money to spend on luxuries and peasants from the villages had barely enough food to eat and rarely came to the city to shop for gold jewelry as they had before.
During the war, like most people in Indonesia, Heng's family had to

make do on vegetables, tofu, and rice, since meat was expensive and nearly impossible to come by.

So, during his first two years of life, Sin had never tasted meat.

After Indonesian Independence had been declared, Sui Chin decided to celebrate Chinese New Year in a special way to cheer everyone up. She carefully saved up and bought a chicken to roast! It was thin and tough, but still, it was the first meat they had had since the war began. Sui Chin gave Sin the drumstick as a special treat. Sin had never eaten chicken before and thought it, with its crisp roasted skin and juicy dark meat, was the most delicious thing he had ever tasted! In fact, he liked it so much, he refused to let his mother throw the drumstick bone away, even after he had chewed off all the meat!

For two whole days and nights he clung to the chicken bone as if it were made of solid gold! He even stubbornly slept with it clutched tightly in his tiny fist. Only on the third night was his mother finally able to pry it loose from his grasp while he was sleeping!

It was his parent's first indication that their son had a will of iron, which would one day serve him in good stead when he undertook the challenging rigors of Kung Fu.

7

-

SIN'S GRANDPARENTS

MUI MUI, SUI CHIN'S FATHER, LOVED his firstborn grandson, Sin. Mui Mui would often come to visit Sin's house and would take little Sin out for a ride around town on his bicycle. Sin loved to ride on the back of his grandfather's bicycle and enjoyed the interesting sights and sounds they always encountered along the way.

They both had a love of animals and this helped forge a deep and loving bond between grandfather and grandson. It was his Grandfather Mui Mui who first introduced him to the joys of sharing your life with a loving pet companion.

One day, for a special treat, Grandfather Mui took his grandson to the local tropical fish market, sure he would find it enchanting. He was right. The market was a delight for the boy, stocked as it was with exotic aquariums filled with exotic tropical fish, each one more colorful and beautiful than the next!

Sin was especially drawn to a Fighting Beta Fish that circled fiercely around and around in a small glass bowl, defending its tiny territory against all comers!

Seeing how enthralled his grandson was by the feisty fighting fish, Grandpa Mui bought it for him. Sin was thrilled to have his very first pet! Every day, he carefully fed and tended his Beta Fish. Most children his age tended to overfeed their fish, which would only foul the water and kill the fish. But Sin was smart for his age and took special care to follow the instructions the store clerk had given him. He was rewarded with a healthy and thriving pet that lived for a long time.

Several months later, Grandpa Mui took Sin to a bird market. As before, one beautiful animal caught Sin's eye. A large, elegant, snow-white parrot with a regal yellow crown. It was a stunning creature and what's more, it could speak!
It said to Sin, "Hello, my name is 'Kaka'. What's your name?"

Sin was thrilled! He had to have this delightful creature!
Again, his kindly Grandfather bought him the parrot, which Sin immediately renamed 'Kakatua'. Sin fed it fresh corn and played with it every day.

Happily, after the war ended, the economy began to revive as farmers from the countryside flooded into town to buy clothes and jewelry. Heng's jewelry shop, which had struggled all through war, started doing well. Within a year, Heng was able to buy the entire building the shop was in.

Because they now had more living space, Sin's parent's thought Sin was ready for more responsibility, and they let Grandfather Mui take him out to get a dog! Sin was beside himself with glee!

At the pet market, he saw all type dogs – big and ferocious, little and cute, expensive pedigreed dogs, but none of them really caught his eye, until he spied a little yellow mixed breed puppy that leapt on him with joy and licked his face.

Sin fell in love with him on the spot!

Sin called him 'Yellow' and the puppy quickly became Sin's inseparable companion and best friend. They played together all day long. Yellow was eager and friendly and followed Sin everywhere he went.

Sin's neighbor owned a Rhesus monkey, which they kept chained to a post in the yard. As you might imagine, a Rhesus monkey kept chained up it entire life can turn mean and nasty. There were no fences between the two neighboring yards and one day Sin wondered too far into the neighbor's yard by mistake and the monkey leapt right at his face to attack him!

Luckily, Yellow was with the frightened boy and, even though he was still just a gangly young pup, the brave little dog leapt in front of little Sin and saved him from the snarling monkey! The monkey recoiled from the dog's ferocious barking and Yellow became Sin's hero in the truest sense of the word.

When Sin was five, their father was doing so well in his shop he was able to build a second story above it for their family to move into for their new living quarters. Three more boys and a little baby girl had been added to the family - his brother Tze, 4, his sister Yu, 3, brother, Seng, 2, and his one-year-old baby brother, Hiang.

Their old house was now too small for their growing family. By building an addition over the shop to move into, the whole family would have more room and be able to be together all the time.

On moving day, all their furniture, kitchenware, and clothing was piled into a big truck, and headed out first with their servants. The family came behind in a horse-drawn carriage.

Because there was no room in the carriage, Sin's little dog, Yellow, had to follow along behind the carriage, with Sin whistling to him to keep him close.

Their old house was situated in the suburbs and the shop was in the city center, so the whole family enjoyed the sights as the carriage traveled into the city. As they neared the neighborhood of the shop, Sin got excited and turned to look ahead in the direction of the shop. Suddenly, Sin heard a terrified yelp from behind him and turned just in time to see Yellow being lassoed by a dogcatcher! The terrified little hound fought with all his might to escape the strangling noose around his neck… but he could not break free!

Sin screamed at the dogcatcher to let his puppy go, but the dogcatcher ignored him. By the time the distraught boy got his parents to stop the carriage to go back to save his beloved pet, the dogcatcher was long gone and Sin's beloved pet was lost forever!

Young Sin sobbed himself to sleep for weeks. It was the first time he had experienced the agonizing loss of a best friend and a deep sense of grief assailed him that would haunt him for a very long time.

The layout of the family's new home was spacious. It had a living room on the ground floor behind the jewelry shop and continued upstairs into the sleeping quarters. As the shop grew more prosperous, and the family had more money for luxuries, they decorated the walls with beautiful landscapes done by the famous Indonesian artists, Lukeman, Rudyat, and Soejono. Between the paintings hung exquisite Ming dynasty china plates that Heng had brought with him to Indonesia when he'd emigrated from China.

Like Sin, his father loved tropical fish and had beautiful tropical aquariums installed in the downstairs living room and the upstairs bedrooms as well. Heng would sit for hours into the wee hours of the morning, watching the fish circle their tanks, lost in contemplation. Kakatua's parrot house was installed in pride of place next to the aquariums. The house had a lovely rooftop garden of fruit trees in giant containers and a gorgeous quilt of bougainvillias, gardenias, and roses planted in large clay pots. The containers lined the walls, leaving the center of the roof open for the children to play in. This garden became their favorite spot to play in as the years went by.

Heng set a high standard of how family members should treat each other, with courtesy, kindness, and integrity. He had an unusual way of achieving this too. He made a rule, that anytime there would be fighting amongst the brothers, that Sin, as the eldest would get a whipping first. Then the ones actually involved would get a whipping too. His reasoning was that since Sin was the eldest, it was his responsibility to prevent the fight from happening in the first place. And since Sin Thé was the only brother who was an expert fighter and Kung Fu Master, the other brothers had a healthy respect, even intimidation, for Sin and did not want to earn his ire by getting him whipped!

So, as strange as his rule had been, it worked! Their family always treated each other graciously, which had never ceased to amaze their friends. Their school buddies said that if there was one piece of fruit left, everyone in their friend's family would be squabbling over it, wanting it for them themselves, but in the Thé household, everyone would be offering it to someone else first!

But, that was yet to come.

When they first moved in, Sin was deeply traumatized by the loss of his beloved dog, Yellow, and, combined with the stress of moving into an unfamiliar house, he began to have a terrifying, recurring nightmare…

It always began the same way: a beautiful young woman of about 18 years old would appear and hurl herself at a strange wooden dummy with a man's face painted on it.

She would pummel and kick the dummy, screaming, "Die! Die! Monster, die!"

Then the dream would morph to a scene of a group of violent kids screaming as they stoned a shaggy-haired madman who huddled in an alley.

In the dream, Sin would approach the children and yell at them to stop, but they wouldn't listen. The madman would stagger up and charge them, screaming. The violent kids would laugh and scatter in all directions, leaving the madman chasing after Sin, the only innocent one who had never laid a hand on him!

Sin would scream, "I didn't do it! It wasn't me!" and try to run, but his legs would suddenly be paralyzed! Helpless and unable to save himself, Sin would be brutally beaten by the crazed madman!

The terrified boy would wake up screaming, afraid for his life! His mother would have to run to his room, night after night, and try to soothe him back to sleep.

8

-

AN OLD STORY (Part 1)

SIN'S TERRIFYING BOUTS WITH NIGHTMARES WORRIED Sui Chin. One night when Sin had had the nightmare again, Sui Chin came back to her room after calming him down and slumped onto their bed in despair.

Heng was still up reading his book. He put the book down, concerned, "How's our boy?"

Sui Chin shook her head, a worried look on her face. " I don't know what to do. His nightmares are getting worse, not better."

Heng considered a moment, then said, "What if Sin had a secret Kung Fu hero built into his imagination that he can turn to in times of need who could fight this madman for him?"

Sui Chin was impressed. "That's a great idea! But how do we go about suggesting one?"

Heng smiled, "I have one in mind: Sin's own Great-great-great-Grandfather, the famous, Zheng Yen Zi, who had defeated the reigning Shaolin Grandmaster in a deadly duel to the death!"

Sui Chin listened wide-eyed as Heng recounted the exciting true story of his ancestor. Her eyes lit up, "Perfect! I'll tell Sin the story the next time he has a nightmare and tell him can call upon the Spirit of his great-great-great-grandfather and Kung Fu fighting champion to protect him!"

Sui Chin smiled, pleased with this solution, and Heng was happy he'd been able to help. He turned off the light and cuddled up to his wife.

True to her word, the next time Sin had a nightmare, his mother sat down beside him and told him this story:

"Your great-great-great-grandfather, Zheng Yen Zi, was a prosperous land-owner in Fukien province. He loved Kung Fu and used his wealth to hire the best Kung Fu masters from all over China to come train him. As his skills improved, he eventually became known as the best fighter in China.

One day, a prodigy from the Shaolin Temple, Ah Wang, came to challenge him. Thinking that such a young man could not possibly have earned a significant enough reputation to deserve to fight him, Zheng Yen Zi dismissed the challenge. He snubbed Ah Wang and had his servant tell him to come back when he had earned his own status as a renowned fighter.

Bitter at not having been granted an audience, Ah Wang left angry and dissatisfied.

The next day, Ah Wang disguised himself as a transient searching for work. The head servant in Zheng Yen Zi's household employed him as a gardener, but Ah Wang was cunning and bribed his way up to become Zheng Yen Zi's valet.

One day, Zheng Yen Zi instructed him to give him a shave. As Ah Wang wrapped a towel around his neck, Zheng Yen Zi proudly pointed to his long mustache and warned Ah Wang to be especially careful not to touch it.

When the shave was done, Ah Wang handed Zheng Yen Zi a mirror and waited for approval.

Zheng Yen Zi nodded to indicate a job well done, when suddenly Ah Wang grabbed the razor and sliced off one side of the mustache!

This was his way to force Zheng Yen Zi into a duel. But instead of accepting the challenge, Zheng Yen Zi, still sitting, looked in the mirror he was still holding as a guide and jabbed his other hand backwards to hit Ah Wang in Death Point #9, a pressure point located in the neck.

Ah Wang dropped to the floor like a rock. Zheng Yen Zi stood up roaring, and threw down his towel. He looked down at Ah Wang and told him that he had three days to ask for forgiveness or else he would die.

Ah Wang struggled to his feet and as he stumbled out of main gate, he yelled that he would rather be dead than ask Zheng Yen Zi for forgiveness!

Ah Wang barely made it home. His wife shrieked when she saw how badly he was hurt and quickly helped him to bed. Ah Wang told her what had happened and she immediately wanted them to go back to see Zheng Yen Zi to ask him for forgiveness, but Ah Wang stubbornly refused. Instead, he asked her to take him to the Shaolin Temple to see his teacher, the Grandmaster, who he believed could release him from the death touch.

Worried that the long journey ahead might prevent them from making it in time, his wife hastily complied and they set out for the temple immediately in a small horse-drawn carriage.

But, by the time they reached the temple, Ah Wang had passed away. His devastated wife presented his lifeless body to the Grandmaster and told him the story, sobbing inconsolably.

The Grandmaster was livid.

A few days later, Zheng Yen Zi was in the middle of his daily training when he heard a street vendor pass by his front gate shouting, "Onde... Onde...!"

Onde, or sugar dumplings, were his favorite food. He ordered two of his servants to go out and buy some. The servants opened the heavy stone gate and went out, closing the gate behind them.

Moments later, the gate was flung open and in stalked an old man in a monk robe with piercing eyes. He held a bowl in his left hand. He walked into the courtyard, bowed to Zheng Yen Zi, and handed him the bowl of Onde.

With great caution, Zheng Yen Zi took it, but when he did so, the monk levitated into the air and flew back a few feet and dropped into a fighting stance.

Zheng Yen Zi applauded the old man for his skill and said, " I don't think you've come here to sell me food… Who are you? And why are you here?"

The old man replied, "I am Shu Shi, the Grandmaster of Shaolin. I am here because you killed one of my students and that I must set straight."

The Grandmaster ordered Zheng Yen Zi to donate half of his fortune to the widow of Ah Wang and the other poor people in the village. He also said Zheng Yen Zi had to spend seven years at the Shaolin Temple to redeem himself.

Zheng Yen Zi readily agreed to donate some of his money, but not half of his fortune, and he refused to spend seven years at the temple.

The Grandmaster insisted that the offer was not negotiable, so Zheng Yen Zi asked him how he proposed to solve the issue.

The Grandmaster smiled, "I will challenge you to a match, paralyze you in the fight, and carry you back to the temple for your just punishment."

At this point, numerous people had gathered in the courtyard in the hopes of witnessing some excitement.

Zheng Yen Zi laughed out loud, "Old man, I don't think you can hold your own in a fight against me, let alone carry me back to the temple against my will!"

The two men faced each other, bowed, and started the match. A lightning fast exchange of blows took place, their movements becoming a blur. Both skilled masters, they each switched easily back and forth between diverse fighting systems, including the animal styles: tiger, white crane, monkey, snake, and golden leopard.

They were very evenly matched.

The Grandmaster understood that being the elder of the two, time was not on his side. He made a drastic and unconventional move.

He jumped out of the fight as if to quit, raised his arms up high above his head and thundered out an ear-piercing yell. He then shot up into the air, like a rocket. His body suddenly made a 180-degree rotation like a hummingbird and came down headfirst, blasting toward his opponent.

Caught by surprise, Zheng Yen Zi was unable to block the powerful attack in time and got hit directly on the head. Summoning all of his might, he retaliated like lightening, striking the Grandmaster in the stomach before they both fell to the ground, unconscious.

A huge commotion broke out amongst the crowd, who did not know what to make of this epic battle!

Suddenly, all their jabbering stopped, as the Grandmaster and Zheng Yen Zi both regained consciousness and stumbled back to their feet.

The Grandmaster spoke first, "I used Dim Mak and struck you in Du Meridian #20. You have forty-nine days to live. Come see me before it's too late."

He bowed and headed toward the gate.

Zheng Yen Zi shouted after him, "One moment. I struck you in Ren Meridian #6! You have ninety-nine days to live."

The Grandmaster turned and said, "Then I shall look forward to my next reincarnation." He walked out through the gate and disappeared down the road.

Zheng Yen Zi and his entire household stood there, stunned.

Sin The´'s mother concluded her story, "Your great-great-great-grandfather became paralyzed on the forty-seventh day. Just before he died on the forty-ninth day, as the Grandmaster had foretold, he whispered a private message to his son, your great-great-grandfather. Many years later, we discovered that his last words were a plea for his son to make up for the sins that he had committed, so that the bad luck would not pass on to future generations. To honor his wishes, your great-great-grandfather devoted the rest of his life to meditation and charity. The Shaolin Grandmaster returned to the temple and lived out his last days resolved and in peace with himself. When he passed away on the ninety-ninth day, the monks commemorated him with a big celebration."

Sin was mesmerized by the story. His eyes were aglow with wonder and determination.

"Next time you have a nightmare, ask the Spirit of your Great-great-great-Grandfather to come and fight the madman. He will protect you and keep you safe."

Sin turned his big, serious eyes on his mother and slowly shook his head, "Mother, I would rather learn Kung Fu myself and become a champion fighter like great-great-great-grandpa did. Then I can protect myself!"

Sui Chin was stunned. Most boys would have leapt at having a big hero to protect them, but her brave little boy wanted to learn to protect himself! Her heart warmed with pride.

"Why yes, My Little Warrior, what a wonderful idea. Now go to sleep!"

9
-
GRANDMASTER E

WHEN SUI CHIN WENT BACK TO her room after talking to Sin, she told her husband about Sin's request. Heng smiled and told her that Lao Wong, the father of one of his former students, knew a Shaolin Grandmaster who taught in the area. The master's name was Grandmaster E Chang Ming.

During a school event, Lao Wong had told Heng all about about the time the Shaolin Grandmaster had had to kill eleven Yang Warlord's soldiers in unarmed combat in self-defense to escape from China. That same Grandmaster had settled in Indonesia and happened to live right here in town.

Heng told his wife that he would ask his student for an introduction to the Shaolin Grandmaster and see if there was any possibility of enrolling Sin in his Kung Fu class.

Sui Chin had reservations about it. She was worried that, boys being boys, if Sin learned Kung Fu, he might accidentally use his fighting techniques to hurt other children.

But Heng assured her that would not happen. He had faith in his son's character and also knew that along with instruction in fighting techniques, Kung Fu students had to learn the important underlying philosophy that went along with it of never using one's skills for evil or against another unless your life was in danger.

A good Kung Fu teacher always made their students understand and swear by this oath.

So, Sui Chin reluctantly agreed. That night, after another of Sin's nightmares, Sui Chin told Sin that they were going to try to introduce him to the current Grandmaster of Shaolin, E Chang Ming.

Sin was so excited, his mother had to tell him all she knew about the Grandmaster E to calm him down enough to sleep.

"During the warlord period in China in the 1920's," she said, "The Bei Yang army had invaded Southern China. One day, after a hard workout in a neighboring field, Grandmaster E decided to take a shortcut through the woods on his way home. Along the trail, he stumbled onto a newly set up army camp. The flags around the camp revealed it was the base camp of the fierce warlord, Sun Chuanfang.

Grandmaster E turned to leave quietly, but was spotted by a sentry, who ordered him at gunpoint to stop and put up his hands. The sentry called for reinforcements and the leader was a brawny sergeant, who ordered the Grandmaster to come forward.

Thinking he was surrounded by a large army, Grandmaster E saw no alternative but to comply. To humiliate him, the Sergeant demanded that Grandmaster E kowtow to him and polish the soldiers' boots. Grandmaster E was quietly obeying this degrading order, when he overheard the sergeant laughing with another soldier, saying he couldn't wait for the rest of the men to return to camp so they could have more fun with their new plaything.

That sounded ominous and Grandmaster E realized there was little hope he would ever leave the camp alive. By then he had also realized that the few soldiers he had seen were the only ones in camp at the moment, so he took some time to consider his options.

The sergeant waved his prisoner over and barked out that it was his turn to get his boots polished.

Again, Grandmaster E obeyed, but when the job was done, the sergeant attempted to kick him in the face. Wrong move!

Quick as lighting, the Grandmaster blocked the sergeant's kick, grabbed his leg, and yanked it toward him, dropping the shocked sergeant into the mud on his butt! One of the other soldiers immediately grabbed for his rifle to shoot the prisoner, but Grandmaster E grabbed the rifle barrel and re-aimed it so that when it went off, it accidentally hit one of the other soldiers in the head - killing him instantly!

After a moment of shocked silence, several soldiers charged Grandmaster E at once, intent on overpowering him and beating him to death!

The Grandmaster saw that there was no way out but to fight to the death. He had not started this fight, but he vowed to finish it. In a blinding blur of motion and skill, he danced and punched and kicked his way through the murderous soldiers surrounding him, until all eleven fell dead to the forest floor.

The Grandmaster took a moment to bow at his fallen adversaries with great sadness and respect, then hastily made his escape before the rest of the army returned.

Back at the Shaolin training camp, Grandmaster E could not sleep. The unavoidable deaths of the soldiers weighed heavily on his mind. He cursed himself for taking the shortcut that had caused the encounter with Yang's volatile soldiers in the first place.

Realizing that the other soldiers could eventually track him down, putting his Shaolin brothers' lives at risk, he packed a few items and fled in the night.

His long journey eventually brought him to Indonesia, where he established his own Shaolin Kung Fu school."

10

-

SIN'S FIRST KUNG FU LESSON

A SHORT TIME AFTER SUI CHIN told Sin the story of Grandmaster E, Lao Wong, the father of Heng's student, brought Sin to meet the Grandmaster.

Grandmaster E was a strong, rough-looking man with a long tobacco pipe that rarely left his mouth. He carefully looked Sin The´ over with clear, assessing eyes. He must have liked what he saw, because he went on to explain the process of what it would take for Sin to be accepted as one of his students.

In accordance with Chinese tradition, potential students had to first be recommended to him for consideration. Then there would be a probationary period in which the Grandmaster would evaluate which candidates deserved to be accepted for training.

So, during Sin's probationary period, Sin came to class every night and observed the other students doing their Kung Fu routines. He was fascinated!

Three weeks later, Sin was still watching, still fascinated and itching to join in. Many of the students were in their teens or older. At only five years-old, Sin was the youngest one there. The student group was led by a 16-year-old assistant instructor, who came over to Sin after class to tell him that the Grandmaster wanted to see him.

Holding his tobacco pipe in his hand, the Grandmaster pulled out a lighter and lit it while sizing Sin up out of the corner of his eye. He took a couple of big puffs and blew out. When the smoke hit Sin's face, the boy began to cough.

He asked Sin how many weeks he had come to class. But before Sin had a chance to answer, the grandmaster 'accidentally' knocked over a bowl of uncooked rice sitting on the floor.

Grains of rice scattered everywhere across the clean cement floor.

"Oh, there goes my meal for tomorrow!" Grandmaster E exclaimed. "I have a very special diet, which requires me to reduce my intake of rice by ten grains each day."

He explained tomorrow's meal should have 800 grains of rice and slyly asked if Sin would count the grains for him and put them back into the bowl.

Sin wanted more than anything to accommodate him, but in a quavering voice the little boy admitted that he did not know how to count to 800.

Grandmaster E smiled. "But surely you know how to count to ten,?"

Sin eagerly agreed that he could count to ten.

Grandmaster E handed Sin a piece of paper and a pen and told Sin to count ten grains of rice and mark a line on the paper. When Sin had ten lines, he was to cross them out and write 100. When Sin had eight 100s, then he had 800.

"See how simple it is to count to 800?" the Grandmaster asked.

Sin was thrilled to be of help with such an important task and, with great concentration, started counting. Grandmaster E quietly left the room.

It took a whole hour for Sin to finish his task. With a big smile on his face, he took the bowl of rice to Grandmaster E's room next door to the training hall.

The door was ajar, so Sin peeked in to see if the Master was there. He was taken aback to see the Grandmaster sleeping between two benches, suspended in mid-air with his legs on one bench and his neck on another. There was nothing in between!

Hearing someone outside his door, the Grandmaster abruptly stood up and beckoned the boy to come in. Sin handed him the bowl and proudly told him that there had been 836 grains of rice, but he had removed the extra thirty-six.

Grandmaster E smiled and told Sin he had done a good job and had passed his test. He would take him on as a student.

Sin was ecstatic to learn that he had been accepted! He eagerly asked when he could start classes.

He was told to meet the Grandmaster in his garden at 4pm the next day. As Sin left the room, he caught a glimpse of Grandmaster E gazing down at the bowl of rice and shaking his head, a big smile wreathing his face.

It wasn't till Sin was much older that he realized that making him count the rice was Grandmaster E's way of teaching him to be patient and meticulous. And seeing if he had the commitment to follow up on difficult or tedious tasks. Most importantly, it was also an important lesson on how to tackle a seemingly difficult problem by breaking it down from an overwhelming large one to more easily solvable parts.

Later on in Sin's life when he hit a difficult patch and started to feel overwhelmed with a seemingly insurmountable obstacle, Sin would think back to the very first lesson he had learned from Grandmaster E, and it would help him work it through.

11
-
A ROCK IN A GARDEN

THE NEXT DAY, WHEN SIN CAME to see Grandmaster E, he found him sitting on a bench puffing on his omnipresent pipe while admiring his beautifully-arranged garden.

Still sitting, the master instructed him, "Given all the tools you can find in this garden, move that rock." He pointed to a boulder embedded in the dirt by a banyan tree.

The boy looked confused and asked shyly, "I do not understand Grandmaster... I thought we were going to start Kung Fu lessons today, not work in the garden."

Grandmaster E smiled and explained that in order for someone to move a large rock, they would have to understand the basic principles of physics. Knowing these principles could help a smaller person, such as Sin, overcome a much larger person, the rock.

Sin blushed and began his attempts to move the rock, but no matter how he tried, he wasn't able to move it at all. After numerous unsuccessful attempts, Sin spotted a rod by the house and ran to fetch it, and tried to push the boulder with it. When this also failed, Sin started to dig the rod underneath the rock to pry it up. To his great elation, the rock gave way slightly, but as he could not hold it up, it dropped right back down. After a few more exhausting tries, Sin reluctantly gave up.

Grandmaster E saw how discouraged the boy was. He walked over to him and placed another rock the size of an orange under his rod and said, "Now try again."

Sin found renewed strength and pulled the rod down. This time the rock toppled over easily, and Sin jumped up and down joyfully over his accomplishment.

Grandmaster E took a puff from his pipe and smiled. He stood up and faced Sin. "Son, that is physics."

He went on to explain that the force exerted on an object multiplied by its length (or distance) equals the size of the torque it creates.

"I know it is above your head right now. But you need to understand this principle in order to take on an opponent that is much bigger and stronger than you. How? Firstly, by minimizing the distance between you and him. Then the torque that he produces will be less able to hurt you."

Sin nodded, but Grandmaster E saw the uncertain look on his face.

"Let me give you some examples." The Grandmaster suddenly grabbed Sin's right wrist with his left hand and gently lifted it and turned it so that Sin's palm was facing up. Then he twisted it to his left.

Responding to the pressure, Sin automatically moved back and tried to pull his hand away, but couldn't. The pain caused the boy to bleat out, "Ow! Ow! Ow!"

Grandmaster E released Sin's hand and smiled. "What's wrong with this picture, Son?"

Sin was still shaking his hand in pain. He stared at his teacher blankly.

Grandmaster E prompted him, "When you found the rod and used it to pry up the rock, did you succeed?"

Sin shook his head.

"Then I placed a small rock between the rod and the ground and what happened?"

"I was able to topple the boulder."

"Yes! Now think for a minute about what I said about force, distance and torque. What was the distance?"

Sin thought for a moment, then hesitantly pointed from the tip of the rod to the little stone underneath it.

"Very good, Young Man. Correct. Now when I grabbed your wrist and twisted it, what was the distance?"

Sin thought hard again, then pointed along the length of his arm.

E applauded, "Very good! Now, what would you do if you wanted to minimize the amount of pain?"

Sin showed how he would minimize the distance by bending his elbow and pulling his hand in close to his body to shorten the length of his arm.

E nodded. "Very good, Son. Correct again. You see it's not too difficult to understand physics, is it?"

Sin glowed, basking in his praise.

"The only thing I would change is, don't try to pull your arm back, because you may not be able to do so if your opponent is big and strong. Instead, move your body toward him to shorten the distance of your arm. That is always within your control."

This key lesson taught Sin an important principle that he would find invaluable in the years of Kung Fu training to come. In Grandmaster E's garden, Sin had used the rod and the smaller rock to create more torque to topple the boulder, but now he realized that the same principle applied to fighting.

When Sin started sparring, he learned that, in any encounter in which his opponent was able to establish physical contact with him, the pain or injury he would be able to inflict would be a direct result of the force he exerted and the length of the body part targeted.

To prevent pain and injury, Sin must learn how to alter the opponent's force or the length of his body part targeted. In most cases, one couldn't depend on being able to manipulate his opponent's force, however, one could always change the length of his own body parts by contracting it.

For instance, if someone were to twist your hand to the side, they would cause you a lot of pain or possibly break your shoulder. Most people's natural instinct would be to pull back or away from their attacker, but this defense would lengthen your arm and create more pain and damage.

However, if you were to step *towards* your attacker, the length of your arm would become shorter and the pain and injury would be greatly reduced. It also becomes very difficult for the attacker to twist an un-extended arm.

This lesson was the first of many valuable lessons Sin learned in the serenity of Grandmaster E's garden.

12

-

THE KOI POND

AT THE BACK OF THE GRANDMASTER'S rock garden was a beautiful Koi pond. The pond was a pleasing oval shape over twenty feet long. Water lilies, water irises and lotus plants graced the pond.

Grandmaster E sat on one end of a bench beside the pond smoking his pipe, deep in thought. In the last several months he had been training Sin, and found the little boy had an amazingly active mind and good strong body.

Sin had learned and grasped his lessons well and had come up with his own answers to cope with the new problems that the Grandmaster presented to him daily.

He had been very impressed with the boy's progress so far. He had never seen anyone so young grasp so quickly the underlying physics behind the study of martial arts. He had learned from the mutual friend that had introduced him to Sin that the boy came from a long line of bright, well-educated people, from Sin's father all the way back to his great-great-great-grandfather, so he was not surprised that he was able to pick it all up so quickly.

The boy's focus and discipline was astonishing for one so young and Grandmaster E felt deep inside him that the boy was special and would go far…

Grandmaster E sat back and mused about his own life… He himself had been very good at science and when he was young he had contemplated going abroad to study physics at one of the great universities in Germany, where Einstein had studied.

But, then he had seen all the suffering that his fellow Chinese people were going through, trying to change their lives for the better, and he realized he could help them more if he stayed in China and took another path.

He had always loved the stories of the great Kung Fu masters and heroes who helped the poor. Some of them took riches from abusive and greedy rich men and re-distributed them to others less fortunate. Others taught the students from all walks of life how to elevate and better their lives through martial arts.

Since Grandmaster E was good at Kung Fu, he decided to take the long and disciplined path to become a Kung Fu master and give his students a chance at a new life – one they could live with pride, self confidence and dignity.

He only regretted the sad twist of fate that had brought him face to face with Yang's soldiers that fateful day, forcing him into exile from the homeland and people that he loved.

Grandmaster E was still deep in reverie when Sin arrived and stood quietly beside him.
"Master, I am here," the boy said quietly, not wishing to disturb him.

Grandmaster E smiled fondly at the boy. He picked up a small container next to him and stood up.

"Come feed the koi with me." He walked Sin to the koi pond and handed him some koi's food pellets from the container. He tossed pellets into the water and Sin followed suit. They watched the lovely, golden fish swarm to the surface to feed, stirring the still waters like bright ripples of vibrant silk.

"You have been doing really well with the self-defense techniques to shorten the distance and minimize the opponent's force. Now we will add another element, *direction,* to the mix."

As he finished speaking, E grabbed Sin's right wrist with his right hand and pulled Sin toward the koi pond.

As he'd been taught, Sin instinctively bent his elbow to shorten the length of his arm to minimize the torque that was pulling his body toward the pond. But, this time it wouldn't be enough for stopping him from being pulled right into the koi pond!

"Aiye!" Sin shouted as he anticipated a plunge into the pool.

But, as he toppled toward the water, suddenly Grandmaster E changed the direction of his move and brought Sin down beside the pond.

"You had the right idea, Son, to bend your elbow, but that alone will not be enough if your opponent is so much larger, like me. You need something else, and that is 'direction'."

The Grandmaster used Sin's hand to illustrate what he meant. He pulled it toward the pond in slow motion. As before, Sin bent his elbow and pulled his arm back tight against his body.

But E pointed out that since Sin's forearm was lying perpendicular to his body, it actually pointed in the direction his opponent was trying to push him!

E showed Sin how to bend his forearm tight back against the rest of his arm, so it was pointed up toward the sky. Then he instructed Sin to bend his wrist down so his fingertips were facing the ground and squat low the next time he tried to pull him.

So, the next time E tried again to pull Sin toward the pond, Sin did as he'd been told and Voilà, it worked! Sin saw right away that when he bent his forearm toward the sky, not only was it shorter, it also did not point at the pond, so it could not be used by his opponent in that way. And he could resist the force of pulling much better when he bent his fingers toward the ground and squatted down. Sin was ecstatic to learn this new principle of self defense!

He was practicing bending his forearm upward and curling his wrist down, when E handed him two buckets full of water.

"Here, use these to practice your technique." He showed Sin how to start out by standing straight, his feet wide, about two shoulder-lengths apart, with the buckets hanging down beside his body. Then to squat down low while lifting the buckets up, curling his forearms toward the sky and his wrists in. Then repeat. And repeat. And repeat…

After ten repetitions, Sin got tired and stopped. But Grandmaster E told him to continue the exercise. When Sin finally could do no more, E told him to walk around the koi pond holding the buckets in his hands. A few minutes later his teacher told Sin to do the exercise again.

When Sin finally could do no more, E told Sin to walk around the koi pond again. Eventually, Sin lost count of how many times he had done the exercise or how many times he walked around the pond. All he knew was that he couldn't even hold the buckets anymore, much less lift them up. The buckets finally fell from his swollen fingers and spilled all over the grass.

The Grandmaster calmly massaged Sin's shoulders and arms. Sin was so sore he felt like crying in pain, but he fought with all his might to repress his tears.

His teacher gave him a glass of cool water and, before he sent the boy home, invited him to sit beside him on the bench overlooking the koi pond. E held his pipe, but did not light it. They sat for a time, just watching the fish gently fanning back and forth beneath the glassy surface of the water.

"Everything in the Universe revolves around force, distance and direction, Sin. The Sun, the Moon, the rain and the wind are all influenced by these three elements. The next time the wind blows, close your eyes and feel it's force and try to determine it's direction, but above all, see if you can turn your body in a way that does not block it's path. If you can do that, you are learning to become one with nature."

The encounter by the koi pond was to have a profound influence on Sin throughout his life. His quest to become one with nature could truly be said to begin there, by the gentle, still waters of the little koi pond.

13

-

BOUND FEET, LAMB & PIGEONS

THE LOVING BOND BETWEEN GRANDFATHER MUI Mui and Sin deepened, as did the little boy's love for Grandmother Ah Ma, Mui Mui's wife. The elderly couple loved Sin so much that they asked Sin's parent's, Heng and Sui Chin, if they could adopt Sin and have him move in with them.

OF COURSE SIN'S PARENTS REFUSED. THEY loved their eldest child too much to let him go. But they also knew Heng's parents were lonely and they came up with a different plan. They let Sin stay overnight at his grandparents place as much as Sin wanted.

Since Sin loved both his parents and his grandparents, he chose to spend half of the week with his grandparents and the other half with the rest of his family. His grandparents's house was much smaller and simpler than his parent's house, but Sin loved the attention and love they showered on him and the quiet he experienced there.

Sin had always been amazed at how tiny his grandmother Mui Mui's feet were compared to everyone else's – they looked like the little petals of a flower. But, she walked with little, hobbling steps, as if she was in constant pain. One night when he was staying over at his grandparents' house, Sin saw Ah Ma slowly unwrapping the tight strips of cloth that were usually bound around her tiny feet.

As she slowly uncoiled each strip of cloth, she would suck in her breath and grimace in agony. As soon as the bindings were off, she hastily thrust her feet into a bucket of warm, soothing water and gently massaged her feet.

Sin was shocked to see that her naked feet looked shriveled and deformed, with her toes snapped in half so that they lay folded completely under her soles! Mortified, Sin asked his beloved Grandma what had happened to her feet!

She shook her head sadly and told him a story...

"Many years ago Emperor Li Yy of the Southern Tang's Ten Kingdoms had a beautiful concubine who had very small feet, that she made even smaller by binding them at his request into the shape of a lotus flower. As she danced for him, he found her tiny feet so exciting, he insisted she always bind her feet to please him. Soon, the fashion had spread to the rest of the Imperial court, including the daughter's of the aristocrats. Even though it crippled their children forever, the father's all insisted on binding their daughter's feet in the hopes that they might one day be chosen by the Emperor to be his concubine.
Eventually the brutal practice spread to the families of wealthy tradesmen, who felt it proved they were wealthy enough that their women did not have to use their feet to work. It became a symbol of being high-class and women with bound feet came to be considered more desirable in marriage."

Sin was appalled. "Grandma, does it hurt very bad?" he asked with tears in his eyes. She turned her face away and slowly nodded her head.

Sin bent down and gently pulled her feet out of the basin and kissed each one. "Kisses make it feel better, Grandma."

"Yes they do, Dear Boy," she murmured and stroked his hair with her soft, gnarled hand.

Sin felt a fierce sense of protectiveness and anger rise up in him. Young as he was, he deeply believed in keeping one's body healthy and fit. How could an Emperor, who was supposed to protect and care for his people, force all the innocent girls of his realm to brutally bind their feet and grow up crippled and in constant pain? What *right* did he have to impose this kind of cruelty on his loyal, innocent subjects? And how could their supposedly loving parents allow this to happen to their beloved daughters? It was beyond Sin's comprehension.

"Did your parents make you do this, Grandma?" Sin demanded angrily.

Ah Ma forced out a sad, bitter smile and nodded, "My father had my feet bound when I was just a little girl."

"What happened if you said 'no'?"

"Girls weren't allowed then to refuse anything a parent or husband told them to do. We had no choice in those days, Little One, not even over our own bodies. Our father was the patriarch of the family. He had absolute control over all of us. He could even force a disobedient son or a daughter to commit suicide if they displeased him."

Sin was stunned into silence. How horrible!

"That's the real reason why your grandfather and I decided to leave China and come to Indonesia. In this country, it was less rigid and strict, we had more choices. And there was more opportunity for us to pursue our dreams and make our fortune."

Sin thought carefully about this. What would his life have been like if he had grown up somewhere besides Indonesia?

"I am glad I was born here, in this time, Grandmama, when I can do what *I* want with my own body. I would hate to be born in those olden times. He kissed her and said, "And I am so sorry about your poor feet! I wish it had been different for you…"

Ah Ma hugged her grandson, her eyes red with tears. "You are wise beyond your years, My Son."

Sin had been heart-broken for months when his beloved dog, Yellow, had been taken away and hoped to have another dog one day. But their new home over the jewelry shop had no grassy yard in the back for a dog to play in, so his parents refused his pleas for another dog.

His grandfather wanted to do something to raise his spirits, so he took Sin to a street market that sold live animals, so Sin could see all the little baby farm animals. Sin was curious about everything and enjoyed seeing all the piglets, calves, goat kids and ducklings, but he stopped dead in his tracks when he reached the sheep pen.

Inside, kippering about on its spindly little legs, was a snow-white, baby lamb! Sin smiled for the first time in months, and his heart warmed to another little creature.

Sin begged his grandfather for the little lamb. Grandfather Mui hesitated. Neither their house nor Sin's parent's house had a yard for it. He looked doubtful and asked his grandson where in the world they would keep it?

Sin knew his parents would not let the lamb stay in their house, but he hoped he could prevail on his doting grandparents.

Thinking fast, Sin replied, "Why, in your living room, of course! That has a concrete floor, so he can't hurt anything. Can I, please?"

When his grandfather hesitated at this outlandish idea, Sin grinned at him and wheedled, "Please, please, Grandfather, then I can come stay with you more often!"

This promise touched Mui Mui's soft spot reserved for his first-born grandson, and he relented and bought the lamb for Sin.

At his grandparent's house, Sin had a wonderful time playing with the little lamb, who frolicked and gamboled playfully around the room with Sin. For months, as it grew, the little white lamb filled the empty space in his heart left by the loss of Yellow.

In the corner wall of Sin's parent's rooftop garden stood a metal lightning rod that soared twelve feet up from the roof. Sin and his brothers and sister all loved to play in the garden and often would fly kites from the roof where the breeze was brisk and would carry their kites aloft with ease.

Late one afternoon, a big storm was brewing. Ominous, black clouds began massing overhead and the air crackled with electricity. From an early age, Sin had loved that special moment just before a big storm hit, when the air itself seemed to come alive, dancing with electrical ions that seemed to fill him with energy too. Eager to experience the storm, he raced up to the rooftop garden to drink in the energy dancing around his head.

The clouds had an eerie, bruised look and hung low in the sky. As he stood on the roof enjoying the feeling, he noticed his favorite kite had gotten tangled up on the lightning rod and, without thinking, went to retrieve it.

But the second his hand touched the rod, a massive bolt of lightening zapped through his body! Sin's body arched back in a mighty spasm and he fell to the ground! Groggily, he picked himself up, amazed to find he wasn't hurt!

But just then, his little brother, Tze, ran up on the roof behind him and also saw their favorite kite tangled up on the rod.

Before Sin could yell out a warning, Tze reached out to retrieve it too! The moment he touched the rod, his little body contorted in a massive electrical shock as another bolt of lightening coursed through him! Desperate to save his little brother, Sin lunged and grabbed his arm to wrench him free.

Wrong move!

That only sent another massive electrical bolt jolting through Sin's body too!

Luckily, their legs collapsed and they both fell away from the pole. Dazed and groggy, they looked at each other for a few seconds, too stunned to speak.

Suddenly, realizing they had survived death by electrocution, they both bust out laughing! They had both been zapped by lightning and lived to tell the tale – how many boys could say that? They would be heroes in school!

They laughed and laughed, giddy with relief, and only stopped when the clouds opened and pelting rain drove them back inside.

The family's house had a pigeon coop tucked into a corner of the rooftop garden, in which Sin had installed two mated Messenger pigeons, that were dove grey with sprinklings of white. He was fascinated by science and had gotten the pigeons when he learned at school that they used the *electromagnetic field* of the Earth to orient themselves and could find their way home unerringly from over one hundred miles away.

He was anxious to test this himself. One day, his father took all the kids to Jakarta, the capital city, for a fun visit. Sin got permission to bring the male pigeon with them in a little wicker cage, and he was filled with excitement at the chance to see if the pigeon truly could find it's way home!

After seeing the sights and sounds of Jakarta, Sin released the pigeon as they started their journey home - almost 100 miles away. He was anxious the whole way home, worried that he had made a mistake and had just lost his dear pet, stranding it somewhere far from home. He was despairing by the time they got back home and walked in with a downcast air. Imagine his delight when one of the family servants told him that the clever bird had beaten him home by an hour!

A few years later, Sin's brother, Tze, who had picked up an interest in birds from Sin, learned in biology class that animals that were *crossbred* produced stronger offspring. Tze decided to experiment and he sucked out part of a pigeon's egg through a syringe and replaced it with part of a chicken's egg, then sealed the tiny hole with a tape. He was convinced that this would produce a bigger pigeon.

Later, when Sin asked what the outcome of his experiment was, one of the servants swore that the egg had hatched a pigeon that was larger than normal, but Tze just smiled his quirky, charming smile and refused to either confirm nor deny it.

14

-

RACIAL DISCOMFORT

Since Indonesia, the fourth most populous country in the world, did not produce enough cotton to supply its own needs for fabric and material, it had become a very lucrative business to import cotton from Japan and Korea and weave it into textiles in Indonesia using the cheap labor available on the island.

Indonesians were predominantly employed in agriculture, so it was usually the overseas Chinese who swept in and started to dominate the textile industry and who profited considerably from it.

Even though many Chinese immigrants were extremely poor, the common notion was that all Chinese people were rich and prosperous. Both the Indonesians and the Chinese were very conscious of class differences, and the rich tended to consider those less affluent than them as inferior and, unfortunately, treated them as such.

As the economy deteriorated drastically in the 1960's, with inflation going through the roof, the Indonesians felt like demeaned citizens in their own country and increasingly perceived the Chinese population as greedy outsiders.

When Heng's jewelry shop had thrived, he had used his profits to start a textile factor, handing the jewelry shop over to Sin's mother to run. The textile factory did so well that Heng opened another one and had over 1200 employees working for him in each factory.

One morning at breakfast, when Sin was about ten years old, Sin's father had a worried look on his face and told them that one of his factory foremen had warned him about a radical group of Indonesian Muslims, who were targeting Chinese people and their businesses. He urged everyone to be aware of their surroundings and be careful about going anywhere alone.

This was the first time Sin realized that some Indonesians might perceive the Chinese as a threat.

Sin was very close to the family driver, Rudiyat, whom he spent a lot of time with, because it was Rudiyat who took him to school and Kung Fu class. Sin regarded him as a good friend, and whenever Sin went somewhere to eat, Sin would invite Rudiyat to join him for the meal. Sometimes, people in the restaurant would look at them funny, as it was very unconventional for servants to dine with their employers.

One day, as they were going to lunch, someone they passed on the sidewalk called Sin a 'Chinese pig!' As they sat down to eat, Sin asked Rudiyat why he thought Muslims did not like the Chinese. He explained that many of them perceived the Chinese as impure for eating pork, drinking alcohol, not circumcising their boys, and so on, and that many of these negative impressions got exaggerated by the leaders in the mosques during their religious sermons, so the ill will kept building and building.

Later, as Sin became friends with some of the older Kung Fu students who studied at the university, he would often hear them talk about how ridiculous it was that some of their Indonesian professors would lecture in a way that insinuated the Chinese were to blame for the country's economic problems. When things became more and more expensive, one professor had argued that it was because the Chinese merchants were holding back their goods to create the appearance that there was a lack of commodities, so that they could raise the prices and make more money. Sin knew his parent's didn't do that, but had no idea what others might do.

Religious and cultural differences, aggravated misconceptions, poverty, hunger, and desperation, all fueled the chaos looming ahead. A volcano ready to explode...

15
-
CURRICULUM OF SHAOLIN

THE CURRICULUM OF SHAOLIN UNDER THE tutelage of Grandmaster E was organized and comprehensive. He credited that to the contribution of his legendary teacher, the great Grandmaster Su Kong Tai Jin, about whom Sin knew very little.

Some afternoons after one of those strenuous trainings which left Sin barely able to move his arms or legs, as a reward, Grandmaster E would take the opportunity to tell Sin wonderful stories of the great Shaolin heroes of the past.

Sin loved these stories and on that particular day, he was especially excited that Grandmaster E chose to tell him the story of his great Grandmaster Su Kong Tai Jin, who had trained Grandmaster E and whose teachings he was passing down to Sin The´.

Su Kong Tai Jin was born in Fujian Province in 1849, but was abandoned as an infant because he had a genetic condition called hypertrichosis languinosa, a rare affliction which caused an unusual amount of hair to grow over his entire body, even as a child.

Back then, local people were very superstitious. They thought a baby born like that was the result of a demon planting his seed in the unsuspecting wife, so it would be better off to abandon the baby in the woods where cold or predators would finish it off.

His mother was reluctant to abandon her own child, no matter how odd he looked, but in China at that time, the father was the head of the family and he insisted that keeping the baby would only bring bad luck and disgrace on the whole family. His will must be obeyed. So, they bundled up the unfortunate babe and snuck off into the woods that night and left him there, alone in the woods. Trying to give him a fighting chance, his mother left him on the trail, where he would be seen by passersby, in hopes that some kind soul would take pity on him and save his life.

It so happened that that trail ran by the Shaolin Monastery and was the one that the monks took for their morning run. Imagine their surprise when they heard a baby crying in the middle of nowhere! A young monk found the baby and took him back to the Temple for the Abbot to decide his fate.

Despite the baby's odd appearance, the Abbott believed that if they saved the abandoned child, then the monastery would reap the intangible reward of spiritual satisfaction that such kindness can bestow on the giver. So it was that the odd, hairy child, Su Kong, came to be raised in the Shaolin Temple amongst the warrior monks.

Life was not easy for Su Kong growing up in the Temple. He was considered a freak by most of the other young monks and had to endure their taunts and abuse. They would make fun of him when they all took a shower, pointing and shouting, "Eyu....who let the monkey in here?"

The other children would burst out laughing and little Su's feelings would be crushed. Worse still, they knew Su had been abandoned by his parents and often one of them would add, "Who would want to raise such a freak? No wonder his parents left him in the woods to die!"

Often at night, Su would cry himself to sleep. But there was no relief for him in his dreams either: he would see himself being left in the forest and stalked by a pack of vicious wolves with giant fangs and red devil eyes. They would surround him, lick their lips, bare their fangs and attack!

Su would wake up screaming! Because he dared not sleep for too long, he began to spend his nights practicing Kung Fu, and as the years went by became the best fighter in the monastery!

Aside for his love of Kung Fu and the martial arts, he realized very early on that he would never be accepted by the normal society outside the gates, so he vowed to make the most of the life that had been granted him inside the monastery.

So, he pursued the knowledge of Shaolin Arts with unrivalled passion and, over the years, mastered over one thousand Shaolin Kung Fu forms and a very high level of Nei Kung training.

Grandmaster E told Sin that he had the good fortune of witnessing Su Kong's Nei Kung ability: one hot summer day, Su rubbed a dead fish all over his body then sat down and meditated. Soon the smell of fish attracted flies from everywhere, eager to feed on him.

But, Su Kong had other plans.

Witnesses heard a strange humming sound coming from his body and saw the hairs on his body stand up. They felt an electrical current in the air surrounding him as he became electrically charged.

When the first fly tried to land on him… ZZZT! It got ZAPPED like a bug light!

Soon "ZZZT, ZZT, ZZZT…!" sounds filled the air, as more and more flies got zapped. Within fifteen minutes, hundreds of flies lay dead in circle around Su Kong, burned to a crisp!

On another occasion, Su Kong walked through the courtyard in a heavy rain heading toward the dining room. The doors were not yet open for the meal and many of his fellow monks huddled under the porch roof out of the rain, waiting to get in.

They wouldn't let him join them under the dry canopy and forced him to stay out in the pouring rain.

"I prefer to be dry," he said quietly. He took a deep breath and exhaled forcefully, tensing all his muscles at once. Suddenly, all the moisture in his clothes shot off his body like bullets, striking several of the bullies hard enough to make them cry out in alarm! It hit the dining chamber door hard enough to chip paint!

But his most legendary feat was the use of his superhuman senses to save the lives of an entire Imperial delegation.

Rebellion was sweeping the land, threatening the reign of Emperor Quangxu of the Qing Dynasty. Su Kong, by then a master well-respected for his wisdom and sharp understanding, as well as his legendary Kung Fu skills, was commissioned by the Emperor to meet a contingent of high-ranking rebel leaders who had been fomenting rebellion against him in a last-ditch attempt to negotiate a peace settlement with them.

This top-secret meeting took place in an out-of-the-way house owned by one of the rebel leaders. When Su Kong entered the Hall, the twelve rebel leaders were already waiting for him, arranged around a long table in the middle of the room.

As he approached the table, the rebels stood up and bowed to him to show respect.

Everything looked fine, but Su Kong paused, his senses suddenly alert to danger. Something had triggered his awareness and set off alarm bells, but nothing seemed amiss. So he politely bowed back to repay their respect in kind. He moved to take his place in the chair reserved for him, where a knife, bowl and chopsticks had been placed in readiness for the meal.

In a blur of motion too fast to follow, he snatched up the knife from the table and hurled it at the ceiling! The others leapt up, fearing treachery, then gasped in shock as a body tumbled down from the rafters and crashed onto the table!

They later discovered that it was a Ninja assassin sent by the powerful Empress Dowager Cixi, the Emperor's aunt and regent who was secretly plotting to overthrow him.

How had Su Kong noticed the Ninja's lurking presence, when twelve other, highly-trained warriors had not?

He had heard *thirteen* people breathing, when only twelve were in the room!

So it was that his special Nei Kung skills enabled a humble priest to save the day.

Sin was so entranced by the story that he felt transported to another world! As the story ended, so did Sin's aches and pains. He felt rejuvenated and ready to take on any other grueling tasks that Grandmaster E threw his way.

16
-
BELT LEVELS

GRANDMASTER E HAD MASTERED MANY OF the Shaolin Arts and Nei Kung training. For his own students, Grandmaster E organized them into different levels to make them easier to learn and enhance the student's sense of accomplishment. As was customary, for each level of mastery, he assigned a color belt to denote a student's achievement and proficiency in the Arts.

When a prospective student passed the screening test and was accepted as a beginner, he would be given a white belt. He would then be taught the arts of self-defense and some simple forms.

A form was created over the years by compiling various fighting techniques into a set. For instance, a simple beginner's form might be comprised of twenty-four relatively simple fighting moves and techniques. And though not difficult for advanced masters, even the simple techniques would be difficult for new students to master as they learned the best applications for each move.

More advanced forms might consist of hundreds of fighting

techniques. But as a beginner, students start by learning short forms that consisted of only a few moves. Students typically learn ten of these short forms. Then each student would begin learning ten basic *sparring techniques*.

As each student progressed in the study of self-defense, learned the sparring techniques and martial arts forms, they had only to pass the test to become a *yellow belt*.

At the yellow belt level, students began to study animal forms, like the popular Tiger form. Also, one simple weapon, like a staff, was introduced.

After mastering more self-defense techniques, more sparring and fighting techniques, plus five more short forms, bringing their total form count to fifteen forms, the student was ready to pass the next test to become a *blue belt*.

At the blue belt level, other animal forms, such as the Eagle would be introduced, along with another weapon, such as *nunchaku*. The student also had to master seven more short forms – for a total of twenty-two forms, plus five more sparring techniques.

Once he passed the test, he would become a *green* belt.

At the green belt level, he might be introduced to a *Praying Mantis* form, along with another weapon such as the *short stick*. He must master another eight short forms to make at total of thirty and five more sparring techniques and fighting aspects for a total of twenty.

Then he was ready to pass the test to become a 3rd-degree brown belt.

At the brown belt level, students are required to learn three White Crane forms, including: White Crane Spreads its Wings, White Crane Spins its Wing and White Crane Spins its Legs. Another weapon form is added, usually the broadsword, plus a more in-depth study of sparring and the Iron Man form called, San He or Three Unity must be mastered.

At this point a beginning level of Nei Kung Meditation, called Hou Tien Chi or Breath of Yesterday, is also introduced. Nei Kung students will also be taught Yang Chi (loosely translated as Positive Circulation of Chi breathing technique). The main objective of this level of Nei Kung training is to make the body strong and immune to sickness. When students become proficient in all these, they are ready to pass the test to become a 2nd degree brown belt.

As a 2nd degree brown belt, the student will learn three Hawk forms: The Hawk Descends from Heaven, The Hawk Spread Its Feathers, and The Dance of The Hawks.

Two new weapons will be introduced, plus *The Sai* form and *The Sea Dragon Cane* form. In *Nei Kung,* students will learn the *Yin Chi* or *Negative Circulation Of Chi* breathing technique. The main objective of this technique is to make a person more alert and able to concentrate harder when he works his mind. This opens the mind more readily to new, positive things and new knowledge and information.

When they have mastered all that, plus a more in-depth study of sparring, the student is ready to pass the test to become a *1st degree brown belt.*

At this level, the student will learn three of the Black Tiger forms: *Mount Ching Kang Tiger, Five Directional Tiger Palm, and Tiger Connecting Fist.* Plus, they must master another staff form and a long weapon called, *General Kwan Kung's Knife,* plus the *Yin Yang* Chi or *Negative and Positive Chi breathing* technique.

After more a in-depth study of sparring and fighting aspects and when student has become proficient at all these elements, he is ready to pass the test and become a *1st degree black belt.*

The requirements climb exponentially for each successive level of *black belt* testing. It may not be for the faint of heart, but the pursuit of mastery in martial arts is an incredibly rich and powerful tradition that can change anyone's life for the better.

17
-
SNAP, WHITE CRANE & TIGER

THE YEARS FLOWED QUICKLY PAST AND by the time he was eleven, Sin had survived Grandmaster E's tough and grueling training to become a 2nd-degree brown belt. He had perfected the three White Crane forms and was concentrating on the three *Hawk* Forms.

One day, while Sin was punching a sand bag after all the other students had left, he was so absorbed in his training, he was not aware that Grandmaster E had crept up behind him to watch.

Suddenly, the Master snapped a handkerchief at Sin's leg, causing him to leap back with a yelp of pain. Sin looked at the handkerchief, shocked. Who knew a soft cloth handkerchief could hurt so much?

Grandmaster E admonished him, "Snap! Snap! That is the *secret* to destroying your opponent! A harmless handkerchief becomes a deadly weapon when I *snap* it with sufficient force."

To spark Sin's interest, Grandmaster E told him the story of Wang Pang Fu, a gifted circus performer and brilliant fighter....

"When I was about your age, the world famous Hong Kong Acrobat Circus was in town. Everyone was excited and wanted to see them and I was fortunate enough to get a ticket. One performer in particular impressed me greatly - Wang Pang Fu – he really understood the power of the *Snap*.

Wearing only a thin pair of silk trousers, Wang picked up a staff and began twirling it faster than the eye could see! He twirled it so fast, it formed a shield around his body. The Master of Ceremonies invited the entire audience to try to hit him with their peanuts. The stadium went wild as everyone shouted and hurled handfuls of peanuts at him, trying to breach his shield.

Then the announcer commanded them to stop and Wang stopped twirling his staff, they saw an entire ring of peanuts piled around Wang … and not one peanut had made it inside the ring!

Next, stagehands manacled Wang's arms and legs with four thick chains, which they locked to four large carriages drawn by four powerful steeds. The Announcer snapped his whip over their rumps and the four horses charged off at top speed in the four directions of the compass!

The audience gasped! Wang would be torn apart in seconds!

But the powerful acrobat was so fit and powerfully-muscled, he accomplished what no man had done before: he held four charging horses in place without being torn to pieces!

For his next feat, Wang's assistants littered the stage with brittle shards of broken glass and, with a flourish, Wang lay down on them! But he didn't stop there – next his assistants placed a thick board on his stomach, and before the audience knew what was happening, one of the horse-drawn carriages, packed with a dozen people, raced right at him!

Everyone gasped! The daring performer would be crushed to death before their very eyes! The whole theater watched in fascinated horror as the horse and carriage trampled over his prone body! A shocked silence blanketed the theater.

Just when they were sure Wang would never get up again, the board flew into the air and he leapt to his feet, completely unscathed, and raised his arms over his head in victory!

The audience went wild, cheering his amazing feats!

When Wang's astonishing performance was almost over, out of nowhere, a huge white man burst out onto the stage! He was blonde, blue-eyed, and as big as a mountain. Two stocky helpers struggled in behind him carrying a massive Roman shield.

"I am Stanley Stromberg," he roared, seizing the shield and beating his chest with it, "The Strongest Man in the World!"

He strutted across the stage and ridiculed Wang's daring feats, dismissing them as *cheap tricks!* Then he challenged Wang to a bare-knuckled duel to see who really was the strongest. They would trade punches and the last man standing could justly claim the title as the "Strongest Man in the World!"

Though he felt it was beneath him, Wang saw no honorable way to refuse the foreigner's rude challenge. He gravely accepted, then turned to the audience and informed them that he would demonstrate the superiority of Chinese Kung Fu, by allowing the *Kwai Lau* (the

Foreign Devil) to punch him three times first before he punched back. But when he *did* retaliate, with one punch, he would send him back to *hell* where he came from!

The Brit and the Chinaman, two of the strongest men in the world, faced each other.

Stanley, using the British fighting style, made small circles with his fists to stimulate the energy to flow from his body into his fist.

Wang, on the other hand, focused inward, using his training to concentrate his will and activate powerful internal meridians to marshal his *Chi* to protect him. He stood erect, fearlessly facing his opponent, ready to receive his mighty blow.

Stanley drew back his massive fist and slammed it into Wang's chest! A mighty impact took place! But instead of striking Wang down, he stood unmoving, while the recoil from Stanley's blow hurled the British fighter back several yards!

Stanley was stunned! What on earth had just happened? He was the Strongest Man in the World! Yet, how could this little Chinaman force him backwards without raising a finger? Impossible!

Unable to believe his own eyes, Stanley punched Wang again – with the same results! He was confused and furious. Desperate not to lose to a man half his size, he decided to try a more devious tactic…

For his last punch, he cagily waited until Wang had turned to the cheering crowd and raised his arms triumphantly, then sucker-punched him in his solar plexus with all his might!

Stanley's blow caught Wang unprepared, and hit him with devastating impact! Blood surged into his throat, but he clamped his mouth shut and kept it in.

As fast as lightning, Wang countered and punched Stanley in his solar plexus as well, using a *snap punch* so fast it could not be seen by the naked eye.

Stanley never saw it coming. He vomited a fountain of blood onto the stage and fell rigid to the ground. He died on impact, never to rise again!

The crowd fell silent in awe, trying to make sense of what had just happened.

Wang, the last man standing, staggered off the stage and made it back to his room. He sank into a deep meditation, trying to heal himself, but too much damage had been done.

Wang passed quietly away, seated in the lotus position, with a gentle smile on his face, knowing he had upheld the honor of his people and died possessing the undisputed title of "The Strongest Man in the World."

Grandmaster E summed up his story lesson, "When you punch someone without a snap, the force that you deliver into him will bounce back through your hand as a reaction force. This reaction force will cause both of you to be pushed apart. Only 20 percent of your force is delivered to your opponent, while the other 80 percent recoils against you and goes to *waste*. But, when you *snap* your punches back, your hand will not be there to receive the reaction force, and 100% of the force of your punch goes into your opponent where it belongs."

Sin grasped the concept immediately and changed his punches to include snaps from then on. Grandmaster E stood and watched him for a while until Sin began to feel more comfortable with the snaps.

Then Grandmaster E directed him to practice his kicks on the sandbag using the same snap technique and Sin happily did as instructed.

Eventually, Sin exhausted himself, so he quit the sandbag training, and was about to head home, when Grandmaster E asked him to do one more exercise.

The Grandmaster positioned Sin in a horse-stance, a posture in which the knees are slightly bent and aligned with the shoulders. He laid a 25-pound rice bag on each of Sin's thighs then raised his palms in front of Sin's face and instructed him to use the back of his finger tips to strike the palms as if they were an opponent's face.

Half an hour later, Sin's uniform was drenched in sweat and he was ready to collapse from exhaustion. Grandmaster E dropped his hands, nodded in satisfaction, and removed the rice bags.

"This was white crane finger strike training combined with tiger leg stance training, and that is a good beginning. It is vitally important to develop your finger *strength* using this White Crane training so that they become an iron weapon to use to strike your opponent's eyes and incapacitate him."

But Grandmaster E still wasn't finished with Sin. After a quick break, he had Sin lean against the back wall at an angle with just his fingertips supporting all his body weight.

Sin knew this would be good for his finger-strength training, but what a price to pay! The pain in his fingers was excruciating - every fiber in his being begged him to stop this excessive training and go home to a nice quiet dinner!

But he managed to resist the temptation to give up.

His fingers were still numb when Master E strapped one-pound wrist weights on each of Sin's wrists and set the twenty-five pound bags of rice back on each of his thighs and had him repeat the combined White Crane and Tiger training.

When Sin's entire body was convulsing in pain and he was on the verge of collapse, Grandmaster E finally relented, removed the bags and helped him stand up.

Sin thought his training was done for the day, but Grandmaster E had *one* more lesson to squeeze out of him. "Show me some kicks and punches, Sin."

Worn out, Sin managed to throw a few weak kicks and punches, but was interrupted by Grandmaster E.

"No, no, you are doing it all wrong! You must put your whole body into it."

He demonstrated how to use his back and hip to drive the punches and kicks home with maximum strength.

Sin tried several times, but was not able to imitate his movements. Seeing this, Grandmaster E picked up a chopstick and stabbed Sin in the arm with it. Though it didn't really hurt, it startled Sin.

But then, Grandmaster E fastened the chopstick to a piece of wood and before Sin could react, he hammered Sin's arm with the chopstick on the wood. This time, a sharp pain shot through Sin's arm, and he jumped and cried out.

"You see?" Grandmaster E exclaimed, "Using your arms and legs alone is like poking at someone with a single chopstick. Not effective. But, if you put your whole body into it, it is like fastening the chopstick to that piece of wood. You have much more force and can do many times the damage."

That put it all in perspective, forcing Sin to realize the importance of making this key change, and from that point on, Grandmaster E drilled him until it became habit.

While Sin shook his agonized hands and legs, trying to get enough control of them so he could make it home, his master instructed him that he must do the White Crane finger-strength training every day from now on and practice his snap and punch technique as well.

After Sin had left for the evening, Grandmaster E lit up his pipe, took a puff and sank into contemplation.

He never thought young Sin would be so resilient and master everything he threw at him. Who was his great–great-great grandfather again? A smile spread across Grandmaster E's face as he remembered Sin's gifted forebear had become the greatest Kung Fu fighter in all China before he died.

Later that night, Sin tossed and turned in his bed, every muscle in his body on fire. Finally he fell into an exhausted asleep and had a strange dream.

In his dream, a beautiful, young lady was angrily kicking and punching a rough, wooden dummy, which had a face painted to look like a middle-aged man.

With each kick and punch, she screamed, "Die, you evil bastard!"

Sin woke up in a panic. He couldn't seem to get her image out of his mind. It was so real! It was as if he could touch her - as if he had seen this scene before.

The next morning, Sin was in the middle of an essay exam at school, when his hands started to go into spasms and he could no longer hold his pen properly. He resorted to biting his fingers to loosen up the muscles, but he had to finish the essay pretty quickly and didn't think he answered well.

When class was over and everyone got up to turn in their essays, Sin's legs also began to tremble uncontrollably when he tried to put weight on them! With enormous determination, he managed to wobble up to the teacher and hand in his paper.

The teacher gave Sin a funny look and asked if he were all right.

"Fine, fine," he reassured her, but as soon as she left the room, tears rolled down his cheeks as he fought back the pain that racked his body.

This was to become the pattern of Sin's life for many years to come.

18
-
FIELD EXPERIENCE

ONE NIGHT, IN HIS DREAM, SIN found himself in a dark and crowded funeral parlor. As he walked down the aisle towards the casket, Sin passed by rows of grieving people, their faces unrecognizable, shrouded in mist. They all stared at him as he approached the dreaded spot where the open casket lay.

Inside, lay a beautiful young girl.

Sin looked at the girl, but did not recognized her. Just as he was wondering who she was, suddenly a strange young man, also dead, appeared lying next to the dead girl!

With his peripheral vision, Sin noticed a young girl standing next to him, mourning the passing of the young man.

Sin turned to look at the girl just as she looked at him. This startled them both and they, cried out in unison, "Who are you?"

Sin awoke in a sweat. He had no idea who the dead girl was, nor the dead man lying beside her, nor the pretty girl who mourned the dead man, but something told him they would play a significant part in his life.

So Sin lay awake and contemplated the dream for a while. Soon he fell asleep again and slipped back into his dream, and again saw the girl that had been standing next to him at the funeral.

In Sin's dream, the young woman he'd seen earlier was enjoying a savory breakfast in a lovely, Sechuan-style garden sitting with an elegant older lady dressed in exquisite silks. Her mother.

The lady raised her delicate teacup, "Mother," she said, "Last night I had a strange dream. I dreamt I was crying in front of a casket, mourning the death of a young scholar I'd never met before. Suddenly a beautiful young girl, with cold marble skin appeared in the casket next to him!

Hua, the young woman, hugged her arms around herself, as if feeling the chill of death. "I heard someone crying. I turned and saw a young man dressed in strange clothing, crying over the beautiful young woman. It sounds foolish, but I-I think he was from the *future.*" She glanced at her mother, "What do you think it means, Mother?" Her mother looked thoughtful, "I don't know, My Sweet. But I believe our minds can travel through time. Maybe you did catch a glimpse of the future."

The older woman paused and shot her daughter a nervous look.

"My Dear, I know it is an uncomfortable subject, but your father has asked me to talk to you about marriage. Ever since you were fifteen years old, you attracted suitors from far and wide to ask for your hand in marriage. But you have turned every one of them down. You said none of them passed your 'test'. But Daughter, you are one of those rare natural geniuses who can do anything – from poetry to Kung Fu."

Hua modestly shook her head.

"And what has come from your exacting standards? Nothing! To this day, I have never seen a man to match you, and at eighteen, you are still unmarried! Your father is beside himself and begs you to lower your standards ever so slightly so you can settle down with a rich, handsome and able suitor before it's too late!"

Hua shrugged uncomfortably, feeling pressured. "Please, Mother, I don't feel like talking about it today. Can't we just enjoy the gorgeous scenery?"

She stood and walked down a garden path, trailing her hand along the colorful blooms.

Her mother flapped her hand at her retreating back and muttered, "Stubborn girl."

The following day, after her mother had left, Hua took a ride in her carriage through a little valley to enjoy the fresh country air and the glimmering rice paddies on the valley floor. As her carriage approached the rice fields, she saw a young farmer reclining under a shady tree, reading a book! This was a very odd thing for a farmer to be doing in the middle of the workday. She looked more closely at him and something about him attracted her interest. She craned her neck to get a better look at him.

What an odd place to find a scholar, she mused.

Although the man was dressed in worn robes, she could tell there was something refined and educated about him that marked him as a scholar, rather than a farmer. Yet, his body was trim and fit from tending the rice paddies and his hands rough from manual labor. She found herself curious about a man of the soil who clearly loved to learn. Wasn't there something familiar about him?

The man didn't notice her carriage approaching. When she drew abreast of him, Hua ordered her driver to stop. Only when she had gathered her silk robes about her and descended from the carriage on slippered feet to stand before him, did he snap out of his reverie. His eyes flew wide in astonishment to find a beautiful, aristocratic young lady standing before him, dressed in regal robes. Gathering his wits, he bowed low and sputtered out a greeting, "My lady."

Hua regarded him intently, mesmerized by his warm, intelligent eyes. She collected her thoughts, "I-I saw you reading... Er, I too love to read. May I?" she asked, gesturing toward the tree where he was sitting .

"Please!" he agreed, hastily brushing crumbs from his meal off the grass beside him.

Hua sank gracefully down beside him and, feeling slightly nervous, looked at the book in his hand. "What are you reading?"

Before he had chance to respond, she reached out and playfully pulled the book from his hand and turned it to see the cover. "Ah yes, Su Tung Po. A very good poet. Did you know he was the one who suggested that Sung Emperor build West Lake in Hangzhou?"

The scholar was surprised at both her boldness and her knowledge. "N-No, I did not know that. How did he persuade the Emperor to do that?"

Hua chuckled, amused, "Oh, it's scandalous, he had an affair with the Empress and she was so in love with him, she agreed to persuade her husband to build the West Lake."

The scholar was a little shocked at her openness. "Oh...," he faltered.

Hua looked up at him from under her lashes, "Startled, she gets up, looks back with longing no one sees..." She looked at him expectantly. Her companion looked back at her in confusion. *What could she mean? Was she trying to seduce him?* Suddenly, embarrassed, he realized she was quoting one of Su Tung Po's poems!

"And will not settle on any of the cold branches along the chill and lonely beach," he replied with a faint blush, quoting the next line.
She smiled. "I roam through ancient realms, absurdly moved, turn gray too soon..."

He smiled back, "A man's life passes like a dream... pour out a cup then, to the river and the moon."
Time flew by as they amused themselves, trading quote for quote. Eventually, Hua ran out of Su Tung Po's poems, so she switched to Li Bai, a revered poet of the Tang dynasty.
"Before my bed, the moon is shining bright—"

The scholar's eyes rounded, startled, then he effortlessly recited the next line, "I think that it is frost upon the ground..."
The young man seemed to know Li Bai's poems better than she did! Before a word or two escaped her lips, he would finish the poem. What kind of farmer could do that?

"I raise my head and look at the bright moon..."
"I lower my head and think of home."
The poem complete, they beamed at each other, unguardedly, and a special moment passed between them.
Something about the way he'd recite those well-loved words stirred her memory... Suddenly her face lit up and she clapped her hands in delight, staring at him.
"Little Li Bai! It's you, isn't it? I wore through the soles of my shoes searching the length and breadth of China for you! Yet here you were the whole time, right under my nose!"

Ever since she was a young girl, she had heard the story of 'Little Li Bai' from her tutors. Little Li Bai was a child prodigy who could recite every poem of his namesake, Old Li Bai, when he was only four years-old. People thought he was the *reincarnation* of Li Bai, hence the name.

He was a sensation every time he performed and by the time he was twelve he became a big celebrity who travelled all over the country performing the poetry of Li Bai and other famous poets.

By the time he reached his twenties, his lifestyle had become a luxurious and decadent one, full of dancing girls and wine.

One day, without warning, he simply disappeared. How or why, no one knew. And he was never heard from again. Some said he was tired of the fast life, while others thought he had been secretly murdered by a jealous husband.

Hua stared at the handsome man before her and continued in a rush, confessionally, "I-I developed a little girl's crush on him. I fantasized that I would find Little Li Bai someday. My parents were well off and travelled a lot, so everywhere we went, I would ask everyone if they had seen him. For six long years I looked and looked...and found nothing."

Hua stopped to catch her breath and looked sideways at the scholar. His expression was enigmatic.

"Well?" she asked, dying to know, "Have I fulfilled my quest? Are you Little Li Bai?"

Never taking his eyes off her face, the scholar stood up. And bowed. "Not-so-little Li Bai, at your service, my lady."

Hua crowed with delight! She leapt to her feet up and returned his bow, ecstatic. "And I am Pai Hua, Good Sir."

"Ah, '*White Flower*'," he mused, rolling the sound of her name on his tongue. "A beautiful name. White is the symbol of purity, while the flower is the essence of beauty."

He gazed at her lovely, animated face, "How appropriate."

Hua blushed, suddenly shy. "We both share white or purity in our name. Perhaps there is a special meaning there."

Li Bai nodded in agreement. "In your case, the purity remains, but in mine, after a dissipated life of dancing girls and too much wine, there is little still 'pure' about me."

Hua shook her head, agitated, "No, no! I can see your spirit – and it remains pure and good. Why else would you have come here in nature, away from the worldly temptations of riches and fame?"

Li Bai gave a bitter laugh, "I was 18 years old and had the world at my feet. Fame, money, position, anything I wanted, I could have. But soon, the endless procession of wine and women and meaningless evenings with empty-headed officials and sycophants left me wondering if *this superficial existence* was all there was to life? Surely there is something important I have yet to discover?

Hua regarded him, wide-eyed, unconsciously nodding in agreement. "With the wealth I had amassed, I decided to travel the length and breadth of China to seek a more meaningful life - but not as the famous Li Bai. As a nobody. So, I dressed in inexpensive robes and took to the road anoymously..."

They were quiet for awhile, sharing the moment.

Li stirred and continued, "Then three months ago, just as I was running out of money, I, er, saw a sign asking for a tenant farmer to farm this land, and I knew that I was 'home'. So, for the time being at least, I am a farmer, and I find that this simple, honorable way of life agrees with me. I till the soil, I eat, I read and I sleep. That has been enough for me...."

He cocked his head to shoot a glance at Hua and said under his breath, "Until now..."

Hua dimpled and busied herself with straightening her already perfect robe unnecessarily. Suddenly Li's stomach growled and they both laughed, breaking the tension.

"Er, it is apparently time for lunch, Milady. Would you do me the honor of sharing my humble meal?"

Hua nodded and Li pulled his lunch basket toward him and began setting the contents out on the grass beside them.

"Nowadays, I eat mainly vegetables, nothing fancy, but I did learn how to cook them from the very best chef in China."

He was looking vainly for another pair of chopsticks, but had none. Hua pulled a set out of a pocket in her robe.

"I always carry my own chopsticks. They are made of silver, so I can detect if my food has been poisoned or not. They turn green if it is poisoned."

Lee shook his head ruefully, "I used to have someone taste my food before I ate it to check for poison. But that was ten years ago, when I lived a life of luxury and might be a target for such enmity and envy."

Ten years ago? Hua did a little mental arithmetic and concluded that Li Bai must be about twenty-eight years old, exactly ten years her senior. Perfect! She beamed at him and began sharing his tasty meal. They were both astonished to find the meal was the most delicious meal they ever tasted! For Hua, that could have been attributed to her joy at finding her Little Li Bai and for Li Bai, that could have been because he was sharing it with the most beautiful, intelligent women he had ever met. And though the lunch he brought would normally have served as his dinner as well, today he shared it all to the last bite with the amazing woman beside him.

When they had eaten their fill, Hua thanked her host for the wonderful meal and praised him over and over again for his culinary skill. Lee was extremely pleased and proud that his guest had enjoyed his cooking that much.

When the sun was slanting low in the sky and it was clearly time for Hua to leave, they stood awkwardly near her carriage, not wanting this magical day to end.

Suddenly Hua had a strange notion: "I've never been a farmer before, would you mind if I joined you as an apprentice?"

Li chuckled, envisioning this beautiful lady, dressed in the finest silks, standing up to her knees in the mud with him. But he answered solemnly, "As you wish, my lady."

She beamed at him, "Then I will see you tomorrow, Sir, and my apprenticeship shall begin in earnest." As her carriage pulled away, she turned and waved to Li with a sweet smile.

Li waved back, hardly daring to believe what was happening. All these years he had been searching for the meaning of life and he wondered if he just had a taste of it today?

Though Li Bai had barely dared to hope, the next day as he rose at dawn to tend his rice paddies, Hua returned.

When she alighted from her carriage, he saw that she had exchanged her fine robes for simple homespun clothes more suitable for farm work. And she was carrying a cloth-wrapped package as if it was full of precious gems.

Li came to greet her. She held the bundle out to him shyly and he took it, overcome with curiosity. He unwrapped it and found precious books inside! Books by the famous social critic, Li Ping. One of them told the story of Su Tung Po, the Empress's secret lover, who had gotten her to persuade the Emperor to build the famous West Lake of Hangzhou. But, eventually, Li Ping had become such a blatant critic of the ruling class that even the Empress could not protect him and he had to go into hiding to escape imprisonment or worse.

Li Bai thumbed through his book that criticized the ruling class for its excesses, "What would a high-born noblewoman like yourself see in these books?"

Hua cocked her head, giving his question some thought, "I think that there is a brutal truth to what he says about the unfairness of our society, where the rich can use their wealth corruptly to bend the laws to their will. What do you think?"

Li Bai nodded, "That was exactly what drove me to remove myself from society years ago. All around me, I saw corruption and abuse. Yet, when I pleaded with the noblemen, royals, and high-ranking officials who flocked around me to reform the system, none of them wanted to have anything to do with it. They were all too comfortable in their own, well-feathered nest to give a thought to the many others less fortunate than themselves! At last, when I saw I was getting nowhere, I couldn't stand it any longer and took myself away."

Hua was moved by Li's words. She knew then that he was a genuinely righteous man and silently thanked the gods above for leading her to him.

They set the books aside to look at after their working day was over, and Li led her into the rice paddy. She giggled in surprise when she took her first step into the shimmering water and the warm mud squished up between her toes!

They worked side by side all day, laughing, talking and telling each their life experiences. She would burst into delighted laughter when Li told her stories about the funny things that happened to him along the way, and Li would double over in hysterics at the witty tales she recounted of the silly antics the nobility got up to.

Before they knew it, it was time for their lunch, and Hua proudly told him that this time she had made lunch. She pulled out the big basket of gourmet foods she had made with her own hands. Li was astonished at what a good cook she was and his heart grew even fonder.

After lunch, they worked until sunset and, again, found it difficult to part from each other as they reluctantly said goodbye. Li examined his feelings and realized he had never felt this way about any other woman. So, on Hua's next visit, he took her to see his parents, anxious to see what they thought.

On the way there, he confessed that he hadn't been completely honest with her when he'd told her that he'd seen a wanted sign for a tenant farmer. In fact, it was his parent's farm and, overcome with homesickness, he had finally returned home after ten years of wandering.

Hua nodded, accepting his apology, though she was surprised to learn his parents were still alive, since he had never spoken of them. But, she was glad he had been able to return to a place he was loved for who he was.

When they arrived at Li's parents house, Hua looked around curiously. The house was large and roomy with high ceilings criss-crossed by rough wooden beams. The walls were hung with rice-paper scrolls depicting famous scenes of China and the main room was furnished with hand-carved, black shellac furniture that glowed in the firelight. Not as elegant and expensive as her parent's house, but it was pleasant, well-appointed and well-cared for.

Li's parents were delighted to meet Hua. Li had been talking about her non-stop about how beautiful, how smart, and how educated she was, and now they could see for themselves that their son had not been exaggerating. If anything she was even more beautiful than they imagined. They were bursting with happiness for their son!

Though Li's parents were farmers, they were relatively well-to-do and Hua could tell they were highly-educated. They were also excellent hosts and offered her a generous selection of dishes and dim sum, a custom usually limited to the more affluent families.

In spite of everyone's initial nervousness, they all hit it off and ended up talking animatedly for hours. Everyone had a lovely time and Hua left later that night feeling like she had a second family.

From then on, Hua came to see Li every day and their friendship slowly turned into love. Every day they enjoyed each other's company and shared more and more of their life stories and every night when they parted, they couldn't wait to see each other the next day.

One day, it struck Hua that she had finally found her one true love - without having to put him through the elaborate and strenuous testing regimen as she had done with all her other, unwanted suitors. With Li, the feeling in her heart was the only test she needed and he had passed with flying colors.

Li also realized he had found what he had been missing in all those long years of traveling. His questions about the meaning of life had been answered... and the answer was: *Love.*

Neither one of them had worked up the courage to talk of their feelings or marriage, but it was clear from how they comported themselves that they would never have eyes for anyone else again.

So it came as a shock when Hua returned home to her parent's house one day after seeing Li and found her father waiting to talk to her in their spacious living room about another suitor!

She stepped into the room with its familiar walls, decorated with expensive, multi-colored tiles of jade and lined with antique showcases brimming with exquisite figurines made of the highest quality jadeite. Her eyes flew to her father's face, because he was practically dancing with excitement.

"Guess what suitor came to pay his respects to you today? None other than Master Siung, the Governor's eldest son! Such a prominent, wealthy family. And what a handsome and educated young man he is! And a martial arts master as well! He told us he has been heralded far and wide for his scholastic achievements and renowned as one of the best Kung Fu fighters in all of China! His teacher, Master Tasu, is well-known in the Chiang Pu and Kung Fu community. He knows he must best you in Kung Fu, and I dare say, from the look of him, he probably can. So at last, my beloved daughter, here is a match worthy of you! Isn't it wonderful?"

Hua was stunned. A month ago, before she met Li, this would indeed have been exciting news. But now that Li had stolen her heart, this was a serious problem.

She didn't dare blurt out she'd fallen in love for a farmer's son, no matter how famous 'Little Li Bai' used to be. So reluctantly, she stalled for time until she could figure out what to do. She told her father she hadn't trained in Kung Fu in over a month and wanted to be in tip top form before she accepted the Governor's son's challenge. Her father hid his disappointment that she didn't seem more eager, but also understood that her and the family's honor was at stake. She had built her reputation on her skill as a martial artist and would protect it until the bitter end.

He nodded his assent, "But don't take too long, my Dear. We don't want such an esteemed young man to lose interest."

Hua nodded. Her stomach did a few flip-flops. She bowed her head to her father and hurried off to her room.

That night, Hua tossed and turned, but sleep eluded her. What was she to do?

She could try to persuade her parents to agree with her choice, because, although it is not as glamorous as having the Governor's son as an in-law, someone as famous as Li Bai was still very honorable.

But before she could do that, she needed to know if Li Bai would be willing to rejoin society and move in the circles that she and her parents moved in.

She didn't know if she could convince Li Bai that it was time for him to come back to society and all the demands and constraints and hypocrisies that would entail. Even if she could convince him, it would take time, and time was the one thing she didn't have.

Hua chewed her lip, thinking. Why couldn't she just run away with Li Bai? She had saved a lot of money over the years and was a wealthy woman in her own right. Each suitor had been required to pay her family a handsome fee to qualify to be tested by Hua and her parents had given it all to her. With her savings, she and Li Bai could afford to travel together for years and that would gave her the time it might take to convince him to return to her parent's social sphere.

But, before she could do that, she needed to know if Li Bai even wanted to marry her! Did he feel the same way about her as she did about him? She couldn't tell and he certainly hadn't proposed yet!

When the dawn spread across the horizon, Hua leapt out of bed, threw on some clothes and quickly rode her favorite horse to Li's house. Once there, she flung herself off and pounded on the door.

Li Bai opened the door, shocked to see Hua in such an agitated state. "My Lady... whaa--?"

"Oh Li, I have so much to tell you!"

He quickly ushered her into the living room where his parents were sitting, and she blurted out the whole story to them all, starting at the very beginning, telling how, reluctant to marry, she had set a difficult challenge for every suitor to dissuade them, and had bested them all. Listening to Hua's story - how she had defeated one suitor after another since she was fifteen years old - only increased Li's respect for her. And when she told them of the Governor's son's pursuit of her hand, he felt his blood grow heated.

Li's parents looked at Li hesitantly, then asked what she thought the solution might be? Hua explained the two options that she'd come up with last night.

Li's parents turned to look at Lee, their eyebrows asking the question they respectfully chose not to ask out-loud.

Li sat back. If he understood Hua correctly, she seemed to be saying she would rather choose a faded old scholar, then accept the hand of the Governor's son!

Li's heart began to sing. He looked at Hua, sitting in his home with such grace and ease. How could he not have seen earlier how much he loved her? Ever since she had come into his life, he'd had a much happier outlook on life. And he wasn't about to lose that feeling – ever! He loved Hua and wanted to protect her, even if it put his own life at risk.

Li took a deep breath, "First, my lady Hua, I am honored that you would choose me over the Governor's son. I would love nothing better than to marry and spend the rest of my life with you!"

Hua blushed and gazed down at her hands clenched tightly in her lap, a relieved smile on her face. He loved her!

Li raised a cautious hand, "But, you must think it over *carefully*. Do you truly understand what it would mean to give up the wealth and privilege that the wife of the governor's son would enjoy? What can I give you that would compare with that?"

"There is no one in the world I would rather marry than you!" Hua burst out, standing up abruptly to punctuate the strength of her feelings.

They beamed at each other. Li's parents smiled indulgently and cleared their throats to bring the love-birds back to earth.

"I will go home and tell my parents," Hua said decisively. "And send the good news as soon as I can."

"But, don't get too excited yet," Li's father cautioned her, "It might not be as easy as you hope to convince your father. Expect an uphill battle. It is his duty to protect his daughter…"

Hua nodded, sobering slightly. Li walked her to the door and for the first time, shared a joyful kiss.

When Hua got home, she broke the news to her parents - she had fallen in love with the distinguished scholar, "Little Li Bai" and intended to marry him, not the Governor's son.

"I know Li is not as glamorous or wealthy as Siung, but I love him deeply and want to spend the rest of my life with him! I know we will be happy together and have a lot of darling grandchildren for you!"

She looked at her parents pleadingly, hoping for their understanding. Her mother smiled tentatively, with a sympathetic look on her face. Her father hesitated, deep in thought.

"My daughter, I want your happiness… But how can we put off the Governor's son now without causing grave offense? His family could do us much harm. Remember, you declared to the world that you would accept the hand of the worthiest challenger who defeated you. But, now you plan to reject only Siung? He would lose face completely!"

Hua looked striken. She couldn't put her family in danger.

"We must think of a convincing excuse for you to beg off the challenge. Perhaps we can put it around that you are ill and must go away to recover. That way Siung could save face. Give me a couple of days to put a plan in place."

Hua threw her arms around him. "Thank you, thank you, Dear Father, from the bottom of my heart! I hoped you would understand!"

That night, Hua tossed and turned and couldn't sleep. She tried to come up with a good excuse to tell Siung, and by daybreak, she thought she had an idea that might work.

Suppose her parents announced that their daughter had had enough of the lifestyle of the rich and famous and had decided to disappear into the world of Chiang Pu Kung Fu. She would write a letter to her parents to that effect, so no one would blame *them* for her eccentric behavior.

It was not uncommon for children of wealthy parents to run away from home and join the World of Chiang Pu, so no one would question it this time.

Meanwhile she and Little Li Bai would disappear far away and start a new life as husband and wife. Many years later when things had cooled down and the Governor's son had found another wife, they'd return with their children to visit. What a perfect plan!

Hua's mother was saddened at the prospect of Hua leaving them for many years, but her father saw the silver lining in Hua's proposal and readily agreed to the plan.

Hua hugged them both and whispered in her mother's ear, "Don't be sad Mom, I'll be back before you know it."

Her mother started to tremble and broke down in tears. Hua held her gently and wept with her.

Her father left the room and returned carrying a sack of gold. Hua told him it was not necessary, that she had plenty of money. But her father insisted that it be the only wedding present he would be able to give her, and in the end, she graciously accepted.

During all the commotion, unbeknownst to them, someone had been eavesdropping at the door.

Chang, a disgruntled family servant, had been listening from behind the jade-panel room divider. What shocking news! With a face reddened and pockmarked by a disfiguring birthmark, he had always been jealous of Hua's family's wealth, beauty and happiness.

Chang leered in excitement. The tables were about to turn and his employers' entire future would be in *his* hands! He could destroy them with a word in the ear of a certain party...! He felt a tinge of remorse - maybe he shouldn't hurt them, since they had given him a job when no one else would and always treated him well. But, the thought of the huge reward that the Governor's son would surely give him washed away any lingering trace of loyalty.

After Hua left to return to Li Bai's, Chang slithered slyly away unseen. Twenty minutes later, he was surreptitiously knocking at the door to the Governor's mansion. When the butler opened the door, he asked to speak with Siung, saying he had some very important information for him. Fifteen minutes later, Chang walked out of the Governor's house with a sack of gold.

Back at Li Bai's, Hua told him and his parents about the plan. They all agreed that it was a good plan and were excited for Li Bai and Hua's happy future together.

Hua told Li Bai they must be very vigilant and keep their plans a closely-guarded secret so no one would suspect a thing until they were long gone.

"How soon can you be ready, my love?" she asked Li Bai, impatient to be off to their new life together.

"I must finish a few things on the farm for my parents before I can leave, but I can finish them all and be ready to leave in three days time.

Hua beamed. "Wonderful! Then I will meet you in three days at the Lotus Garden in town. It's an out-of-the-way restaurant in a small town midway between your place and mine. We can slip away from there unseen."

Three days later, Hua said a long tearful goodbye to her mother, who couldn't stop crying. Her father gave her a loving hug and wished her all the happiness that life had to offer. He couldn't help shedding a tear himself as he watched his only child walk out his door to be wed without him in some far-flung place.

Hua had dressed in a comfortable Kung Fu outfit, and strapped a double-edged sword on her back. She took nothing with her but a few books, a few clothes and a trinket or two to remember her parents by. And two strong leather sacks heavy with gold. With such largess, she and Li Bai could start their new life together wherever they chose. Hau swung up onto her beautiful white horse and trotted out, leading another strong, black horse for Li Bai behind.

She took one last long look at the only home she had ever known and brushed a tear from her eye. She was elated, but saddened at the same time. Big changes bring with them big emotions...

She arrived at the Lotus Garden promptly at noon and tied her horses to the hitching pole outside, lugging the sacks of gold in with her. The restaurant was packed with people, but Li Pai was not there yet. She ordered some tea and waited. Two hours later, all the lunch customers were gone and there was still no sign of Li Bai.
Had he misunderstood her? Did he think they were supposed to meet here later in the day? Worried, but uncertain, she continued to wait. But, by four o'clock, when Li still had not shown up, Hua sensed something was terribly wrong.
She rushed out and galloped off to his place.

When she got there, it was already dark. She heard a terrible wailing coming from the house and her heart thundered in her chest in terror. She rushed to the house and pounded on the door. It was opened by Li's father, who looked at her sorrowfully, his eyes red from crying. There, in the middle of the living room, was an open casket. Li's mother was hunched over it, sobbing hysterically.

Hua's throat closed up. Her legs trembled as she approached it and she saw, to her horror, Li's body lying in it. Her legs buckled as she collapsed to the ground.

When she came to, she crawled to the coffin and broke down. She sobbed for hours. Li's father tried to console her, but to no avail. When she finally managed to dry her tears, she demanded to know what happened. Li's mother explained that Li Bai had gone that very morning to the Lotus Garden to arrange for a special private room to celebrate their coming marriage and to try some of their dishes to choose the perfect ones to please and impress her.

"He was gone for a long time and finally reappeared, but was so ill and weak that two of our neighbors had to support him to get him into the house. He spoke a few words to us, then lost consciousness as soon as we laid him on his bed. A few minutes later... he was gone." Li's mother took a ragged breath, "The neighbors said he'd told them he'd gotten food poisoning at the restaurant from one of the dishes he sampled."

"This was not accidental food poisoning!" Hua raged, "Someone *murdered* my dearest beloved! And I swear to you on my life, I will get to the bottom of this and whomever did this to him will rue the day he was ever *born*!"

Before she left, Hua told Li's parents that for their own safety, they must get out of town as soon as they could and disappear for awhile, because whoever did this to Li might come back to finish them off as well. Hua tried to press one of her two sacks of gold into Li's mother's hands, but she and her husband protested and would not accept it. Hua insisted, explaining that since they would have to leave this very day, they would have no time to sell their property. What would they live on? Seeing the wisdom in this, they reluctantly accepted and thanked her profusely, kowtowing to the ground over and over again. Unable to bear a single moment more in the house where she had spent such happy moments with Li and his family, Hua bid them a hasty, tearful goodbye and ran out the house.

She was mounting her horse when Li's mother ran out after her. "Wait! Wait! I am so sorry, dearest daughter, but I have something more to tell you. On his deathbed, Li Bai told us something else, but begged us *not to tell you*. But, for the love you bore my only son, I must tell you or regret it for the rest of my life."

She shuddered and continued, "At the restaurant, after eating, he felt ill almost immediately and knew something was seriously wrong. He doubled over in agony, holding his stomach, then collapsed to the floor. He said a large man with a big red birthmark on his face loomed over him and kicked him while he was down!"

Hua gasped! She recognized the man by his descriptio n- her father's head servant!

"The horrible man said to Li, 'Remember my face. I am the head servant for Hua's father and it was he who ordered me to poison you for daring to consort with his honorable daughter! She is meant for the Governor's son, not for the likes of you!' Then he kicked Li Pai again and spit on him before he left."

Hua's knees turned weak and she felt the ground spinning around her. Could it possibly be true? Could her own father have betrayed her so utterly and crushed any hope for happiness to try to force her into a loveless but prestigious marriage?

Her stomach heaved and she had to hold on to her horse for support, so intense were her emotions. When she straightened up, she was shaky and pale and thanked Li's mother for telling her the truth. As a parting gift, knowing her life had changed forever and that she would never see Li Bai's parents again, she gave the heartbroken woman the beautiful black stallion she had bought for Li Pai.

Then, shedding no more tears, she set her jaw in murderous determination and rode back to her parent's house.

Hua burst into the house and dragged Chang into the living room. He cowered at her feet, begging for mercy. She shouted angrily for her parents, demanding they come immediately. Her parents rushed into the room, shocked at her rude and inexplicable behavior, but they loved her and realized she must have a good reason to behave as she did.

Hua screamed at them, "Li Bai is dead! Dead!"

Hua's parents expressed genuine concern and tried to comfort Hua with a hug but Hua slapped their hands away in a rage. Her father was stunned by the look of hate in her eye and just stared at her, speechless with shock.

"And here is the swine who murdered him!" She threw Chang down on at her feet. He tried to scuttle away, begging for mercy. She slammed him to the floor with her foot. "Didn't you?" She applied more pressure until he squirmed in agony, "DIDN'T YOU?"

Chang buckled and nodded his head in admission, as he was cowering away from her.

"And you told Li Bai that you did so on the order of my father! Is that true?"

Chang nodded his head vigorously, hoping to shift the blame to her father and thus save his own life.

Hua's father recoiled in surprise and indignation. "No! How could you think-!"

Hua refused to listen, " SIT DOWN!" she screamed!

Her father was so shocked and feared she might fly into a fit that could stop her heart, so he sat.

"But, dearest daughter, I assure you- "

Hua snapped her head around in time to see Chang slither from the room. Ignoring her father's protests, she ran after Chang, determined to grind his bones to powder, but she was met at the door to the kitchen by a tall stranger holding a dagger in each hand.

He flew at her, slicing for her throat! Only her championship reflexes saved her life, as she dodged away from the flickering blade.

Li's parents recoiled in horror, but were helpless to intervene, as the fighting skills of Hua and her attacker were far beyond anything they could match.

Her attacker was good – very good – but Hua was better. It took her awhile to defeat and kill him and, by that time, Chang had fled.

Hua returned to the living room to confront her parents. Her father stood to face her, to plead his innocence of this heinous crime, but she was too enraged to listen.

Hua used her *Nei Kung speed* training to cross the room to her father's side in a split second and deliver a brutal series of crushing blows to vital acupuncture points.

Paralyzed, he regarded her in open-mouthed horror as he buckled to the floor. He began to quiver, shake and spasm violently. His fingers curled into rigid claws, his neck twisted to the side, and his back became crippled and bent.

Her mother screamed and hurled herself between her vengeful daughter and her husband. "Stop, no! NO! you mustn't – he—"

"How could you defend a man who would destroy the happiness of his own daughter and lie about it!?" She spun to face her father, "You are not going to die. Far *worse*, you will live a long and miserable *crippled life*! And every day you live, you will remember what you *did to me* and it will haunt you to your grave!"

Eyes blazing, Hua stalked toward the door. She turned on the threshold, "My life is over, Mother. I am as good as dead. If I am to continue living and not follow my beloved to the afterlife with a steel blade this very instant, I must do something *worthwhile*. Henceforth, I shall defend the poor and helpless and protect them as no one protected me!"

She stormed out, never looking back. Her mother collapsed over her father's twitching body, wailing in shock and sorrow, her and her husband's life in tatters.

But before she left town, Hua paid a return visit to the Lotus Garden, bent on revenge. It was jammed with diners enjoying their meals and four chefs were working non-stop in the kitchen. Suddenly, the kitchen door flew and open and Hua burst in, dressed in a full Kung Fu combat outfit.

The chefs stopped and looked at her in astonishment. Hua flew at the biggest cook in the house and struck his neck at a Nei Kung pressure point. He screamed in pain and his body numb! He tried to stagger away, but couldn't move!

Hua ripped his belt off and let his pants slide down, exposing his genitals. She seized a huge carving knife and held its razor-thin edge to his privates.

"One of you poisoned a customer here two days ago who was near and dear to me. Was it you?" She jiggled the steel blade, drawing a crimson line of blood from the one place no man could bear to see blood. The cook gasped in horror and vigorously shook his head.

"Well, if no one wants to tell me who did it, then I'm going to cut *all* your penises off, starting with yours."

Hua looked the head chef in the eye and raised her blade to slice. The big cook started babbling wildly and pointing to another cook on the other side of in the kitchen.

"H-he did it- please spare me!"

Hua's eyes fastened on the culprit like a hawk to prey. Without another word, she pounced.

The guilty cook screamed in agony as the deed was done!

Hua leaned over him as he writhed on the soiled floor holding his bloody groin, "I promise you, every time you go to the bathroom, you will feel the pain you have caused me and the innocent life you destroyed! For the rest of your pathetic, eunuch days, every step you take, you will be haunted by the ghost of a man one thousand times better than you! He will torment you for the rest of your miserable life, until sleep eludes you and you long for death! Good Bye, Worm, *Hell* awaits you!"

And, as suddenly as she had appeared, Hua disappeared like a coil of smoke.

Back in real life, Sin awoke, unsettled by such a sad and disturbing dream. He didn't understand what it meant or why Hua kept appearing to him. He went down to have breakfast with his family meaning to ask his parent's about it, but forgot when he remembered this was the day he was going on his first field-trip with Grandmaster E!

Sin's mother told him over breakfast that she was worried about him going, because she had had a dream about him being attacked by a group of farmers the previous night. Then Sin's father urged him to be extra careful of where he went and who was around, because anti-Chinese sentiment was running high.

One Indonesian politician had been quoted in the newspaper saying that though the Chinese only made up three percent of the Indonesian population, they controlled over 90 percent of the country's wealth. This had spurred a lot of anger and discontent amongst the native Indonesians.

Sin told his parents he had to go or Grandmaster E would be very upset, but that he would be very careful.

Reluctantly, they consented.

Grandmaster E took Sin on a beautiful hike through the lush Indonesian countryside. They talked and laughed throughout the entire trip. Toward the end of the day, Sin finally opened up and told Grandmaster E all about his weird dreams and asked him if he knew what it all meant.

E was silent and thoughtful before he replied. He said that *dreams* worked mysteriously and could have multiple meanings. It could mean that Sin had traveled into the future while dreaming and seen something that was yet to happen, such as the unfamiliar girl in the casket.

Or, since in this case it also involved the story of Hua and Li Bai, it might mean something entirely different. He asked Sin if he was familiar with the Chinese concept of a Spiritual Guardian?

Sin shook his head.

Grandmaster E then told him that a *Spiritual Guardian* in Chinese worked the same way as a *Guardian Angel* in the West.
Sin listened attentively. He had always been fascinated by the spiritual realm, and was intrigued to think that he might have been experiencing something so ethereal and exotic!

E continued and told Sin that he thought Hua might be Sin's Spiritual Guardian and that she was showing him her life story because she thought that Sin might need to learn an important lesson from her that would enable him tackle his own challenges in the future.

Sin was quiet for a while. "So, whatever future I will be facing might be a gloomy or sad one, since Hua revealed her sad life to me?"
Grandmaster E took a long puff from his pipe, then gravely nodded his head. "Perhaps."

Grandmaster E and Sin continued their walk through the rice paddies. They passed a group of farmers plowing the rice paddies, and out of the blue, Grandmaster E snuck up behind one of them and kicked him in the butt for no reason!

The farmer fell facedown in the mud! His friends turned to see what was going on and stared angrily at Sin. When Sin saw that they were all staring angrily at him, he looked around and discovered that Grandmaster E had mysteriously disappeared, leaving Sin to face the music!
The farmers started to come at him all at once, shoving him with their hoes from all sides! Sin dodged left and right and managed to escape their attacks by a hair. He knew he was a much better fighter than any of them and didn't want to hurt them, so instead of fighting back, he took off as fast as he could as soon as he found an opening.
His clothes were torn and he was covered in mud from head to toe.

He kept running and running until he spotted Grandmaster E way down the road.

When he finally caught up to him, Sin exploded, "What did you do that for? You almost got me killed!"
Grandmaster E grinned, puffed his pipe, and said, "You have studied many fighting systems and yet you cannot know if they are effective until you try them out."

Hurt and angry, Sin stopped walking and let Grandmaster E continue down the road without him.
A few moments later, Sin heard him yell back, "Coming?"

Swallowing his pride and anger, he ran to catch up with him. After a while of walking in silence, Grandmaster E snaked out his hand and lightly struck Sin in the back of his neck in a specific pressure point. Sin dropped like a log.
Grandmaster E caught him before his head hit the ground and dragged him under a tree. Then he hit Sin in a different pressure point and Sin snapped awake.
Sin looked puzzled and asked him what had happened and how he got under a tree?
The grandmaster hid a smile and told Sin that he must have been so tired from all the running that he had fallen asleep while walking! Sin was very confused, but got up and started to walk again. Barely a moment passed by before Grandmaster E struck Sin on a different pressure point in his back. This time, as Sin started to collapse, he struck another pressure point and Sin snapped awake. The Grandmaster repeated this several times, hitting different pressure points each time.

As a result, Sin stumbled down the road like a drunk! When he finally staggered to a stop, he burst out, "What the heck is going on?"

Grandmaster E smirked, "Nothing. I think you're just exhausted. Come, let's go home."

Many years later, when Grandmaster E taught Sin the secret Dim Mak, *Death Touch,* technique, he finally told Sin the truth of how he had pranked him on their first field-trip! Some joke!

19
-
CONSEQUENCE OF DAYDREAMING

Sin was just thirteen when he got his first-degree black belt. He was so into Kung Fu, he spent every waking hour doing it or meditating about doing it. And spent every sleeping hour dreaming about it.

His mother had put him to work in his mother's jewelry shop when she learned how good he was at selling merchandise. This earned him a nice commission. Since the fees at the Kung Fu school were voluntary and students could pay whatever they could afford, Sin started to put all his earnings into the school and ended up paying about fifteen times as much as the average student.

Grandmaster E was impressed with his dedication and started to teach him privately in the afternoons after the regular class. Soon he became the most advanced student in the class and was entrusted with teaching many of Grandmaster E's beginner classes.

Grandmaster E explained to Sin that, in order to advance into his second degree black-belt, he would need to master quite a few more advanced forms, plus an in-depth form of *Nei Kung* called *Shien Tian Chi* or *The Breath Before You Were Born* technique, and more heavy sparring training.
The Grandmaster told Sin that the enhanced curriculum and

training would have an unexpected benefit. It would make Sin excel in his academic studies at school, because the training would make him smarter.

Sin was happy to hear this, but didn't quite believe it. He smiled and nodded at Grandmaster E.

But, to Sin's surprise, his master was proven right! After just a few weeks of intensive Kung Fu training, it seemed like a light bulb had gone off in Sin's head and he suddenly began to excel in his academic classes!

His mind began working so fast that his teacher's lectures that used to challenge him now seemed too easy. He had a great interest in science and foreign languages, so more often than not, when the teacher was lecturing, Sin would secretly read a scientific journal or a foreign language textbook.

When Sin was fourteen, he had learned the theory and science behind nuclear fission and by the time he graduated from high school, he had taught himself to speak three more foreign languages: German, Fu Chang Hua, and Malaysian.

His Kung Fu mastery had also accelerated. He was able to learn and master a new Kung Fu form every single day - averaging seven forms a week. That was an extraordinary pace.

One day when he was sixteen, he was cruising around on his motorcycle with his 15 year-old brother, Tze, on the back. They were driving home from a scenic little town called Lembang. The drive was mainly downhill, with gorgeous rice terraces stacked on the hillsides around them.

Sin's mind was far away, preoccupied with reviewing his Kung Fu material, when a car by the side of the road pulled out in front of him without warning!

He snapped out of his daydream, but too late to avoid the car. They slammed into the car, going about thirty miles and hour! Sin hit the door, so he didn't travel far, but Tze was thrown over the top of the car and landed on the pavement on the other side with an ominous crunch!

Sin staggered up and limped over to Tze and found him unconscious. The owner of the car rushed out, saw the situation, and quickly offered to take them to the hospital.

Sin was beside himself with worry and gratefully accepted. He and the driver carefully carried Tze into the car, trying not to move his neck and raced off.

When they arrived, the doctor rushed Tze into the emergency room, while one of the nurses examined Sin. The nurse put some ointment on his head wound and told him that he had been very lucky not to have suffered any serious injuries.

As soon as she was done, Sin called his mother at the shop and told her what had happened. The whole family rushed to the hospital, desperately worried. Sin's mother was devastated, and his father, trying to express his concern, scolded Sin to pay more attention to the road while driving.

Sin felt so guilty he could barely look them in the eye. After an agonizing wait, a young doctor came out leading Tze, whose head was wrapped in sterile surgical bandages. The doctor informed them that Tze had a bad concussion, but was otherwise fine and ready to go home. They were all so relieved!

If only they had known what was yet to come…

Two weeks later, Tze and Sin were soaking their feet in the local swimming pool surrounded by large bamboo trees. Sin asked Tze if he really felt all right after the accident.

Tze said, "Fine, fine…but do you believe in Heaven and God?"

Their family wasn't particularly religious, so this question got Sin wondering why he was asking.

Tze went on in a serious voice, "While I was unconscious, my soul flew up to Heaven and I was met by beings that told me the accident was of my own choosing – it was pre-determined in my prior life! I didn't really understand what they meant, but when I tried to ask them what they meant, I was zipped back to Earth!"

Sin pondered this extraordinary thing for a while. He saw that Tze was getting agitated just thinking about it, so he told him not to dwell on it, because it had all worked out all right.

"Relax and enjoy the lovely view," Sin said, pointing toward a beautiful girl who was playing splash games in the pool with her girlfriend.

"Now that's a beautiful girl. I would love to have her as my girlfriend!" Sin breathed appreciatively.

The two brothers sat companionably side by side, enjoying the day, lost in their own private thoughts...

MASTER WU

Since the day a bulb had gone off in Sin's brain that Kung Fu would be his future, he had devoted himself to the art in a passionate and incredibly disciplined way. His absolute dedication and natural ability had enabled him to progress exponentially in Kung Fu training.

Part of learning everything he could about Kung Fu meant that he also loved to visit other Kung Fu schools and spar with their senior students to hone his technique. The more he did this, the better he did and his confidence and mastery continued to grow.

One day, he heard a new Kung Fu Master had come to town. Chi Tiong, a fellow student fifteen years older than Sin, who had been taking lessons from Grandmaster E a lot longer than Sin, found out where the new Master lived. He asked Sin if he wanted to come with him to check him out.

Of course Sin wanted to go! He loved fighting too much to let a new opportunity pass him by!

Wu's residence and his hardware store sat side by side, only five minutes walk from Sin's house. So, that Sunday afternoon, Sin and Chi Tiong went to visit him. The store was closed for the day, so they rang the doorbell on his home next door. A maid answered and politely asked what they wanted.

When they said they were there to see Master Wu, she ushered them into his living room. The maid went to get Wu and a moment later a rather chubby, middle-aged man appeared and greeted Sin and Chi Tiong.

The boys looked at him in astonishment. This is not what a Kung Fu Master was supposed to look like!

He invited them to sit down and the maid served tea. Wu asked them the nature of their visit and Chi Tiong answered that they heard the rumor that a great fighter was in town. They had heard that this fighter had beaten all the local Kung Fu experts and people had begun to call him "The World's Greatest Fighter." They said they were here to find out for themselves what all the fuss was about.

Wu laughed at this, heartily amused. Then he stood up and pointed to his stomach, "Look at me! I am a fat old man! Do I look like the 'World's Greatest Fighter' to you?"

He sat down, smiling. "What I am is an expert in meditation and maneuvering.. I can maneuver *directional forces*. One day when I was meditating, I suddenly felt that I understood what birds and dogs were saying. I also felt immortal and indestructible. That afternoon, a man came into my shop and shook my hand. At that instant, I instinctively *knew* the direction and magnitude of his force of motion. I thought to myself that if I slightly diverted his force in another direction, it would compel him to fall in that direction. Before I could stop to think, I acted on that impulse! I was elated when he fell just as I had imagined! Naturally, I caught him in time to avoid any injury, but he left with a very puzzled look, unable to understand why he had suddenly fallen."

Wu shrugged, "Soon it became an amusing game for me. Everyone was different and not everyone could be uprooted so easily, so some of them took a lot more maneuvering. But, in the end, they *all* went down. After a string of successes, I upped the ante and instructed my male servants to attack me unawares. But, even when they sprang at me at the most unexpected times, as soon as any of them punched or kicked me, all I had to do was touch their arm or leg to maneuver their energy and motion in the direction I wanted them to go, and, just like that, I was able to control them too!"

Wu sat back complacently in his chair and chuckled. Sin and Chi Tiong exchanged skeptical glances.

"After that, I was confident enough to begin to seek out real Kung Fu fighters and, low and behold, I was able to do same thing with them! In fact, Boys, I haven't encountered a fighter yet that could *best* my special maneuvering technique."

Throughout their host's whole story, Sin and Chi Tiong had remained unconvinced. They looked at him with barely disguised contempt! Who had ever heard of a fat Kung Fu master? He probably had never faced off against any really good Kung Fu fighters who knew what they were doing.

Wu asked Chi Tiong how old he was and what Kung Fu style he had studied and for how long.

Chi Tiong replied, "I am 28 years old and have studied Shaolin with Grandmaster E for twenty years now."

Wu nodded. He didn't bother to ask Sin, because, though he was fifteen years old, he looked much younger for his age. Wu assumed the boy had just a come along to watch. He had no way of knowing that this little kid knew twice as much Kung Fu as his older friend, Chi Tiong did, and was twice the fighter he was too!

So Wu was surprised when Sin spoke up too, "I am fifteen years old and have studied with Grandmaster E since I was five."

Wu cocked his head at them, eyeing his visitors appraisingly, "Well, as I said, I am a meditator and maneuverer, not a fighter. I have nothing to prove to you guys."

Sin and Chi Tiong were silent, considering this. Chi Tiong finally said, "With respect, I do not believe your story. I think you bested everyone so far because you haven't met anyone really good. We came here to check you out and cannot leave until we do."

Wu regarded him skeptically, "I might have considered it, but as I say, I have nothing to prove. My interest is in meditation, not in fighting, so you have nothing of value to give me."

Chi Tiong was stymied, but Sin, an avid student of meditation techniques and Nei Kung, interjected politely, "Then let's discuss meditation first. In *Shien Tien Chi* Breathing, what Meridians and what pressure points should one channel their *Chi* through for the *Eight Pathways To Immortality*? One would begin with the first pathway, the *Small Circle of Heaven*, would you not?"

Wu was astonished. He had been learning and practicing meditation for forty years and it was only in the last couple of years he had begun to practice the advanced techniques for *The Eight Pathways to Immortality*. There was no way that this little kid could know as much as he did about such a high level of meditation!

Chi Tiong flicked a surprised glance at his fellow student, impressed. He heard the rumor that Sin's mind had somehow 'clicked on' a few years ago, enabling Sin to absorb everything Grandmaster E taught him like a sponge.

Clearly, the rumor must be true. He began to pay attention to the interesting exchange between Sin and Wu.

Being cautious, Wu did not want to reveal the secrets of his own meditation technique, so he turned Sin's question back on him and asked what *he* knew about the *Small Circle of Heaven* meditation.

Sin calmly replied that it entailed two meridians, the *Ren* and *Tu* and cited the different pressure points the *Chi* passed through.

Wu was very impressed. They carried on discussing meditation for a long time, until Chi Tiong finally got inpatient.

"That's all fine," he burst out, "But we came here to fight and you have just been talking nonsense about Nei Kung the whole time!"

Wu and Sin both smiled at his outrageous statement. Any one who understood the forces of energy-flow through the body understood the vital importance of Nei Kung techniques.

"I told you I am not interested in fighting—" Wu began.

"Of course you are not interested in fighting. You don't want to get your fat ass kicked!"

Sin was shocked at Chi Tiong's rudeness, but Wu just nodded.

"All right, Big Shot! If you insist. No reason to be rude."

Chi Tiong turned red.

Wu called his servants to move the furniture out of the way and Sin settled back excitedly to watch the bout. Chi Tiong was an excellent fighter and had never been beaten by anyone outside of Grandmaster E's school, so Sin anticipated a swift victory.

Wu and Chi Tiong stood opposite each other and ritually bowed to start the fight. Chi Tiong struck a heroic pose. Wu smothered a smile and just stood there, nonchalantly, like he was waiting for a bus!

Chi Tiong launched a lightning fast series of attacks and though Wu moved slowly and even awkwardly, he managed to block all Chi

Tiong attacks without getting hit!

Both Chi Tiong and Sin were astonished! How was that possible? The guy was fat and slow, yet Chi Tiong could not land a punch! To make matters worse, Wu suddenly reached out and made contact with Chi Tiong's hand and was able to push Chi Tiong's hand back into his own body and maneuver Chi Tiong's body back toward the wall! Chi Tiong tried hard to resist Wu's pushing touch and slip away from it, but somehow Wu's hand seemed to be *glued* to him! And with little apparent effort, Wu succeeded in pressing Chi Tiong into the wall and pinning him there. Then Wu pummeled him with his other hand!

Chi Tiong was helpless to resist! Wu let go of him and they faced off again. The same thing happened! No matter how fast Chi Tiong attacked Wu, Wu, in his slow, awkward way, managed to block all his attacks and then, crushed him back into the wall like a tidal wave! Chi Tiong eventually gave up, mortified.

Now it was Sin's turn. He took Chi Tiong's place on the floor and bowed to Master Wu. Wu hesitated for a brief moment, because he did not expect such a little boy to try to fight him. He thought he already bested their champion, so what is the point to fighting an inferior one?

Wu did not bow back. Instead he said, "Little Boy, like a baby chick, you still haven't shed your yellow feathers yet. Why don't you come back in a few years?"

Sin looked at Wu and smiled sweetly, "Why don't you humor me and grant me my death wish?"

Hearing this, Wu acquiesced, "It's your funeral."

They bowed to each other and started the fight. Wu had been impressed by Sin's knowledge of meditation, but assumed Sin was one of those people who was obsessed with meditation and book learning, but had had little skill in the way of real Kung Fu training. So he was relaxed and willing to play along with Sin to humor him. But Sin had seen what happened to Chi Tiong and realized that it was only when you stopped attacking Wu that he had a chance to trap your hand and do his killer maneuvering. So as soon as they bowed, Sin didn't waste any time posing, instead, he lunged for Wu and showered him with a flurry of meteoric attacks!

Catching Wu unprepared, Sin was able to land several hard strikes to his body and face, shocking his opponent!

But, eventually, Wu was able to trap one of Sin's hands and started to maneuver him back toward the wall. But Sin managed snap his hand loose from Wu's and again showered Wu with a barrack of attacks, landing several more powerful strikes!

When Wu finally managed to touch another one of Sin's hands, this time he did not underestimate his young opponent's abilities. As soon as his hand touched Sin's, he used his astounding maneuvering ability to glue his large frame to the boy's.

Sin tried to break loose by retreating quickly away from Wu, but the heavy man seemed to know where Sin was going before he did, and effortlessly followed his movements in sync. They moved back and forth across the room for quite a while before Wu was finally able to pin Sin to the wall.

Pinned by Wu's massive bulk, Sin could not move. Wu held him tight against the wall and raised his right hand beside Sin's face and smacked it in a symbolic blow.

Chi Tiong had been mesmerized by the exchange. Initially, he'd been thrilled to see that Sin's blazing speed had enabled him to score a few points before Wu even knew what hit him. But his frustration grew when Wu wised up and stayed glued to Sin. He shared Sin's horrible frustration at the overwhelming feeling of helplessness he felt when he was pinned to the wall, unable to move.

Wu let go of Sin. Anxious to find out how Wu had done his maneuvering and eager to try another tact, Sin asked for another try. Wu smiled and nodded his head.

This time around, Sin had a new strategy. He realized that when Wu had glued his hand to his and he had tried to break Wu's grip on him, he made the mistake of moving back in a *straight line*, making it easy for Wu to follow. This time, he had a better plan.

For Wu's part, he realized he had seriously underestimated his young opponent and was mortified that *he*, who had not been hit in *years*, had allowed himself to be struck several times by a child before he had been able to defeat the boy!

This time he was ready too. No way was this little sucker going to touch him again! On full alert, his adrenaline pumping, Wu faced little Sin.

As before, Sin showered Wu with a barrage of attacks! But this time, Wu moved faster than he ever had before to block them all. But, because he was so busy blocking Sin's attacks, he had no chance to do his maneuvering! This went on for a long time until Wu finally saw his chance and glued his hand to Sin's.

But, he was astonished when Sin was able to break his hold by twisting to Wu's blind side, instead of moving back.

Wu suddenly realized Sin was a brilliant fighter who had been able to assess his defeat and come up with a new strategy on the fly. He was genuinely impressed.

As soon as Sin broke Wu's hold, he immediately executed another flurry of attacks that kept Wu busy blocking him. When Wu got another chance to do his hand-gluing-maneuvering technique, Sin again moved to his blind side, but this time Wu anticipated Sin's move and quickly turned his body to match Sin's moves, and continued his maneuvering.

Not willing to be bested, Sin again moved to Wu's blind side, but before Wu had a chance to turn his body, Sin pushed his whole body against Wu's using all the strength he had to try to push Wu off balance.

Wu felt a tidal wave of force hit him, but he quickly sunk his Chi into his feet to become immovable.

Sin felt as if he had hit a solid mountain! While Sin was still reeling in shock, Wu maneuvered him into the corner wall and pinned him.

Sin turned red, quivering from anger and frustration, too embarrassed to ask for a rematch.

But Wu tapped his shoulder gently and said, "Come on, Young Master, let's do it again."

They bowed to each other and started the bout again, which proceeded much the way it had before, with Sin trying new tactics and gaining ground, but still getting pinned in the end.

Sin was finally convinced that he must acknowledge defeat and he bowed to Wu. Wu accepted graciously, but was so exhausted himself, he collapsed on the couch and invited Sin to join him.

Sin sat down besides him and they were all very quiet for quite a while, lost in their own thoughts.

Wu sensed Sin's an Chi Tiong's frustration and spoke kindly to them. "What are you so sad for? I am the one who has earned the title of the "World's Greatest Fighter", yet, in all those years of fighting, not only have I never lost a fight, but no one has ever even touched me! Today, a thirteen year-old kid ran all over me!"

Sin demurred, "Fifteen."

Wu waved away this minor point. "Thirteen, fifteen! *I* am the one who should feel disgraced and defeated!"

Chi Tiong hung his head and asked, "But Master Wu, we are frustrated because we can't figure out how you did it. How can you move so *slow* compared to us, yet still defeat us?"

Wu broke into a long laugh and shook his head sagely, "Trade secrets!"

Chi Tiong and Sin left soon after, licking their wounds. Sin was so devastated by losing, that he could not bring himself to go back to Kung Fu practice right away.

He was in turmoil and felt like the rug had been pulled right out from under him. Before his fight with Wu, everything in the Universe appeared black and white, governed by rules he had come to understand and respect. If one practiced martial arts religiously and learned every aspect of it to the highest level, one would be rewarded with mastery within themselves and against others...

Now it seemed like the world had been turned upside down and no longer followed the Laws of Nature as he knew them!

How could someone so slow, awkward and overweight like Wu, who had never taken a day of Kung Fu training in his life, defeat a twenty-year veteran like Chi Tiong and worse, beat Sin, whose whole *existence* was Kung Fu?

Did it really make a difference how hard he trained or how dedicated he was...?

That depressing thought devastated him. It sapped the ambition and drive right out of him and made him question his commitment to devoting his life to Kung Fu and Nei Kung so he could be the best martial artist in the world one day.

Sin struggled to make sense of it all, but only grew more despondent and depressed by the day. Soon, he made himself ill with worry and frustration.

One night, another strange dream occurred to him while he was in this confused and despairing state:

He fell asleep and found himself standing by the gates of an opulent mansion, in a city far, far away... Inside the mansion, dogs began barking ferociously, heralding an intruder. Bright, handheld lanterns began to light up everywhere, as servants rushed out into the courtyard to see what was the matter.

Suddenly, everyone's gaze swept to the roof as a violent fight broke out on the rooftop! Four of the mansion's best fighting guards were battling a masked intruder! They were all master Kung Fu fighters and they kicked and punched and parried with supreme skill, intending to dispatch the intruder instantly. But to no avail! Even four-on-one, they were no match for the masked bandit, who moved like lightning and seemed to be in four places at once!

One by one, the expert Kung Fu Masters were struck unconscious and slid down the roof to be caught by the gaping spectators below, while the masked intruder escaped.

Meanwhile, inside the house, a huge clamor arose when the owner of the mansion discovered he had been robbed - his family treasures and gold stolen clean away!

"For generations we have hired the best Kung Fu masters in all China to guard our house and not once have we been robbed!" The owner wailed, "How could this happen now?!"

A short time later, not far from the nobleman's estate, a lone figure climbed high atop a mountain above a quiet village below and gazed down upon the sleeping town.

As blue morning light crept across the horizon, sleepy villagers began to come out of their dwellings rubbing their eyes to prepare for another day of backbreaking labor trying to save their crops from the deadly drought that was plaguing their area.

They stopped in surprise to see small leather bags lying on every doorstep! What ecstasies of delight they felt when they each opened their bags and found them filled with gold!

The drought had been so severe that year, they had been living in fear for their very lives. Now, a guardian spirit had spared their lives! They threw themselves down on their knees and bowed in humble thanks to the Heavens above.

High atop the mountain, Hua pulled off her mask and smiled. Another good deed accomplished! The wealthy nobleman she had robbed cared nothing for the people of his village and had been prepared to let them starve rather than share an ounce of gold with them. She had righted that grave injustice.

She watched as the villagers ran to and fro showing each other their newfound wealth with cries of delight. Absentmindedly, she pulled an unusual leaf from her pocket and began to blow a beautiful, haunting melody – one that she had composed in honor of Li Bai. It was a poignant counterpoint to the joyous cries echoing up from the village.

Suddenly, Hua and the entire village froze in time:

A mysterious bearded man with long dark hair *appeared* beside her. He walked up to Hua, still frozen, and sized her up. Nodded in satisfaction.

"Ah, my Lady, the 'Champion of the Poor'. What a noble idea! Your heart is also made of *gold*. I will leave you a small token of my regard - some day you will need it."

He put a tiny gourd into her hand that was decorated with elegant, engraved swirls and patterns. Then *vanished*.

The world spun back into motion once more.

Hua snapped out of her strange paralysis and exclaimed to herself, "Whaaaat was *that*...?"

She sensed something *very strange* had taken place, but had no idea what had happened. She was astonished to find she was holding a small, engraved gourd that had not been there seconds before! What was the meaning of this unusual gift and where had it come from? Sensing it was important, she hung it from her belt and went on her way.

The next day, Hua found herself strolling through a busy marketplace, jammed with people buying goods and supplies. She munched contentedly on an apple as she wove through the stalls chock full of livestock, baskets and mats, cooking implements, leather goods, etc.

Suddenly a commotion broke out and everyone started running toward the noise to see what was happening. Hua pushed her way through the crowd and found a father clutching the hand of his pretty young daughter with one hand and holding a traditional Chinese wedding dress in the other.

The father and daughter were surrounded by six Imperial Guards. An arrogant youth dressed in the multi-colored silk uniform of the Imperial Guards taunted the father, "Well, well, Old man, What's the special occasion for such a pretty dress?"

The old man timidly replied, "Tomorrow is my daughter's wedding day, Sir".

The youth looked the pretty girl over, "Isn't she a little young for marriage?"

"In our village, it is the custom for girls to marry young," the old man mumbled.

The youth raised an eyebrow, "How interesting... So your daughter will be ravished tomorrow night by her new husband?"

The old man flushed and tried to back away through the crowd.

The youth sized the girl up with a lecherous gaze and saw that underneath her grubby farmer's clothing, she was a real beauty.

"I have tasted all sorts of beautiful women, but never a girl as young as her. Say old man, what if I pay you a lifetime's worth of wealth for one night with your daughter?"

The old man backed away clutching tight to his frightened daughter's hand, pleading, "Please, Sir, she will be dishonored and live the rest of her life in shame with no hope of a husband."

"Bah! A handful of gold will take care of that! Pay the man and take the girl!" he ordered his second-in-command.

One of the guards tossed a small sack of gold at the father's feet and grabbed the girl's hand. The terrified girl fought him and clung to her father, sobbing.

The guard raised his hand to strike the desperate girl when suddenly a hand came out of nowhere and blasted him in the chest! He sailed through the air and crashed to the ground twenty feet away!

Hua appeared from out of the crowd and stood protectively in front of the girl. "No one touches her," she said calmly. She motioned for the girl and her father to leave, but the commander and his guards blocked their way.

Seeing the situation, Hua laughed, "So you and your guards are looking for some fun, eh? Well, you'll have more fun with me, I assure you."

With that, she flew at the guards and, despite being greatly out-numbered, she quickly dispatched them, one by one.

The young commander watched this one-sided fight with keen interest. When he saw the mystery woman had felled the last guard, he slowly began to clap his hands.

"What a show!" he said approvingly, looking Hua over. He glanced at the father and daughter cowering behind Hua and said, "You may leave now. And keep the money, consider it your daughter's wedding gift."

The dazed father and daughter quickly disappeared into the crowd.

Hua cocked her head at the commander, "Why the sudden change of heart?"

The youth strolled toward her casually, "She was only an ordinary girl. I prefer a spicy Lady who knows how to handle men."

Hearing that, Hua smirked, "In your dreams! I despise arrogant rich pigs like you!"

"What's wrong with being rich?"

Hua replied heatedly, "Because men like you think they can *buy* everything. Honor is nothing to you."

The youth reddened.

She turned and started to leave when he yelled after her, "Stop right there! I'm not through with you yet! You have displayed magnificent Eagle Claw techniques, but let's see how good you really are!"

Light as a feather, the youth soared up onto the rooftop of a nearby building, challenging Hua to follow him. She smiled and flew to the top of the building like an eagle. There, they flew at one another in a spectacular series of advanced fighting moves! They struck and parried and smashed through walls and roofs, flying back and forth from the ground to the rooftops! Before long, the Market Place had been turned to rubble and people ran everywhere as fruit and vegetables, pots and pans, flew through the air!

Seeing what destruction they had wrought on the innocent villagers, Hua stepped back from the fight. "You are better than I imagined," she said, "Your skills are superb. But we cannot destroy this village to suit ourselves. Let us agree to meet again some other day where we will do no harm to anyone's property."

She was turning to leave, when the young commander launched a sneak attack on her! It caught her partially by surprise, since she never expected that a gentleman warrior would stoop so low to deliver a cheap shot while her back was turned. So, though her reflexes were lighting fast, one of his blows landed on her ribs. She heard a snap of her rib breaking! Fighting through her pain, as fast as lighting, she lashed out with a barrage of Eagle Claw techniques and succeeded in hitting the youth's numbing points that would have normally rendered him paralyzed.

But, unbeknownst to Hua, the young commander had mastered the technique of using his Chi to *block* the paralyzing effect of her numb points!

So, while Hua was expecting the youth's knees to buckle, instead he was unfazed. He pulled out a pair of metal *Pan Kwan Pi* (Judge's Pens, the size of chopsticks), which were deadly weapons used only by an *elite* group of Kung Fu practitioners. He launched a flurry of attacks against his unarmed opponent with them clenched in his fist.

Hua succeeded in blocking all of the attacks aimed at her body, but she sustained a minor cut on her arm. Immediately, she felt a burning itch in her wound and knew the weapons had been dipped in poison! Fury enflamed her and, bent on revenge, she blasted out a barrage of attacks all aimed at the youth's Death Points.

She landed a crushing strike to his Stomach Meridian Death Point number 18 and, while the youth was staggered back, she blasted him with a powerful leg kick that sent him flying off the rooftop to the ground, knocking him out cold.

Without a backward glance, she leapt down and staggered away into the nearby forest.

The poison was fast-acting and Hua wasn't sure if she could stop its deadly progress toward her heart. She dragged herself into the wood and propped herself up against a tree. She rolled up her sleeve to examine the wound and meditated to slow down the onslaught of the poison. But despite all her efforts and skill, the poison was slowly turning the skin around the wound black.

She closed her eyes and sank back against the tree with a sigh, knowing that unless she could find the strength to use her training to nullify the poison, she had just moments to live.

Suddenly, she *felt* a warm, tingling sensation on her arm. She opened her eyes and saw a baby tiger licking her wound! Paralyzed by the poison, she lay as still as a stone, unable to shoo the sweet baby tiger away.

Weakly she urged, "Please, Little One, don't lick my wound, it is poisonous. I have to use every ounce of energy to nullify the poison before it's too late. So be a good boy, run away and leave me alone." But the baby tiger just kept licking her wound.

Hua closed her eyes and went back to a *Deep State of Meditation* in which she manipulated the blood flow in and out of her organs, seeking to isolate the poison in her bloodstream and render it impotent. She rose in and out of consciousness, rising and falling, over and over again, as she struggled to fight off the toxin.

Back in the village, two guards came to and rushed to the side of their unconscious commander. They supported him between them and carried him back to the Governor's Mansion.

The Governor and his wife were summoned and the Lady screamed when she saw the wounded youth.

"My Son! What happened to my son?"

The young man, lying pale as death, was Siung, the very same governor's son who had sought Hua's hand in marriage! The governor ordered the servants to carry his boy to his room and urgently summoned the physician to examine him.

The doctor hurried in, unbuttoned the youth's shirt and took a good look at his wounds. He glanced up at the governor and shook his head gravely.

His mother cried out and rushed to her son's bedside, terrified she would lose her darling boy. She ordered the servants to bring cool water and a compress, which she used to gently bathe his pale, immobile face, while the physician administered a special mixture of herbs with healing properties.

The boy's mother sat beside the bed holding her son's hand, but when he remained unconscious, she began to cry.

The governor strode out of the room and barked at the two guards who had brought his son home.

"I demand to know what happened!" he roared. "Who would dare to attack the Governor's son?"

The two guards nervously mumbled their apologies and took turns telling the Governor what happened. The Governor seethed in rage and dismissed them, vowing revenge.

He turned to the physician and protested, " How is this possible? Tasu, you are the best fighter in China and he is your best student! Yet, here he is seriously wounded - by a woman!"

Tasu gravely replied, "I deeply regret to inform you, your Honor, your son is not merely wounded, he is *dying.*"

The Governor jumped up and roared, "What do you mean? Nothing seems broken, there is little blood--!"

Tasu shook his head and explained, "He has been hit in one of the most deadly Nei Kung pressure points – the *Stomach Meridian Death Point* #18..."

The Governor interrupted, "But you can release that hit, can't you? I have seen you demonstrate it to my son many times! "

Tasu shook his head sadly, "If it was a normal hit, certainly. But this was *not* a normal hit. This mysterious woman put a deadly *curve* on her strike and only she knows the angle necessary to nullify it."

"Why would she do such a thing?"

Tasu shrugged, "Perhaps because your son used the Poison Judge Pens on her first...?"

"Then we must find her and make her release the hit, on pain of death!"

"But, Your Honor, the guards said that with the potent poison your son used on his weapon, she isn't likely to live through the day anyway."

The Governor dropped his head in his hands, hiding his frustrated sorrow.

Deep in the forest, Hua finally woke up. She felt cleansed and refreshed and pleased to be alive. When she sat up, she was surprised to see baby tiger lying beside her, fast asleep. A puddle of black blood and vomit lay splattered on the ground beside the sleeping beast.

"What a smart little fellow you are! You licked the poison out of my wound and then spit it up."

Hearing her voice, the tiger cub woke up and regarded her with its big, solemn yellow eyes. Hua reached out – slowly - and patted him gently on the head. He nuzzled against her hand.

"If it wasn't for you, Little One, I might not have made it. You're my hero!" She stood up gingerly and stretched her aching body. "I'm getting hungry. You must be too. How about I find your mama to take care of you?"

She started searching through the woods for the cub's mother, and the cub trailed along behind her. But after an hour of fruitless searching, there was no mother tiger to be found.

"Well, Little One, since I can't find your mama, I'm going to get enough food for both of us. Stay here and I'll soon return."

She began to walk through the woods toward the village. But, she sensed movement and turned to find the tiger cub following her!

Hua stopped. "No, no, no, Little One, you can't follow me. I don't know what the villagers would do if they saw you!"

But she couldn't shake him off her tail. Finally she gave in, "Alright, you win. You did save my life after all, so letting you accompany me is the least I can do."

When they entered the marketplace, the villagers stared at them. Hua smiled as if nothing was amiss and plucked a ripe peach from a vendors cart and threw him a silver coin, not waiting for change. Munching the peach as she walked, she stopped by a clothing stall and bought new clothes that weren't stained with blood. Next she bought a pile of meat for the tiger cub, who fell on it ravenously. She looked around as it ate and noticed one of the vendors was in the middle of his midday meal. Hua watched as his wife fed him a tasty piece of steamed bun and laughed at something he said.

An image of the lovely, companionable meals she had shared with Li Bai flashed through her mind. Subdued and aching with longing for her lost love, Hua decided to pick out all of his favorite foods and return to the woods to prepare them in his honor just as he liked them.

Before she left, she gave money to all the vendors as a way of compensating for the destruction she and her opponent had caused during their battle. Money meant nothing to her and she longed to do something more meaningful for the poor and needy.

When she had left her parents house, never to return, she had vowed to devote her life to stealing from the evil rich and powerful who had gained their riches through corruption and avarice, and give the spoils to the deserving poor.

For her, it was justice on a personal level.

She had not realized how much her act of charity meant to so many of the destitute villagers, who struggled to live on a pittance per day. It saved their lives. When Hua and her tiger cub left the marketplace, a throng of vendors gathered to wave goodbye.

"I wonder why she brought a baby tiger with her?" mused the fruit vendor.

The vendor in the next booth laughed, "You bring your pet dog with you, don't you, Chu? That's her little pet!" The vendors burst out laughing.

Hua found a hotel in a neighboring village. She paid for the room and received her room key. As she and the baby tiger walked out of the hotel office, the owner of the hotel stood up from his seat and looked over the counter, "Wait a minute! I thought you had a dog with you! That's a tiger! No tigers in my hotel - they might eat the customers!"

Hua threw a gold coin on his desk and went in search of her room.

The hotel owner bit the coin and called after her, "Real gold! Lady, you can burn the hotel down for all I care!"

Hua opened the door to her room and the baby tiger rushed in and sat next to the bed. Hua took some more of the meat she had purchased at the marketplace and placed it in front of the little tiger.

It gobbled it down with gusto.

Hua sat cross-legged on the bed and ate her own meal. She looked down at her new companion and said, "You know, when I woke up this afternoon, I felt so peaceful. And this is the western frontier of China. So from now on I will call you, *SI'AN*, since *Si* means 'West' and '*An*' means Peace, *Peace in the West*. My name is Hua, which means flower. You came along just in the nick of time, my friend!"

The baby tiger looked up at her as if he understood every word she said.

"I have a feeling we are going to get along famously!" Hua joked and petted his silky head.

Meanwhile, back at the governor's mansion, Siung finally awoke and saw his mother and father and his teacher, Tasu, clustered anxiously around his bed.

"I am sorry to cause you so much trouble, honored parents. I have no excuse for what I did. It was foolish and immature."

His mother patted his hand, "Shhh...don't tire yourself, Darling Son." But Siung knew he was dying and he had to get it all off his chest, otherwise he would die without a clear conscience.

The young man coughed weakly and continued, "You see, I knew who she was all along - even though she didn't know me. She is the famous Pai Hua. For years I had heard so many stories about her - how beautiful she was, how intelligent and refined, even what an expert in poetry and literature she was. I was amazed that when a suitor quoted a line of poetry to her, she would immediately know the author right away and could quote the rest of the poem back to him!" he coughed again and his mother anxiously settled his pillow beneath his head.

"But that wasn't even the most amazing thing about her – everyone said her Kung Fu is exquisite! She was so good, most of her suitors lost the match in the first round! Because of her beauty and intelligence she had become a legend, and suitors from all over the country flocked to her door, eager to be tested by her in *person*. I was only sixteen years old and she a year older than I when I disguised myself as a suitor from a distant land and came to see her.

To be fair, she insisted that *all* suitors were tested in front of everyone else. There were twelve suitors that day and she dispatched eight of them before getting tired, so she left the other four until the next day. I was one of those four. Mother," he said with a rasp in his voice, "Truly, it was the biggest day of my life, to see how personable and kind she was toward each of us. I think every man there fell in love with her that day, including me. But, I could tell from the bouts before me that I was no match for her yet, so there was no use for me to embarrass myself in front of everyone else. I left that night, vowing to return when I could beat her.

What I could *never* understand is how could she be better at Kung Fu than everyone else? I had Tasu, the best Kung Fu master in China as my teacher, yet she excelled above me. So, from that day on, she inspired me to train harder at my Kung Fu and to study literature with more diligence. Remember how I was suddenly interested in poetry and asked you, Father, to hire the best teachers in China to tutor me?"

Siung stopped and looked at his father with loving eyes. His father's eyes grew red and filled with tears as he reached out to hold Siung's hand.

"Of course, My Son, I would have done anything for you."

Siung smiled faintly, "For three years, I have been *obsessed* with my studies in Kung Fu and poetry, until finally I knew in my bones I was ready to take her on. That was the day I asked you, Mother, to send word to the Pai's family about my intentions, remember?"

Siung's mother nodded her head and dabbed away her tears with a square of linen.

"I was excited and confident and eager to have her as my bride. But, the Pai family sent word back that Hua was not feeling well and needed some time to recuperate. So I was prepared to wait, but the next day, the Pai family's trusted servant, Chang, came to see me and revealed the true reason I had been put off. Hua had fallen in love with Little Li Bai, the poet, and they planned to secretly wed and run away together to some distant land and I—"

Siung coughed violently, his breath coming in ragged rasps.

"Please Siung, you don't need to-" his father began.

"Yes I do, Father! You must let me atone for my shame!" Siung protested, feeling his strength ebbing away. "I-I did a very bad thing, Father. I realize now that we all have a *good* side and a *dark* side in our souls. And the quality of our life is derived from which path we chose to take... I-I chose the wrong path. I was so jealous and angry at Li Bai for stealing the heart of the woman of my dreams, that I choose the dark side and lie here, dying, because of it."

He pressed his hand to his heart and hung his head, "Honorable parents, *I* was the one who had Li Bai poisoned. Worse still, I told Chang that I would pay him a king's ransom if he would tell him that Hua's father had ordered his death! I foolishly thought that if she felt betrayed by her own father, she would gladly accept my proposal of marriage to get away from him."

Siung stopped and asked for a glass of water and his mother quickly brought him one and held it to his parched lips. He sipped the water and forced himself to continue, despite the stricken look in his parent's eyes.

"But nothing worked out the way I planned. When Hua heard that Li Bai had been murdered by Chang on her father's orders, she crippled her father for life and disappeared into the world of Chiang Pu, leaving me alone once more. I think it was an act of karmic *fate* that she appeared in the village where I was patrolling. But, my misdeeds do not stop there. My shame at destroying her life was so great, that I continued down the darker path and terrorized the women in our villages. I am so sorry for that too... Strangely, I did not recognize her at first as the sadness of losing Li Bai has taken a great toll on her. But as soon as she defeated six of my best guards, I recognized her unique fighting style."

He managed a weak smile.

"My heart sang! I was so excited to come face to face with her again and wondered how my own Kung Fu skills would compare to hers. In my infantile fantasies, my skills were *always* superior to hers and I won her heart by defeating her fair and square. So, I challenged her to a Kung Fu match, believing my dreams would become reality.

To my dismay, even after years of grueling training, her Kung Fu was still superior to mine! She was impressed by my Kung Fu skill, yes, but also knew I wasn't her match and tried to give me a way to save face and avoid killing me."

He coughed again and a trickle of blood coursed down from his mouth. His mother turned away and stuffed her handkerchief in her mouth to keep from crying out loud and disturbing him.

"I should have accepted the out she gave me. B-but I could not let her go! Again, my *dark side* rose up and I launched a sneak attack on her, trying to hit her *numb points* so I could paralyze her and bring her here to our home. I thought that later, when she woke up and found herself in such a beautiful home and learned that I was the Governor's son, she would eventually fall in love with me and agree to be my wife. But, I missed hitting her numb points and broke her rib instead. She was furious and justly scornful of my cheapshot and retaliated by striking my numb points to paralyze me so she could leave the fight with honor. She had no way of knowing that I had had Nei Kung training to *block* my numb points, so I was unaffected – but I was so very angry! How dare she thwart the dream I had nurtured for so long?"

He clenched the coverlet and twisted it in his hands. "Even though she was unarmed, I pulled out my poisoned *Pan Kwan Pi* and succeeded in wounding her. Again, I thought when she succumbed to the poison, I could just carry her home and give her the antidote. She would have to stay here in our beautiful home while she healed, and I would have months to show her that I had loved her blindly since I was sixteen years old and get her to fall in love with me!"

His head dropped back against the pillow and his breath caught in his throat.

"What a stupid fool I was! That was not to be. She beat me once again... Furious at being tricked for the second time and thinking me an unfeeling, evil beast without a shred of honor, she lashed out at my *Stomach Meridian Death Point #18* with a Curved Hit so no one else could release it. So I am marked for *death*, and rightly so. Because it was my own stupidity and poison that killed the woman I loved and the only person on this earth who could have saved me. I don't blame her and I ask you not to either," Siung begged, looking both his parents in the eyes, willing them to nod in agreement, wordlessly. "It was I who made the wrong choice in life and acted dishonorably toward an honorable woman, and now, my *Karma* has caught up to me."

He turned his head weakly toward his teacher, "Master Tasu, remember you once told me there was a Nei Kung Technique for immortality that you would teach me one day if I dedicated my life to Kung Fu? I'm afraid that is one lesson I left too late..."

Tasu looked at Siung with loving kindness and answered with a catch in his throat, "In your next life, I shall return as your teacher again and teach you the Technique without delay."

Siung smiled weakly, knowing his teacher was just humoring him, "Promise?"

Tasu nodded gravely, "I promise."

Knowing his end was near, Siung turned his eyes back to his distraught parents, who were sitting side by side holding his hands to share his last moments.

"Dear parents, I thank you for all your love and generosity toward me. I am sorry that I shall never repay your kindness. When I am gone, please don't shed any more tears for me. I had a wonderful life and I freely embrace my karma."

Having achieved the great wisdom and spiritual transcendence in his final moments that he had failed to achieve in life, the young man breathed his last. In death, his face was peaceful and serene.

His mother burst into deep, inconsolable sobs. The Governor looked like thunder.

He spun to Tasu and spat, "You will take as many guards as you need to search for Hua's body and burn it! If you do not find it, then bring me the best assassins that money can buy - I want her dead!"

"But your son's dying wish...?"

"DEAD!"

Tasu blanched, "Yes, Governor. Your wish is my command."

Weeks later, on a hot, sunny day in China's magnificent but unforgiving Goby Desert, Hua and her tiger, Si'An, were traveling on foot along an immense dune of sand when Si'An suddenly balked and growled low in his throat, sniffing the sand.

Forewarned, Hua pulled out two daggers and threw one into the sand by Si An's feet. Blood spurted into the air and a masked figure thrashed out of the sand and lashed out at Hua with a deadly, curved sword, far longer than Hua's remaining dagger.

As Hua dodged and parried, trying to hold out long enough for the wounded man to lose enough blood and faint, three more masked figures suddenly erupted out of the sand, all armed to the teeth! Assassins!

Realizing she was now seriously outnumbered, Hua feinted to one side then somersaulted back to dispatch the wounded man. That left the other three...

One of them, a giant of a man wielding two huge axes, decided to take Si'An out of the equation early. He charged the giant tiger, his axes whirling through the air like propellers! Despite Si'An dodging and writhing with feline grace to stay just out of his reach, each time the giant's axes sliced closer and closer to the tiger's undefended flanks!

The other two leapt at Hua: they were tall, slender twins, armed with chain-whips and double broadswords. With eerie shrieks, they lunged at Hua and a spectacular battle ensued! They fought feverishly, back and forth across the scorching sands, lunge, parry, stab, lunge, parry, stab, leaping and somersaulting in a dazzling display of murderous virtuosity. Hua's superior skill was the only thing keeping her scant inches ahead of their flashing, razor-edged swords!

Meanwhile, Si'An and the giant had been battling it out as well. Si'An hurled his thousand pounds of pure muscle straight at the giant, his ferocious claws extended like a set of knives to slice his head off! But the man, surprisingly agile for his size, sprang out of the way at the last second! Moving like lightning, Si'An whipped his muscular tail to the side as he passed his opponent by and swept him off his feet!

But, the Giant was fast too! From a prone position, sprawled on his back in the sand, he did a lightning-fast kip-up to a standing position and raised his sword over his head to slice through Si An's exposed belly, just as the angry tiger leapt at him again! It looked like the end for the brave tiger!

The giant began to chuckle as the big cat sailed helplessly through the air right at his deadly sword! But, faster than humanly possible, the tiger whipped its tail around like ballast and twisted its lithe body to make a one hundred and eighty degree turn in midair! It plummeted down on the giant's back, tore though muscle and bone with its deadly claws, while it ripped his windpipe out with its mighty jaws!

The giant's screams were cut short. A gurgling death rattle escaped his lips as his lifeblood pumped out onto the sand.

The murderous twins with their double weapons were startled by his cries - the giant had been the strongest of them and his death unnerved them for a second. That was long enough for Hua to seize the opportunity to take a spinning leap that sent her dagger slicing through their necks, one after the other!

When they toppled to the ground, Hua and Si'An took a deep breath and relaxed their guard. But, as she straightened up and moved toward one of the bodies to search him for clues to his identity, a sword lanced out of the sand right at her heart!

But loyal Si'An, with his hair-trigger, tiger reflexes, leapt in front of her and took the jab in his flank!

As the massive tiger roared in pain, a dark figure writhed out of the sand like a demon, but ran straight into Hua's ready dagger! The figure crumbled to the ground. Hua had jabbed him in a pressure point that would disable him, not kill him right away, because she needed to interrogate him to find out who had sent him. She had no idea who might want her dead so badly that they would pay expensive professional assassins to track her to the far ends of China to kill her! She was astonished to find that the assassin at her feet was a noble-looking gentleman. Hua crouched down beside him, "You have ten minutes before you die a painful death to tell me who sent you."

The figure sighed. "My Lady, there is nothing you could do to force me to reveal what I know, but I feel an obligation to my young master to tell you the *truth*. My name is Tasu. The Governor of your home Province sent me and the other assassins to kill you because you killed his only son, Siung, in the marketplace duel."

Hua retorted indignantly, "Oh was that who that was? But, he tried to kill me first! It was an honorable kill."

"Siung admitted as much. And he begged his father not to seek revenge. You see, he knew that it was *not* your father who sent that servant to kill Li Bai. That was a lie, it was Siung himself."

Hua was rocked to the core as a fiery wave of rage and horror swept through her. "Whaat?! Why would he do such a horrible thing?"

Tasu gasped in a ragged breath, "For the oldest reason in the world... he fell in love with you and couldn't bear the thought of you with another man."

His breathing grew ragged and irregular. "My time is up, but yours is not. Try to live a good life in spite of *all* the dreadful things that have happened to you."

He breathed his last with an expression of peace on his face.

Jolted by his disturbing disclosures, Hua was shaken to her very foundations and sat still as a stone, unable to move. It wasn't until Si'An let out an uncharacteristic mew of pain that she came back to herself and quickly tended his wound.

"My brave, loyal Si An, she crooned, as she cleaned his wound, "What am I going to do with you?"

She was relieved to see that though it was a long gash, it was not deep, so she dosed it with some of her homemade healing ointment and bandaged it with a long strip torn off of her own clothing. She gave the brave tiger plenty of water to drink and then ordered it to lay down for a rest while she tried to marshal her thoughts to consider what she had just learned.

When the horrible truth began to sink in, her legs collapsed out from under her and she sat down hard with a thump. Her emotions ran riot! She saw Siung conspiring with her servant, her servant creeping into the kitchen to poison her beloved, and darling Li Bai clutching his stomach in agony as he breathed his last.

But when her mind ran forward to see herself rushing into her father's house and striking him in his crippling points before she had given him a chance to tell her the truth or even defend himself, she broke down in tears and sobbed for hours. *What had she done?? What kind of a monster would inflict such pain and suffering on their own innocent father?? Was she not as bad as Siung?*

A deep well of loneliness and futility opened up inside her and threatened to suck her down into it. She thought how easy it would be to stay where she was, sprawled on the sand under the unforgiving sun... until she died. It would be a just penance for the devastation she had wrought on her innocent father in her bland anger.

But she knew Si'An would never abandon her and that would mean a death sentence for another innocent victim. No, there had been enough death and destruction in her lifetime and she knew what she must do...

She would have to go home, beg her innocent father for his forgiveness, and atone for what she had done.

It was the only honorable thing to do.

Now that she knew her dearest father had been innocent of the crime she had accused him of, a crushing wave of guilt washed over her as those horrible last moments came flooding back as if they were yesterday, *"You will live a long and miserable life! For every day you live, you will remember what you did to me. It will haunt you through eternity!"*

She shuddered as her damning words echoed through her mind. She saw her father collapsing in agony and watched his limbs begin to buckle and twist in agonizing pain as her targeted blows to his vulnerable pressure points began to take effect. Over the years since she had been gone, he must have become a twisted, helpless cripple. Another horrible thought struck her: what if he had died years ago! He easily could have died from despair if not from the effects of her inexcusable attack. She sobbed again at this horrible thought, her shoulders heaving in wretched despair. Her mother might still be alive – but how she must hate her rogue daughter for what she had done to the man she loved!

Hua dried her tears. No matter how much her mother hated her, she must return to clear her father's name and throw herself on her mother's mercy. Hua jumped up, her entire body trembling with suppressed emotion.

"Come Si An, we must go. Justice calls."

They travelled night and day, barely resting, Hua driving herself to exhaustion before she would stop to snatch a couple of hours of sleep. Poor Si'An did not understand what was going on, but he bore her agitated and single-minded intensity with the same stolid loyalty as he had anything else she had ever asked of him. Some nights, when she lay in an exhausted sleep close to death, collapsed after endless days of hard travel, he would curl up beside her to share his body warmth with her own trembling form, and lick her unconscious, tear-stained face with his warm, raspy tongue.

When at last they reached her parents home, it was late in the day.

Hua stood trembling in the shadows, more afraid then she had ever been in her life. Honor demanded she face her crime and her victims, and so she would...

She wiped the tears from her face, squared her shoulders like she was heading to a firing squad, and stepped forward to knock on the door. An old servant opened the door. He goggled at her incredulously, as she stepped by him, then gaped in horror as a giant tiger followed her in!

Hua found her mother standing in the living room by a tall, hand-painted rice-paper screen. Her mother was deep in thought and had not noticed her come in. Hua gazed at her mother lovingly but was saddened by how much she had aged. Streaks of white threaded through her long black hair and a net of fine wrinkles had settled on her lovely face. Beauty was still there, but youth had long since fled...

Sensing something, her mother turned and saw her. Hua stiffened, expecting an onslaught of recriminations and curses from her once-gentle mother. Instead, her mother just looked at her, her eyes brimming with infinite sorrow and compassion. Then, in the blink of an eye, her mother crossed the room and took Hua in her arms!

They both broke down in floods of tears and clung together like two shipwrecked souls who had been lost at sea, but now saw the promised land rising from the waves.

Hua mumbled into her mother's shoulder, unable to look her in the eye, "I-I have learned the truth. H-How can you ever forgive me, Mother, after what I-I have done?"

Her mother pulled far enough back to look at her, "Dearest Daughter, there is nothing to forgive. We know all. The Governor himself came to confess his deeds and beg our forgiveness. He regretted breaking his vow to his son to forgive you as soon as the assassin's had left his home and tried to recall them. But they were nowhere to be found. I have feared the worse since that time – that you lay dead, unburied and unmourned in some godforsaken land, far from the home of your family and ancestors. How I longed to hold you in my arms just one more time again - and here you are - my prayers have been answered!"

Hua's heart swelled, knowing she was blessed to have the kindest, most forgiving mother in the world! Just then Si An padded into the room and her mother's eyes went round with fright.

"No, no, Mother, there is nothing to fear. This is my loyal friend, Si'An, and he would protect you with his life!"

Her mother's eye's opened even wider, but she bravely stretched out her trembling hand for the beautiful tiger to sniff. It rubbed his massive chin against her palm like a lap cat and she smiled, utterly enchanted.

Hua was so gratified to be welcomed by her mother, but knew she must not put off visiting her father's grave to pay her respects and beg for his forgiveness from beyond the veil of death.

She lowered her head and humbly asked, "M- Mother...May I visit Father's grave?"

Her mother looked at her in confusion, "Grave? There is no grave. Your father yet lives—" She broke off in a soft yelp, as Hua gripped her mother's arms harder than she intended, stunned at what she had just heard.

"What? Father lives?!" Hua stammered, overcome with a wild surge of hope, "Can it be? Where *is* he? Please - I beg of you?!"

"He is right here, Child, as always," her mother replied, pulling aside the rice-paper screen to reveal a sleeping form lying on a daybed.

Hua saw her beloved father, curled up in a crooked ball on the bed. Her heart did a flip!

Her father was alive! She could still atone for the damage she had done! It wasn't too late to make it right!

Afraid to lose another moment, she rushed to his side and gently began to press and massage the correct sequence of pressure points on his back that would release him from his torment.

She was gratified when he awoke in her arms, his eyes wide with wonder, his twisted limbs beginning to relax and straighten, and his pain disappearing completely after all his years of torment! Her mother watched this miracle, hands clutched tightly to her breast, and wept tears of joy.

"Daughter, is that really you?" he asked in a soft, tremulous voice. She nodded mutely, too overcome to speak, and he laid a trembling hand, soft and white as rice paper, against her pale cheek to make sure she was real.

Hua hung her head in shame. 'Father, I am sorry, so desperately sorry for hurting you as I did and believing Chang's evil lies when he said it was you who had..had..." she broke off in shame, unable to meet his gaze.

Her father's voice was gentle, soft, as he stirred and sat up straight for the first time in years. He took her cold, clenched hands in his. "My Daughter, other people's evil has caused this family great pain and suffering for long enough. Now is the time for forgiveness and rebirth. We must put our sorrows behind us and begin again. Can you do that for me?"

Hua still felt crushed with guilt, but knew that there was great wisdom in his words. She could deny him nothing.

"Oh Father, if you would have me, I will work the rest of my life to deserve your love and forgiveness!"

Her mother came to join them and her parents smiled at her. Their eyes, once full of sadness and despair, now shining with hope. Hua bathed in an unexpected glow of happiness. She felt all the horrors of the past slipping away from her in that moment... She was home, she was forgiven, the Fates had blessed them all with the Truth in the end, and an opportunity to begin again. They would be able to forgive and forget the horrors and suffering that the scheming of others had inflicted on them all those years. They had a lot of lost time to make up for...

As she stepped into her parents loving arms, she suddenly felt a strange presence in the room with them. She looked around wildly, fearing the worst, but instead of an intruder, she caught a glimpse out of the corner of her eye of a young Chinese boy, wearing strange clothes not of her time.

He gazed at her with wide, curious eyes, and she felt a strong bond between them, but knew not why...
When she looked again, the vision was gone...

Sin, stayed in bed the next morning and did not come down for breakfast. Normally, he would leave for Kung Fu class at 4am in the morning, but that morning, when the whole family gathered for breakfast, he was missing.
Tze looked around in surprise, "Where's Sin ?"
His mother was concerned, "I think he's still asleep. Can you go and see?"
Tze ran up and returned shortly with Sin plodding along behind him, listless and low-spirited. He was pale and sickly, a rare occurrence for a boy who was hardly ever ill.

Sui Chin placed her palm on his forehead, "Oh Dear, Sin, you look terrible. I'm taking you to see the doctor straight away."

2 0

-

DOCTOR

SUI CHIN TOLD RUDYAT, THE DRIVER, to take the kids to school first, then she took Sin with her to the doctor. At the doctor's office, she sent the driver home, telling him she and Sin would ride a horse-drawn carriage home.

The doctor gave Sin a thorough examination. He checked his eyes, ears, and throat, put his ear to Sin's chest and asked him to breathe deeply and did the same on Sin's back. He had Sin lay down on the examination table and palpated his stomach and checked the rest of his body to see if he felt any pain anywhere.

Finished with his examination, the doctor told Sin to get dressed.

"You are terribly overworked, young man. Exhausted. A few days of rest is all you really need and I'll give you a B12 vitamin shot to boost your energy levels and immune system."

He rang for the nurse and told her what he needed. A moment later the nurse came back with a small bottle of liquid B12. The doctor sucked it into a syringe and administered a shot into Sin's hip.

Sui Chin and Sin thanked the doctor, paid the cashier, and left. On the street, there were several horse-drawn carriages waiting for customers, as that was a common way for people to get around town in those days. Sui Chin hailed one of them and they climbed in.

The doctor's office was miles out of town in a beautiful scenic area called Gedung Sate, so they settled back for a quiet hour together.

Sui Chin quietly noted, "I can't help but notice you seem very depressed, Sin. Did something happen?"

Sin hunched his shoulders, but finally answered truthfully, "Chi Tiong and I went to visit a new Master in town, named Wu. He was a chubby, middle-aged man who knew nothing of Kung Fu classes and moved as slow as molasses - yet he beat both of us! I still haven't been able to figure out how in the world this could be possible? So, yes, I am confused and depressed about it."

"Have you asked Grandmaster E?"

"No, I-I'm trying to figure it out by myself."

"You know, Sin, Grandmaster E did not become Grandmaster for nothing. He understands many things. Talk to him."

Sin sighed, " OK, I will."

The ride from Gedung Sate to Bandung central was a lovely one. The houses along the route were spacious and elegant, with large, manicured yards and gardens. Trees were well-pruned, the lawns nicely cut and the streets wide and clean. It was a treat for the two of them to just sit back and enjoy the scenic ride.

After few moments of quiet reflection, Sui Chen said, "Mr. Huang from school called the other day to say what a brilliant student you have been lately in Trigonometry class. Something about you solving the equation of a triangle…?"

Sin smiled, "Oh yeah. One of the rules in Trigonometry is that the total sum of the angles inside a triangle will always be 180 degrees, no matter what the shape of the triangle is. So as homework, Mr. Huang asked us to prove it. I was so into solving the problem, I actually dreamt the solution! I wrote it down and the next morning when Mr. Huang asked if anyone in the class had solved the problem, I was the only one to raise my hand. He asked me to go to the blackboard and write out the solution. So I did.

Sin paused, reflecting.

His mother prompted him, "And, did Mr. Huang say it was correct?"

"I don't know. I was so absorbed in making sure I hadn't skipped anything or made a mistake that I stood there looking it over until the bell rang. Everybody else rushed out of class, but Mr. Huang and I stood there for quite a while time. He was still looking at it when I left."

Sui Chin smiled and ruffled Sin's hair. "That's my clever boy."

21
-
WU TANG MOUNTAIN

Sui Chin sent one of the servants to tell Grandmaster E that Sin was sick and would be unable to attend his lessons that week. After several days of much needed rest, Sin felt a little better and returned to the Grandmaster for class.

Grandmaster E was pleased to see him. "I have missed you these several days, Son," he said gravely. "I sense your disquiet…What have you wish to tell me?"

Sin hung his head, then blurted out, "My friend and I went to challenge Master Wu and it was a disaster! How could someone so overweight, who has never taken a day of Kung Fu lessons in his life, beat me? I sleep and eat Kung Fu every day of my life? Is it all for nothing? How could he possibly beat me?"

Grandmaster E turned to hide his smile. Collecting himself, he turned back and replied: "Though it may seem a mystery, there is an interesting explanation for it. Let me tell you the story of Chang San Fung…"

"In the year 1100, after studying Kung Fu at the Shaolin Temple for twenty years, a great Kung Fu master named Chang San Fung decided to retire to live on the slopes of the sacred Wu Tang mountain.

Wu Tang mountain was the sacred birthplace of Taoism. Legend has it that 5000 years ago on Wu Tang mountain, a snake and a turtle magically *fused* into one with godlike powers. Called 'Chen Wu' by the local population, this being became a mighty deity that would grant people wishes when they came to Wu Tang mountain and prayed to him.

So great were its powers and reputation, that during the Ming dynasty, Emperor Zhuli himself came to Wu Tang mountain and prayed to Chen Wu. The Emperor prayed to be granted the power to unify China under his rule. Emperor Zhuli had come to power by seizing the Jade Throne and murdering his rival cousin and his entire family to get it, so his position and power were shaky. With nowhere else to turn, the beleaguered Emperor promised Chen Wu that if he would grant him his wish, he would build elegant granite steps from the bottom of Mount Wu Tang to the very top of the mountain in his honor - a distance of 70 kilometers!

When the Emperor's wish came true, he faithfully fulfilled his promise. He set 300,000 laborers to work, bending their backs for thirteen long years to build the steps in Chen Wu's honor and a magnificent Golden Palace Temple at the very top of the mountain.

When their work was completed, Emperor Zhuli declared the Wu Tang Temple to be his official Palace Temple and Chen Wu to be his official deity, thereby establishing Wu Tang as the birthplace of Taoism.

One day on Wu Tang Mountain, the Kung Fu master, Chang San Fung, witnessed a fight between a snake and a white crane. The crane lashed out at the snake with his deadly beak at blinding speeds – yet it never succeeded in striking the snake, which was only a fraction of his size! How was that possible?

Fascinated by the snake's ability to dodge such vicious attacks, Chang collected dozens of snakes and began to study how they moved. He discovered that, unlike humans or other animals, snakes moved in a *curved fashion*, giving them a unique ability to evade the attacks of other animals who moved in predictable straight lines. When the crane's beak struck out at the snake at approximately 100 kilometers per hour, the snake had only to swivel to the side at a fraction of that speed to evade its attack.

Chang San Fung was ecstatic when he discovered this important principal and immediately set about creating a series of Kung Fu movements that would mimic the snake's.

And so the Snake Fighting System was born, over time it evolved into the legendary, *Tai Chi Chuan* or 'The Grand Ultimate Fighting Fist.'

22

-

SNAKE FIGHTING SYSTEM

Sin was mesmerized by Grandmaster E's story. It lifted an enormous load off his shoulders. Everything in the universe seemed to revert back to the way it had been - the way that he was familiar with, when the *rules* he had learned and understood worked as they should. Gone were the mysterious new rules that had weighed his mind down. He just had to learn these new techniques and all would be right with the world.

Relief flooded through him.

With his keen insight, Grandmaster E understood what was going on with Sin. A kindly smile spread across his face.

"It is time for me to demonstrate the wonder of the Snake Fighting System."

Grandmaster E slipped off the top of his robe to prepare to demonstrate the new technique.

Sin had never seen Grandmaster E's torso before and was amazed to see how muscular he was, even at his advanced age.

The Grandmaster handed Sin a spear. "Take this and try your best to hit me."

Sin hesitated at first, but decided to trust that his Mentor knew what he was doing. Plus, curiosity got the better of him! He poked the Grandmaster tentatively with the spear.

The Grandmaster moved like a snake, slithering aside and easily dodging all Sin's attacks. Sin's eyes flew wide in astonishment. He had never seen a human move that way!

Grandmaster E picked up two ropes and handed them to Sin, "Now, tie my hands and legs with these ropes."

Sin did as he was told. When he was trussed up tight, Grandmaster E slid to the ground and began slithering like a giant snake.

Sin was in awe. What an extraordinary ability! He'd never seen anything like it!

E told Sin to attack him again with the spear. Sin obeyed. He tried to spear E, but somehow the Grandmaster always managed to elude his attacks.

Before Sin knew what had happened, E had managed to slither back up onto his feet on Sin's blind side, and used his hip to bang Sin across the room.

Sin scratched his head in amazement.

"Watch," E said, as he hopped over to a light post. He wrapped his bound arms and body around the post like a snake and gradually tightened his grip.

Sin's mouth dropped open as his master slithered up around the post! He slithered a whole meter up off the ground before descending back to the ground. Sin had never witnessed such a thing!

E held out his hands and Sin swiftly untied them. E stooped to untie his legs as Sin tried to digest what he had just witnessed.

"*That* is the snake fighting system. How do you like it?"

Sin shook his head in disbelief, hardly knowing what to say. "I-I love it. I can hardly believe it's possible!"

"Then we shall start your snake training tomorrow," Grandmaster E proclaimed with satisfaction. "Come at your usual training time, but ask your driver to stay and wait instead of dropping you off. Now home you go and rest up. Tomorrow will be a *big day* for you!"

Sin thanked Grandmaster E for showing him the wondrous snake fighting system.

E nodded goodbye and took a big puff of his pipe and slowly blew a thick smoke ring out of his mouth, looking over his beautiful garden and slipping into a *world* of his own.

The next day when Sin arrived at E's place, the Master was already standing outside the door, with some coils of rope and a long pole with hook on it. E went to the car, placed the long pole and ropes inside, then climbed in the back.

Sin was baffled, but quickly seated himself beside him. Grandmaster E gave the driver directions to where they were going, while Sin sat and wondered what was going on.

Grandmaster E directed the driver to a river not too far away. He and Sin got out of the car and headed down the dirt road to the river bringing the ropes and pole with them. When they reached the bank, Grandmaster E asked Sin to concentrate and look in the water to see if he could spot any fish.

Sin concentrated hard and searched the river with his keen eyes trying to locate some fish. It was hard to do because the current was quite rapid, and that made visibility difficult. Snapping out of his intense concentration, Sin realized that Grandmaster E had tied his arms and legs with the ropes without him noticing!

Before Sin could ask him why, his Mentor pushed him into the river! Sin plunged head first into the rapid current and immediately started struggling, desperately trying to stay afloat without being able to use his hands and feet! He moved his body up and down like a dolphin, struggling to keep his head above water as the current swept him rapidly downstream!

Grandmaster E ran alongside him on the bank, carrying the long pole with the hook, ready to snag him if Sin should falter and go under. He was impressed with how well Sin was moving his body like a snake and kept his head far enough above the water to take in air.

The Grandmaster had to keep a naughty grin off his face watching Sin's antics.

But, eventually, quite a ways downstream, Sin began to tire and flounder, swallowing some water. He was having trouble taking a breath and Grandmaster E immediately used the long pole to hook him in and haul him to shore.

Sin was upset as he coughed and spit up water. E gave him a quick pounding on his back to clear the water out of his lungs. When Sin was able to catch his breath and calm himself down, he turned angrily to E and demanded, "Why did you do that without warning?!"

E cocked his head at him, "You really think Life will always warn you? In life, most things happen with no warning at all – the good and the bad. It is not just my job to train you in Kung Fu skills, it's my job to train you in Life and prepare you for your challenging journey through it."

Sin sat quietly, trying to digest what E had said. He didn't like his approach, but could see his point of view.

E continued, "You were instinctively doing the right thing by swimming like a dolphin. That is the basic premise of snake training, which teaches you how to use your entire body to fight an opponent. In the snake fighting system you are trained to use *only your body* to evade the attacks thrown at you and react defensively, leaving your hands and legs free to *attack*. This way you greatly increase the amount of attacks you can *shower* on your opponent."

Sin suddenly understood the importance of his hands and legs being tied, so he could train his body to fight the currents without relying on his appendages.

He grinned and yelled, "OK!" and jumped in the water! E was surprised, then grinned and chased Sin down the stream.

For the next several weeks, Sin and Grandmaster E held their training sessions at the river and Sin's progress in the Snake fighting System seemed as swift as the river itself.

To Sin's surprise, one day Grandmaster E jumped into the water himself. He held a board about one foot wide by three feet long and positioned the board across the river, against the current. Even though the current was quite strong, E seemed to have no trouble holding the board against it. After awhile, he passed the board to Sin and told him to do likewise.

Sin took the board and said, "A piece of cake!" He held the board against the current like E had done and the current instantly knocked him off balance, tumbling him downstream.

By the time Sin's head popped up out of the water, he was sputtering and gagging.

Grandmaster E chuckled, " A piece of cake, eh?"

Sin's face turned red with embarrassment. He tried again, this time being very cautious. But, still he got knocked off balance, but not quite as badly. The currents were merciless and kept coming at him. Eventually, he was pushed far down the stream.

E shouted in the distance, "*Steer* the currents, Son, don't fight them!"

Sin couldn't quite grasp what he meant and eventually, he exhausted himself still trying to figure it out. He came out of the river to face E, hanging his head.

Grandmaster E handed him a glass of clean water and Sin, parched, guzzled it down.

"Remember how Wu maneuvered you into the wall?"

Sin nodded, wondering why Grandmaster E was bringing it up now.

Grandmaster E continued, "He was steering your forces like you were trying to steer the currents."

Like a bolt of lightning, Sin understood, and felt a surge of renewed energy course through his body.

"Eeee-Ya!" he yelled jubilantly, and plunged back into the river to try again!

E laughed, pleased with his pupil's enthusiasm. The sun was setting, casting a golden light across the evening sky, by the time Sin yelled to Grandmaster E, "I got it! I got it!"

Grandmaster E was laying under a tree with a giant cooley hat covering his face against the sun. He woke up from his nap, and sheepishly looked at Sin in the distance, and saw that he was now correctly steering the wave.

"Excellent, My Son! That's enough training for the day. You have done extremely well."

Sin hauled himself out of the water, proud and excited about his accomplishment.

"The next time I spar someone, I can steer him and maneuver him and send him into the corner wall like Wu did. He won't even know what hit him! WOW! Thanks Grandmaster E!"

Grandmaster E smiled, pleased, and took a puff of his pipe, blowing smoke rings out into the air. "I am hungry. Time to head home."

Sin looked eager, "Grandmaster, all this time I have never had the opportunity to take you out to eat. Would you do me the honor of letting me take you to dinner tonight?"

Grandmaster E inclined his head, "Remember years ago I told you to eat soft shell turtle stew every night so you would have great energy for the training?"

Sin nodded. "I still follow those orders and eat it every night. I remember you told me that the soft shells are loaded with gelatin and collagen that helps to regenerate torn tissues and cartilage. Excellent for repairing and lubricating our joints."

Grandmaster E beamed at him, "Then, take me to your turtle stew place."

Sin gave the driver directions, thrilled to be having his first meal with his Grandmaster.

The next day, back at the Kung Fu school, Sin's lessons in Snake Training took an even more grueling turn.

When he entered, Sin saw an iron bar supported by two seven-foot tall wooden beams cemented firmly into the floor. He approached it warily.

Grandmaster E came to stand beside him and gestured to the bar, "This structure is simple… but you must conquer it or it will conquer you."

He quickly bound Sin's feet together with a rope hanging from the bar, then hauled him up until Sin was hanging upside down seven feet up in the air with his feet resting against the bar.

"You think your stomach is strong, Boy? Vertical sit-ups will reveal your true worth…"

The Grandmaster instructed Sin how to curl smoothly up from a hanging position without jerking, using only his stomach muscles.

Sin looked at the bar and smirked. He could do hundreds of sit-ups, so, how hard could *this* be?

So, on the first set, he breezed through thirty repetitions and felt good. He hung there to rest for a moment, then Grandmaster E ordered him to do several more reps. His stomach began to throb a bit by the time he forced out the last six reps, but he still felt confident he was doing well.

Then the Grandmaster demanded he do twenty more reps and halfway through, Sin knew he was in trouble! He squeezed hard but could only squeeze out more fifteen reps before his stomach burned like fire and he couldn't go on.

With a firm hand on Sin's back, Grandmaster E helped him do five more reps, then he let the boy hang down to rest for thirty seconds. Just when Sin had almost caught his breath, Grandmaster E ordered him to do a third set of another fifteen reps!

Sin struggled to obey, but this time his stomach screamed in *pain* and he could only force out nine reps. Again, Grandmaster E helped him finish the set of fifteen, then let him take a glorious forty second rest! Then he ordered him to do a fourth set!

Sin had nothing left to give. His stomach was spasming and he was sure he couldn't go on. But, he dreaded letting Grandmaster E down, so he forced out five more shaky reps and the Grandmaster helped him to force out another three reps.

But when Grandmaster E ordered him to do his fifth set after a short fifty-second rest, Sin collapsed after only three reps, his stomach muscles writhed in pain and refused to obey his will.

Grandmaster E smiled benignly and told Sin to rest for two minutes. Sin hung limply, his diaphragm laboring to draw shallow gasps of air into his chest.

Before he knew it, the Grandmaster commanded him to do the entire exercise of 80 reps - again!

Sin broke out in a cold sweat when he heard this command. His stomach was writhing in agony, his body was wracked with pain, and he just wanted to curl up and die!

He opened his mouth to ask the Grandmaster to cut him down, when he suddenly *flashed back* to his nightmare of the Madman chasing him.

A magnificent sensation of calm swept over him as the beautiful young woman who had rescued him in his nightmare suddenly appeared again in his mind's eye.

She looked directly at him, her eyes luminous and wise beyond her years and urged him, "You must train harder, Sin The´. Harder than you think humanly possible and one day you will defeat the Madman!"

This *visitation* infused Sin with such a powerful surge of renewed energy and confidence that before he knew what he was doing, he had done the first reps again, the second reps again, the third, the fourth and the fifth!

All in a blur of motion that seemed superhuman!

The Grandmaster beamed at him, "Good, my Son, you are stronger than you know."

Then, Grandmaster E told him that he was going to do a *negative* set! In this negative exercise, the Grandmaster pushed Sin into a crunched position, and told Sin to *resist* as he tried to pull him down.

Sin gritted his teeth and used all his strength to resist E's pull for as long as he could. He did well for the first rep and it took E quite a while to pull him down. And for the second rep, he was also able to resist E's pull for a while. But, by the third, fourth and fifth reps, Sin had hardly anything left to resist E.

This went on and on until Sin couldn't even hold himself up in a crunch and finally Grandmaster E nodded and untied his legs.

Sin was so happy to hear the magic words "Good work, Son, you may come down," that he loosened his legs and grabbed for the bar to let himself down, but his stomach wouldn't obey him and he *crashed* head first into the floor!

He tried to stagger to his feet to save face, but his stomach *cramped* on him and he collapsed to huddle miserably on the floor clutching his writhing stomach and moaning. It took everything he had not to scream in pain or vomit on the floor!

Grandmaster E pierced him with his steely gaze. "This is just the beginning, Sin The´. There are much more strenuous lessons to come."

Before Sin could despair, Grandmaster E ordered him to lay on his back while he rubbed a powerful ointment called, *Tie Ta Chiaow*, into the boy's aching stomach. This was a common and effective "bruise medicine".

To Sin, the massage was initially as excruciating as the exercises, but soon began to ease his cramps. The breathed easier as the pain subsided.

Grandmaster E gave him a cup of cool water and two very ripe bananas. "Eat these. They'll help and you need the energy."

Sin wolfed them down and, surprisingly, immediately felt better.

After a few more moments recuperating, Grandmaster E showed Sin a new technique of how to twist his torso along the ground like a snake. Then he made Sin copy his movements.

Sin was able to train for another whole hour before he got another excruciating cramp in his stomach.

Again, Grandmaster E brought Sin a cool glass of water and two more bananas, then rubbed *Tie Ta Chiaow* on his stomach and massaged the cramp away.

Again, after eating the bananas, Sin felt good enough to continue and they spent another grueling hour of hard training before Grandmaster E let Sin get up from the floor.

Then he told Sin that they were going to do some chopstick throwing as a means of resting. Two dozen chopsticks were tied together in two bunches. Grandmaster E took a bunch on each hand and tossed them to Sin. Sin caught them and threw them back. They did this for about ten minutes and, sure enough, Sin felt more relaxed afterwards.

E pushed him, "Okay you are rested now, and ready for another round of *hard* training."

The Grandmaster handed Sin a five kilogram (eleven lb.) dense, rubber ball. "I want you to use the snake training I have just taught you to throw the ball at the wall with both hands and catch it with both hands when it bounces back."

After all Sin's hard training that day, the ball felt quite heavy, and it took a lot out of him to throw it repeated at the wall and catch it on the rebound. He did this several times before E asked him to toss the ball back to him.

Grandmaster E admonished him, "I asked you to throw it the snake way, not the human way."

Sin scratched his head, not at all sure what his mentor meant. How would a snake throw a ball?

Grandmaster E stood about ten feet from the wall in a small horse stance, took the ball in both hands and rested it on his hip. Suddenly, he thrust his hip and torso out to the side, sending the ball slamming into the wall!

The ball hit the wall so hard with a CRACK, it made Sin jump! As soon as the ball bounced back to him, E caught it with both hands and brought it to his other side and whipped his hip and torso forward again. And again, the ball rocketed from his hip and slammed into the wall like a bullet!

E did this about a dozen times, then threw Sin the ball.

"That is the snake's way. Your turn."

Sin was impressed with the sheer force that Master E had been able to generate using the snake method. So, he mimicked Grandmaster E's movements and began to throw the ball into the wall the snake's way. But he'd forgotten that he didn't have E's strength or technique yet, so when he threw the ball from ten feet away as E had, the ball hit too low on the wall to even bounce. It scudded back to Sin along the floor.

It looked so funny, both E and Sin laughed out loud.

Sin picked up the ball and moved to within five feet of the wall and tried the throw again. That worked much better. He did the exercise a dozen more times, beginning to get the hang of it.

By the end of the exercise, he was huffing and puffing and his uniform was soaked with sweat.

When he could do no more on his right side, Grandmaster E instructed him to switch to his left side.

Sin rested a moment and started all over again with his left side. When Sin could do no more on the left, E let him rest for a moment then again had him switch sides. This went on and on and on until Sin could no longer even raise his arms and his hips felt like cement!

Grandmaster E finally allowed him to collapse and rest while he gave him a demonstration of how to do this exercise using only one hand instead of two.

Even with just one hand, E was able to slam the ball into the wall with amazing force!

Sin was very impressed and longed for the day he too could do the same. Then E showed Sin how to do the exercise alternating back and forth between each hand, using first one, then the other.

Sin was amazed at how much power the alternating hand technique generated. E explained that when his body twisted hard in one direction to release the ball, it was poised and ready to twist back in the other direction and release the pent up energy, like a giant spring that recoiled from one direction to the other, and released an enormous amount of power each time.

E told Sin that after he could do the exercise well with both hands, he should doing it alternating directions with both hands. After he'd mastered that, he would move on to doing it well with a single hand, then do the alternating pattern with each hand.

Sin's eyes lit up. He could see himself in his mind's eye, already imagining himself doing it as well as Grandmaster E.

Somehow that thought gave him more strength and confidence and seemed to lift away the pain he had just endured. Physically, he was a wreck, barely able to stand, but mentally he felt triumphant and alive!

He had survived another day of gruesome Snake Training!

Months later, after much sweat and pain, Sin had proudly mastered the Snake Training. He could slam the fifteen-pound ball against the wall with both hands, one hand and alternating hands, all with forceful, fluid motions. Every time he slammed the ball, he used the secret twist, throwing the torque of his entire twisting body behind it, and the ball " WHACKED! " into the wall with astspnishing force!

Grandmaster E watched his progress, nodding in approval.

As a variation of the Snake Exercise, Grandmaster E next picked up a bundle of chopsticks and used the twist technique to toss them to Sin.

Confident in his newfound snake training, Sin turned his body *away* from the direction of incoming projectile, caught it smoothly, then, with a rapid twist, whipped it back at the Grandmaster E like a shooting star!

Of course, being the real master, Grandmaster E retaliated, and slammed the bundle of chopsticks back at Sin with twice the boy's speed, upping the ante!

The two of them had great fun throwing "shooting stars" at each other until their speed was so fast, it was just a *blur*!

Sin was so into Snake Training, he decided that he should do what the Snake Technique master, Chang San Fung, had done: collect all sorts of snakes and spar with them!

Making up his mind to do it, Sin chose a short bamboo stick about eighteen inches long that would be safer than using a chopsticks, in case the snakes did not see it his way!

One of the servants had told him that not too far from the house was a wooded area with a nice little stream running through it that the locals used to wash their clothes or take baths. The servant said that just upstream, about a quarter mile, was the source of the spring that fed the stream and under the dense foliage at the source, hundreds of snakes would migrate together and form a giant, writhing knot of snakes during the mating season!

Sin was thrilled by this news! He got directions to the spring, and the next day, after Kung Fu class, he asked Rudy, a schoolmate, if he wanted to come and catch some snakes with him.

Rudy felt honored to be asked by Sin, who was Grandmaster E's prodigy. He was excited to share a private moment with him and readily agreed to go with him. They set out and found the stream where a group of women were bathing and washing their clothes.
The boys set off upstream, as directed, and soon arrived at the source of the spring, where they found a big tree trunk fallen across the stream that would serve as a handy bridge for them to cross over and take a look around for the snakes.

They climbed out to the middle of the tree-trunk bridge and peered down through the foliage.

They could hardly believe their eyes!

A few feet below the bridge, just where the spring bubbled out of the ground, they found hundreds of snakes entwined in one big, deadly tangle! It was the scariest thing they had ever seen and made their blood run cold!

They instantly grew more cautious, with so many scary-looking reptiles writhing right below them! They had no idea if they were poisonous or not, but they couldn't help worrying that one false move might mean their deaths!

Feeling like brave, intrepid hunters, Sin and Rudy readied their equipment: they had a snake stick with two prongs at the end and a pile of burlap sacks to put the snakes in - if they managed to catch any!

Excited, Sin said he was going to try it first. He asked Rudy to stand by with the burlap bag, ready to take the snake he planned to catch.

Sin leaned over the trunk to pick his quarry. He planned to bring the snakes home that he had caught and keep them in his terrarium, so they couldn't be all that big. He spotted a smaller snake and caught it on the prongs of his stick. He gave the stick a quick twist to tangle the snake in the prongs and pulled it up, thrashing! He quickly shoved the snake into the burlap sack and Rudy jittered around nervously until he had managed to tie the bag closed tightly. He crowed in triumph – they had their first snake! How easy that was!

Sin spotted another little snake and snagged it too. The little fella tried to slither away, but Sin pressed down on it slightly and within seconds he'd caught it and shoved it in Rudy's sack with the other one.

He quickly caught another snake after that – three in a row!

Rudy was excited to see how fast Sin had caught three snakes and anxious to catch one of his own! So, he begged Sin to let him try.

Sin reluctantly surrendered the stick to Rudy so he could try his luck. But, while Sin had picked little snakes that would fit in his glass terrarium back home, Rudy had no intention of keeping the snake, so he just wanted to catch the biggest one in the pile!

So when he spotted a giant python outside the main entwinement, he went for it! He tried to use the little two-pronged stick to capture him. But, the python was so big around, the prongs couldn't even fit over it!

The giant snake easily slithered out from under the stick and started to escape into the undergrowth.

But, Rudy didn't want to let it get away! Using all his might, he pressed down as hard as he could on the stick to stop the python from escaping.

But, to his horror, the stick broke, plunging Rudy headfirst into the middle of hundreds of writhing snakes! He let out a shriek of terror that could have woken the dead! And Sin looked on in horror!

Fortunately, the snakes were as frightened as Rudy was and in seconds, they were slithering away from him in all directions!

Rudy was wearing shorts, not long pants, so he was hysterical batting snakes off his legs and thighs as he desperately tried to climb back up to the bridge.

Seeing that none of the snakes were actually attacking Rudy, Sin couldn't help bursting out laughing at how funny Rudy looked, dancing and jiggling around!

Who knows how many snakes Rudy stepped on before he finally managed to reach into the tree trunk and have Sin help pull him up.

The miracle of all miracles was: Rudy did not even get *one* snake bite!

Finally, after months of grueling training, the day came for Sin's Snake Training test with the Grandmaster.

Grandmaster E took a long bamboo stick and with savage thrusts, tried to strike Sin's body.

Moving like a snake, Sin succeeded in evading almost all of the attacks.

When Grandmaster E finally stopped, he was well pleased. "Very good, Son. *Now* you look like a snake!"

Sin raised his thumbs in the air and cheered, "Yeaaaah! Our hard work has paid off!" Impulsively, he gave E a grateful hug.

The Grandmaster had grown up in a much more formal era, so he was caught by surprise and stood there surprised, not sure how to receive such a spontaneous show of affection.

But his own affection for his favorite pupil won out and he unbent enough to give his prodigy a fatherly pat on the back.

23
-
TAI CHI CHUAN, LEGEND OF YANG LU CH'AN

ONE DAY GRANDMASTER E SAID TO Sin, "Son, the time has come to teach you the first Internal form of Tai Chi, called *Tai Chi Chuan*, The Grand Ultimate Fist. I want to start you with the Yang Tai Chi 64th Form, created in the eighteen hundreds by the great master, Yang Lu Ch'an."

Yang Lu Ch'an was born in 1799 in a small town in China's Hebei Province. His parents were poor tenant farmers and Yang had only a bleak future of backbreaking physical labor toiling in the soil to look forward to, when he followed in their footsteps.

But, since he been a child, he had loved Tai Chi and had, on his own, studied the most popular Long Fist style for many years as best he could.

When Yang was seventeen years old, he heard about the fighting Chen Family of Chen Chia Kou village, who were 14th generation Kung Fu masters, lead by their patriarch, Chen Chang Hsing.

Yang yearned to be accepted by Chen as a student, but knew that because of his humble birth, this was an impossible dream. But instead of relinquishing his dream without trying, he traveled to the Chen Village and managed to get work in the household as a servant.

Fortunately, his modest sleeping quarters looked onto the courtyard where Master Chen taught Tai Chi to his two sons. So, every evening Yang watched them practice and when they had finished for the night, he would practice recreating their moves until the early morning hours.

Over the years, working with unrelenting diligence and discipline, Yang became adept at Tai Chi, while the Master's sons, who were undisciplined and lazy, fell behind.

One day, to his horror, the Master discovered Yang practicing and realized his humble servant has learned his secret movements without his permission! Yang was terrified that he would be imprisoned or even put to death! But instead of having him punished, Master Chen was so impressed with Yang's skill, he welcomed him into the family, elevating him as a brother-pupil who was henceforth allowed to train alongside his lagging sons.

In spite of the antagonism of Master Chen's sons, once Yang was allowed to train in the open, he soared to mastery of his art, making Master Chen proud of his decision to take him in. Years later, when the Master lay dying, he called Yang to his bedside.

As his other sons looked on and scowled, Master Chen gave Yang a brimming bag of silver coins. "You, the *least* of my sons, are the *best* of my sons. Go forth with my blessing, my son, and use this gift to become Master of your own Tai Chi school. You have earned this great honor."

Yang humbly accepted and set off for the capital, where he proudly founded his own school. But sadly, he was so short in stature and no one wanted to study with a man so much smaller than the average Northerner.

At his wits end, just as his money was about to run out, he discovered that Tze Shi, The Dowager Empress of China, was hosting a tournament to find the best Kung Fu fighters in China to become revered Imperial Trainers for her Elite Palace Guards.

Yang knew without a shadow of a doubt that he *would be* one of those elite fighters.

But when Yang stood in line with the tall northern fighters, they all sneered at him. It took him a moment to realize they were all at least a foot taller than him and outweighed him by a good hundred pounds at least!

Yang knew he would have to fight for his life or die trying.

Hundreds of rings were laid out in the arena, surrounded by thousands of fighters itching to display their prowess. While waiting his turn, Yang had the opportunity to watch his opponents fight and quickly memorized their key weaknesses.

When he finally stepped into the ring, he was ready.

Even though he was always matched with large, formidable foes, using the secret techniques he had learned from Master Chen, with one touch of his hand, Yang sent an electrical *jolt* to his opponent's core that sent them flying or struck nerve points that caused his opponents to collapse unconscious just seconds into the bout!

None of the other fighters had ever seen anything like it! They watched in awe as he moved like a vengeful God from out of an ancient myth!

By the time the week was out, Yang ranked amongst the twenty finalists - the 'Best of the Best' from all of China.

When the day of the final competition came, he stood proudly yet humbly to attention, awaiting the arrival of the Empress herself.

The crowd went wild when The Dowager Empress, Tze Shi, entered the court and took her throne. She looked contentedly down the line of tall, strapping warriors, all fit to be elevated to Head Trainer of her legendary Elite Palace Guards.

Until her gaze came to rest on Yang.

He alone was short, slight, and stood with an unassuming humility. Who was this peasant? Nothing about him exuded the aura of a fierce warrior, much less the world's most dangerous one! He was unfit to grace her arena!

The Empress was angry and insulted that a man like Yang had the gall to presume he could become Head Trainer for her 80,000 elite Imperial Palace Guards! What a disgrace it would be to have this midget in charge! *She vowed to teach him a lesson he would not soon forget!*

She called the announcer over and ordered him to pair Yang with a fighter she selected. The announcer bowed and did her bidding as she settled smugly back in her throne to watch the little upstart be pummeled.

Diminutive Yang and the giant fighter the Empress chose came out of the line up and faced each other. Her fighter turned out to be the Mongolian Suai Chiao, a great wrestling champion, who was very, very strong. As soon as the fight began, he came roaring at Yang, grabbed him by the shirt, and, using his hip as leverage, attempted to throw Yang over his shoulder. He had done this move thousands of times and it had always worked like a charm.

Not this time.

Yang used his secret *Nei Kung Internal Power* to literally glue his body into the ground like an immovable mountain. The massive Mongolian wrestler could literally not move him!

When Yang had had enough, he calmly leveraged his huge opponent up into the air and tossed him twenty feet away! When the outraged wrestler struggled back to his feet and threw some combination punches at him, Yang effortlessly blocked his attacks, then struck Suai Chiao's hand using the *Jarring Hand* technique. What felt like an electrical current jolted through the giant wrestler's body and sent him staggering back – again!

To finish him off, Yang *sailed* through the air and struck him on several of his Dim Mak pressure points. The wrestler slumped to the ground, unconscious.

The audience cheered, amazed at this plucky underdog! But the Empress turned red with rage. How dare this little upstart make her chosen warrior look so bad?

She ordered more fighters into the ring, each one bigger than the last, each one with special Kung Fu fighting skills like Praying Mantis, Frog Master, and Sticking Hand that she was sure would defeat the little upstart.

But, Yang handily defeated one fighter after another until there was no one left to fight him! The whole stadium, sensing the Empresses mood, fell silent, anxiously waiting to see what would happen next.

After a frigid silence, Tze Shi's angry voice rang out, "How about *bullets*? Can you dodge them as well?"

She ordered a firing squad of twelve men to line up with their rifles trained on Yang.

"FIRE!" the Empress screamed and twelve gunshots rang through the air. Yang jerked his body to the left and right in a *blur of motion*.

When the smoke cleared, the entire stadium, including The Empress, was stunned to see Yang still standing - completely unharmed!

As the influence of foreign powers grew and she found her armies woefully outgunned, the Empress had been seeking a way to level the playing field and help her to hold them off. Yang's astonishing ability to dodge bullets seemed like the answer to her prayers!

She saw that she had been wrong to loathe the little master. She slowly stood up and humbly raised her head to Heaven in silent thanks, then addressed her subjects, "Today you have witnessed the greatest martial arts demonstration in the history of mankind - performed by Yang Lu Chan. It is my honor to announce that, hence forth, he shall be the Head Trainer for my Imperial Guards!"

The audience went wild and Yang humbly bowed, thrilled to his core at his elevation in rank, but also, just to be alive!

Grandmaster E stopped his story and turned to ask Sin a question. "So, Young Man, do you know how Yang dodged the firing squad's bullets?"

Sin shook his head, mystified.

"The answer lies in the mystery of 720 pressure points embedded in our bodies. By manipulating one's Chi through a special sequence of these pressure points, one can achieve a 'State of Void'. When you reach the 'State of Void', suddenly, time outside your body seems to move in *slow motion* compared to the time you perceive inside yourself. That's how Yang was able to dodge twelve deadly bullets from the Firing Squad."

Sin nodded eagerly, "I see, Grandmaster E! I've been studying physics and Taoism, and they actually agree: our bodies represent the *micro* version of what is going on in the *macro* Universe around us. In our cosmos, time is relative, not absolute, so it moves at different speeds depending on how fast one is moving. So, for planets close to the vicinity of a Black Hole, every *minute* there equals *days* or even *weeks* on Earth. I think the mystery of the human body must parallel the mystery of the Universe."

Grandmaster E was impressed by Sin's knowledge and astute observations. "Very good, Sin. It is true that all things are One and all the mysteries of the Universe are inextricably linked. It is our job to unravel them as best we can. Come, you are ready to learn something new."

Grandmaster E taught Sin the *Push Hand* and the *Sticky Hand* aspect of Tai Chi. Soon Sin had mastered them well enough to perform them well against Grandmaster E, who complemented him on his skill.

Next, Sin was honored when Grandmaster E decided to teach Sin the esoteric *Nei Kung* meditation technique that would enable him to reach the fabled *State of Void* and transform his perception of time at will. But this skill proved to be frustratingly elusive and, initially, Sin got no closer to achieving it, no matter how long he spent trying to master it.

For months he spent hours every day in intense meditation trying to achieve a State of Void, but it kept eluding him. One day, filled with frustration and beginning to despair that he would never be able to master it, he almost gave up. Then a strange thing happened: in sort of giving up, he stopped desiring it so much, and found that it had been his intense desire that had prevented him from clearing his mind!

The very instant he relinquished his desire, something clicked inside him, and suddenly the outside world *changed*.

As he gazed at the big clock on the wall, he perceived that its second hand had *slowed down to a snail's pace*! It appeared to be moving in slow motion, stretching each second into an eternity.

Sin was stunned and woke up from his trance-like reverie elated with his breakthrough!

The next day when he saw Grandmaster E, Sin eagerly told him of his exciting experience.

Grandmaster E regarded his star pupil with approval and nodded. "That's it, Son. You caught a momentary glimpse of the *State of Void*. But to perfect this extraordinary skill will take you many years of hard and diligent practice. But, you have begun well, now practice hard and the rest will follow!" Encouraged, Sin vowed to do just that.

Grandmaster E began to demonstrate the Yang-style Tai Chi Chuan form as he moved across the room with a slow and subtle grace. Sin had been so inspired by Yang Lu Ch'an's story, he watched his master run through the moves with great anticipation.

The 64 moves of Yang's form were divided into 6 sections, each filled with subtle, graceful moves that required one's full concentration in a way that bordered on meditation or more accurately, *meditation-in-motion*. After running through the entire form once, Grandmaster E proceeded to teach Sin Section One.

Grandmaster E broke the silence, "Yang Lu Chang really admired a legendary Kung Fu fighter and giant named Si Gin Kui, who I will tell you about next time. To honor Si Gin Kui, Yang Lu Chang named several moves after the events and characters in Si Gin Kui's legendary lifestories. These include: the *Reverse Smack the Lotus*, which depicts Si Gin Kui on his wedding day demonstrating powerful kicks that made the lotus plants wave to and fro in the pond; *Bend The Bow - Shoot The Tiger* and *Move Back- Ride The Tiger*".

The Grandmaster made a graceful gesture and continued, "Later, when I teach you the *Tai Chi Fan*, you will see that the *Smoke of Incense Reaches Heaven* move depicts the night before he went to his uncle's place. Si Gin Kui, who never prayed to God all his life, decided to pray that night. Instead of lighting up three incense sticks, he lit up a whole bundle, sending a billow of smoke up into the sky. Then the moves: *Climbed the Steps to Heaven*, *Look Up to Heaven's Gate*, and *The Wind Blows, Slipped Foot and Tumbled Down Heaven's Steps*, depict Si Gin Kui's mind floating between life and death when he tried to hang himself from the willow tree. He saw Heaven's Gate but it was not his time to enter it yet. He fell from Heaven's Steps when his future wife found him in the nick of time, and saved his life."

Sin listened intently, loving the exciting, historic details that Grandmaster E always used to liven up his classes.

"Now that you have done so well with the 64 Yang Tai Chi forms, I am going to teach you the 83 Chen Tai Chi forms that Yang Lu Chan learned from Old Master Chen."

Sin found the movements in the 83 Chen forms challenging, as the calm and gentle movements were suddenly followed by a flurry of rapid powerful attacks.

The snapping recoil from his punches were so powerful, his uniform made loud popping noises when he did his exercises! He loved the feel of wielding that much power and that made him practice harder.

Grandmaster E loved to see Sin's excelling himself. For hours a day, while practicing the forms over and over again, Grandmaster E led his pupil into a secret world, previously unknown to Sin.

The gentle, slow motion world of Tai Chi was an epiphany for the serious young man, who was only accustomed to fast, rigorous fighting styles. Sin felt he had experienced an almost religious catharsis by the end of the Tai Chi class and that had a profound spiritual effect on him.

Within a few short months, Sin had mastered the forms so well that he could achieve a deep state of meditation during his practice. He felt he entered another dimension – one that pulsed with a vibrant, life-affirming energy, moving in slow, perpetual motion like the eternal rhythms of the earth.

Deep in his trance, he caught a glimmer of the complex web of energy that coursed between everything in the Universe – linking him the Universe and everyone and everything in it into one radiant, inseparable whole.

Tai Chi changed Sin's perspective on life and he has maintained a deeper awareness of his connection to all living things ever since…

2 4

-

YANG LU CHAN (Part 2)

SEVERAL DAYS LATER, GRANDMASTER E RETURNED to the Yang Lu Chan story. There were more lessons to be learned from him…

"Empress Tze Shi realized Yang could be the salvation of her empire. His techniques could help her Imperial armies to withstand the heavily-armed and combined might of the foreign powers who were gradually imposing their will on China."

So, instead of still seeking his death, she elevated him to be the highest-ranking head of her Imperial Guard and her right hand man.

If Yang felt there was anything strange about this remarkable turn of events, he was too relieved to be alive and too excited about his new position to spare it much thought.

He had wondered, over his years of training, if his State of Void Nei Kung *could* save him from bullets, but naturally he had not wanted to risk testing it out. Now he knew! He could still hardly believe *what he had done!*

The Empress arranged a grand tour for him of the Forbidden City – the gorgeous royal compound where all commoners (except servants) were forbidden to enter. She treated him as an Honorary Guest and hosted him at a lavish meal consisting of one sumptuous course after another.

After dinner, she invited him into the Palace Garden – an exquisite Oriental garden landscaped with fascinating spires of rock and rare species of trees, plants and flowers, all nestled around the serene Tung Ting Lake.

Dozens of gilded birdcages hung from the branches of the trees in the garden, home to many species of exotic birds. Tze Shi proudly showed Yang a little golden cage containing her favorite singing canary.

The tiny bird began to sing a beautiful song, spilling notes of liquid gold into the air. Yang was entranced. When the bird finished singing, Yang asked the Empress if he could pet it.

Tze Shi did not quite understand what Yang intended, but she was so pleased to have found her champion, she was only too willing grant him permission to do as he asked. But she was startled when the next thing she knew, Yang had opened the little door, reached in and gently taken the bird out and opened his hand to set it free!

The Empress was upset, thinking she had just lost her most prized pet.

However, as the bird flew off his hand, Yang began to vibrate his palm and though the bird beat its wings, it could not move away! Yang seemed to be generating some kind of *force field* that held the bird in place!

Tze Shi's annoyed frown changed to one of astonished delight and she clapped to applaud Yang for this unparalleled demonstration of *Sticky Hand Nei Kung*!

For the next twenty years until his death, Yang served as the Imperial Head Trainer for the Empress Tze Shi. He tackled the daunting task of training 80,000 soldiers by dividing them into 80 groups of 1000 soldiers each. He went from group to group, teaching them his style of Tai Chi for 16 to 18 hours every day. It soon became clear that most of his soldiers had mastered the tough, aggressive part of the fighting system but could not grasp the gentle, more elusive part of the fighting system required for the *Sticky Hand technique*.

The original Chen Tai Chi forms that he had learned from his old Master Chen combined both the aggressive and the gentle elements. But, since time was of the essence, he created a new form of Tai Chi that concentrated on the gentle and elusive movements so that the soldiers would be able to achieve a high level of competence in *Sticky Hand* in a short period of time. His troops called it the Yang Style of Tai Chi Chuan.

Yang's ability to judge men's character was so evolved, he could gauge by the way a challenger walked into the room how many seconds that fighter would last against him.

He would set them up for a fall by quietly inquiring, "Excuse me, would you prefer to fall on your face or your backside? Allow me to choose for you – you will fall on your face and kiss my feet!" And down they would go!

Due to the many years of long, hard days spent training his troops, Yang achieved a superb level of *Nei Kung Meditation*, until he required only two hours of sleep meditation each night.

His fighting skills also reached an all-time high, making him a living legend throughout China.

The Empress completely changed her tune and now loved to watch him fight, and in the many long years he served as her Head Trainer, she never missed any of the thousand-plus matches he fought and won against the finest fighters in China.

Until his death at a ripe old age, the diminutive, imperturbable Yang remained undefeated.

25
-
CLOUD HAND OF TAI CHI

ONE DAY, WHILE SIN WAS LEARNING the elegant, Tai Chi *Cloud Hand* movements, Grandmaster E stopped him to ask, "Every version of Tai Chi has a *Cloud Hand* move. Do you know the significance of that?"

Sin shook his head.

Grandmaster E continued, "The name comes from an old Chinese folk tale. The Chinese believe that Heaven is presided over by the thousands of Immortals, who were supreme beings with magical powers. Like Greek Gods, the ancient Chinese believed that gods and goddesses ruled the world by controlling the wind, sun, moon, clouds, ocean and earth.

One night, a goddess I'll call, May Ling, was sent to earth to make sure all was well with the world. She soared through the sky flying over all of China and saw that all was good. But, when she happened to fly over a small hut deep inland, she noticed a strange light she'd never seen before flickering on and off.

Curious, she dived down to check. Peeping in the window, she saw a scholar in neat but worn clothing pouring over a book. But where was the strange, flickering light coming from?

Too poor to buy oil for a lantern, the scholar had devised an ingenious 'natural' lantern – he had caught hundreds of fireflies and put them in a glass jar!

At first they had lit up randomly but in harmony with each other, they soon synchronized and flashed at the same time!

So, when the fireflies lit up together, the scholar could see to read his book. When they turned off, he used the time to memorize what he had read. An excellent system!

May Ling became curious about this resourceful scholar. She used her magical skill to pry into his past and saw his life flash before her eyes in a flash!

The handsome scholar had been born of rich and noble parents. He had lost his parents to the plague when he was still a young man and inherited their vast estates and wealth. He was a brilliant scholar that had produced many excellent poems and writings, but he was too soft-hearted and could not refuse people when they were in need.

When people learned of his good nature, they flocked to see him from everywhere to beg for his help. Touched by their suffering, in less than a year, he had given away the family fortune and lost his magnificent mansion and all his land. Only a small parcel of farmland and the tiny hut he lived in still remained.

The young scholar learned how to farm and by day he worked the land himself with his bare hands and by night, he devoted himself to his studies, reading his precious books by firefly-light far into the night.

In spite of losing everything in life that others prized so highly, the scholar was blissfully happy, leading a simple, fulfilling life.

Touched by his generosity and nobility of spirit, May Ling felt her heart go out to him.

Using her magical power, she materialized another hut not too far from the scholar's. The next day she rose early and found him already up, tending his farm. It was rice-planting season and he was knee-deep in water, pulling individual rice plants from a larger bundle and planting them in long, neat rows.

May Ling shyly introduced herself and invented a story similar to his own: of being born to a noble family, studying with the best tutors in the land, then tragically losing her parents to the plague and finding herself alone in the world. She offered to help him with his tasks in exchange for his company.

The scholar was astonished that a young and beautiful noblewoman would willingly work with her hands in a muddy field, but he gratefully accepted.

While they worked, the scholar asked which poets she liked, and she scanned his thoughts and was happy to discover his favorites were hers too. At noon, she prepared a sumptuous meal that her young scholar marveled was the best he had ever tasted!

Intelligent and happy in each other's company, they talked endlessly about poetry, philosophy and life as the days flew by. A loving bond began to form between them and soon, they fell deeply in love.

May Ling was blissfully happy with him and realized she could not drag herself away back to her rightful place in Heaven with the other Gods and Goddesses. So, when he asked her to marry him, she joyfully accepted, and soon their little family had grown by two beautiful little daughters.

But, all was not well in Heaven. When the King of Heaven realized she was missing, he sent her superior, May Yi, to find her and bring her back. May Yi was shocked to discover May Ling living incognito as a human, married to an ordinary man!

May Yi revealed herself to May Ling, berated her, and dragged her back to Heaven, with May Ling resisting all the way. Her resistance created an awkward diagonal flight into the sky as they flew toward Heaven, and this later inspired the Tai Chi move called "Slanting Fly."

May Ling was so distraught at being forced to abandon her beloved family, she waved to them all the way to Heaven – and her devotion was immortalized forever in the move called gentle, yearning move called "Cloud Hand."

Fortunately, the story has a happy ending.

The King of Heaven felt such pity for the tragic, inconsolable young Goddess brutally torn from her beloved family, that he agreed to reunite her with them! He let her husband and their two daughters take a single bite from the Peach of Immortality that grew in the sumptuous Gardens of Heaven, rendering them all immortal!

And so, May Ling and her family lived happily ever after in Heavenly Paradise.

2 6

THE LEGEND OF SI GIN KUI

After several particularly grueling weeks of training when Sin was making no progress at all, he began to despair. He felt so conflicted and emotionally raw, that for the first time in his life, he thought about giving up his martial arts training. He had begun to doubt about his ability to make it to the end of the long and incredibly difficult road it took to become a reigning Kung Fu Master.

His tutor sensed Sin Thé´s despair and realized the boy was in dire need of help and inspiration to get him through this temporary slump.

He waved at Sin to stop his training and come to sit by him. He pulled out his pipe, tamped in some tobacco, and started to smoke.

"Do you know where the names of the Tai Chi moves come from? 'Move Back', 'Ride the Tiger', 'Turn the Body', 'Smack the Lotus', 'Bend the Bow' and 'Shoot the Tiger?'" Grandmaster E asked casually.

Sin shook his head, so dejected, he was unable to rouse any interest in the subject.

Grandmaster E warmed to his story, "General Si Gin Kui of Tang Dynasty was one of the finest Kung Fu fighters in China, and became one of the most beloved generals in all of Chinese history. You will remember that the founder of Tai Chi, Yang Lu Chan, admired him so much, he named many Tai Chi movements after events in the general's life… But, Si Gin Kui's life wasn't always so grand… "

Si Gin Kui parents were owners of a small shop in a rural village and when their first son arrived, Si Gin Kui was born mute – a very unpromising start. He was so withdrawn, they feared he was also deaf, or worse, touched in the head. But they did not give up on him.

One night, when he was five years old, Si Gin Kui had a bizarre dream: he was transported to the palace of the Great Immortals of Heaven and found them in the middle of what sounded like an old argument!

"He is not ready!" barked one Immortal.

"It is too soon…" cautioned another.

"Enough!" roared their leader, the King of Heaven. "My decision has been made and it is final!"

He picked up a finely-wrought metal pagoda and turned to a huge, intimidating White Tiger that stood beside him, its fierce, intelligent eyes following his every move.

The King of Heaven raised the pagoda over his head and tossed it at the tiger. As it flew through the air, it transformed into a swirling vortex that swept the tiger down to Earth!

The great beast slammed into the floor in the boy's bedroom like a meteorite, rousing Si Gin Kui from his dream with a sharp cry. But, instead of the White Tiger disappearing into the realm of ephemeral dreams, *it remained standing beside Si Gin Kui's bed*!

The boy screamed in terror! The huge tiger got slowly to its feet, and, towering over him, looked deep into his eyes in a soul-gaze…

Suddenly, Si Gin Kui's fear evaporated. Instead a profound sense of completeness, rebirth and selfhood welled up in him, as a vivid, shining spark passed between the boy and the tiger!

Si Gin Kui's screams brought his parents running toward his room. Before they got there, without a sound, the tiger leaped effortlessly out of the window, moving as fluidly as a mountain stream.

When Si Gin Kui's parents burst into the room, they were baffled when their son pointed to the tightly-shuttered window and yelled, "Tiger! Big Tiger!"

To their stunned amazement, their son was no longer deaf and mute! He began to tell them of his dream, speaking as clearly as if he had been speaking normally his entire life!

From that moment on, Si Gin Kui was a normal boy and a great source of pride to his grateful parents.

It was said that Si Gin Kui had been born without a *soul* - until that night. At his birth, the Immortals in Heaven had not been able to agree on what soul he deserved and had argued over it for five long years until the King of Heaven finally intervened and awarded Si Gin Kui a soul so special, only a rare White Tiger could deliver it!

From that point on, Si Gin Kui's mind developed very rapidly and he soon surpassed all the other children in the village. He also grew unusually strong and, by the age of twelve, could carry two 220 pound (100 Kg) sacks of rice, one in each hand, all by himself to distant customers without the need of a horse and cart.

His astonishing feats of strength soon became the talk of the town and people came from all over the land to buy sacks of rice from his parents so they could see Si Gin Kui! The family business flourished and his parents came to expect that their exceptional son had a special destiny to fulfill.

They thought he was on his way when he began to seriously train in Kung Fu, vowing to become a great General one day. Every year the Emperor hosted a Kung Fu tournament to find the finest Kung Fu fighters in all the realm and awarded them with top-ranking positions in his Imperial Army.

Si Gin Kui promised his parents that one day, that would be him! His parents waited with great anticipation for him to fulfill his destiny.

But, sadly that day did not come in time for them. Even though he excelled at his training and his tutor felt he was the best Kung Fun fighter he had ever seen, Si Gin Kui lacked the confidence to compete, certain he wasn't good enough yet. So, year after year, to his devoted parents' keen disappointment, he kept putting it off.

"Next year," he'd say. "Next year, I promise…"

But, tragedy struck and Si Gin Kui lost both his parents within days to the plague. Wracked with guilt that he had not made good on his promise while they were still alive to enjoy it, he retreated within himself and let the thriving family business go to ruin from neglect.

Soon, he had lost everything and was out on the street, penniless.

Lost, despairing and shunned by his selfish Uncle and Aunt, his only surviving relatives, Si Gin Kui lost the will to live. He wandered in utter desolation to a lonely, out-of-the-way spot, tied a rope from a lofty branch, and tried to hang himself!

This was the desperate act at his lowest ebb of the man we now know as the great and noble general revered by all China!

Luckily, a tender-hearted woman was passing by at the time and, touched by his plight, she rushed to save his life. When he came to and they spoke, she was able to sense the unique and exceptional nature of his inner self, hidden beneath his defeated and impoverished exterior. She found herself falling in love with him. Before long, they married and, with a loving and supportive wife at his side, Si Gin Kui found the strength to pull his life back together and finally enter the competition.

Despite the long odds against him, Si Gin Kui vowed he would win the competition in memory of his late, devoted parents.

So great was his belief in himself, and his commitment and determination, it made him unbeatable! Win it he did!

Si Gin Kui rose to meteoric heights and became the most famous general in Chinese history. Imagine such incredible success and accomplishment from a man who had once been so broken and despairing, he had tried to take his own life!

"Imagine the loss to the nation if he hadn't found the strength to carry on and achieve true greatness?" Grandmaster E mused, as he puffed his pipe and cast a meaningful eye at his brilliant young pupil.

"We all have heavy burdens to bear in this life," he continued, "But none will ever be heavier than you will be able to bear, Young One. No matter how bleak your life may look from time to time, know that you hold within you the seed of Greatness, if you can only find the courage and perseverance to see it through…"

Sin The´ bowed to his master humbly and never forgot that inspiring life lesson. From that day on, whenever obstacles seemed too hard to bear, he would remember the story of the Great Si Gin Kui, and it would lift him on wings of hope when he needed it most.

2 7

-

PAKUA CHANG: THE ORTHOGONAL PALM

SEVERAL MONTHS LATER, GRANDMASTER E DECIDED to teach Sin another special fighting system called *Pa Kua Chang or the Orthogonal Palm Hand.* These fluid movements were performed in a circle, designed to enable a fighter to outmaneuver their opponents and attack from his blind spot.

The first form of *Pa Kua* he taught Sin, *The Classical Pa Kua Chang,* had been created one hundred and fifty years ago by Master Tung Hai Chuan…

After years of vigorous training, Master Tung excelled in the *Arts of Chinh Kung* or the *Make Your Body As Light As Feather technique.* So agile and lightfooted was he, before long he was doing his training on the rooftops of his house! To achieve a sense of lightness in ordinary fighting, he trained with extra weights on his shoulders, chest, wrists and ankles. One day to please his adventurous young grandson, Tung put the boy up on his shoulders and took him for a ride on the rooftop too (something one isn't likely to do today!).

His grandson adored the exhilarating ride and invited several of his little friends to join him the next day. Tung good-naturedly acquiesced to the wishes of his grandson and gave all his friends the ride of their lives. Before long, as word spread through the village, all the children in the entire town were lined up front of Tung's house waiting for their turn!

Years of hard training giving children rides on his back as he ran and leapt along the rooftops, honed his *Body Lightening Ability* to exceptional heights. Legend has it, he could move so fast that, with a *flicker,* he could *disappear* before his opponent's eyes, then reappear behind them and tap them on their back before they knew what had happened!

When he had finished telling Sin the story of Tung Hai Chuan, Grandmaster E took a sip of his tea, leaving Sin entranced.

"Just like Tung Hai Chuan's training, we are going to implement weight training along side the *Pakua* form training. I'll start you with weights coupled with plyometrics training to achieve a super explosive power."

He laid an empty bar across Sin shoulders and loaded it with twenty kilos of weight. He told Sin to set his feet wide apart and showed him how to come down slowly into a squat position while breathing in, how to breathe out and *explode* with power as he stood back up.

Sin followed E's instruction and did this exercise until he couldn't do any more. Just as he was going to put the weight back on the rack, Grandmaster E asked him to do one more rep. Sin reluctantly agreed and slowly squatted down. When he tried with all his might to stand up, his burning thighs clenched and he could not rise another inch and almost fell over.

Grandmaster E grabbed the bar and helped him slowly stand up and lift the bar back onto the rack. Sin's legs were on fire and shook as he stood in place.

As Sin huffed and puffed, trying to catch his breath, his master explained to him that power-training needed to be alternated with movement training that used the same muscle group to loosen them up and keep them flexible so they wouldn't get muscle-bound.

For the movement training, Grandmaster E set a two-foot high bench in front of Sin and asked him to jump over it, then jump back to his original position. After twelve jumps, Sin's legs cramped and he could hardly move.

Grandmaster E let him to rest for one minute then bid him jump to the side instead. This time Sin could only make it to ten reps.

Grandmaster E let Sin to rest again for a moment, but it seemed like only seconds before he smiled and barked, "Again!"

Two hours later, Sin had lost count of how many sets of squats and jumps he had performed. He remembered vaguely that at one point Grandmaster E had taken all the weights off the bar so he could do many, many more sets of squats without weights.

Then, when Sin couldn't jump over the bench anymore, the Grandmaster E pushed the bench to the side and ordered him to do frog jumps. Sin's legs were quivering uncontrollably and he suddenly succumbed to a massive leg cramp that left him writhing in pain on the cold stone floor.

Grandmaster E brought him a banana and some cool water to drink. When Sin felt better and was ready to go home, Grandmaster E again ordered him to do some more squats and frog jumps until he could do no more. At the end of it all, Sin sat on the floor and couldn't move. Then he saw E draw a two meter radius circle on the floor with chalk and wave Sin to come over.

Standing on the south end of the circle, E began doing the first sequence of Classical Pakua. Sin could hardly move and, despite his incredible commitment to the craft and respect for Grandmaster E, found himself thinking, *"you must be kidding me!"*

Reluctantly, Sin hobbled over. Another hour passed before E ended the class. By then, Sin was on the verge of passing out.

Never in his life had he felt so happy to be going home and intended to sleep for a long, long time. But when he reached his bicycle and tried to mount it, his leg felt like a lead weight and he couldn't raise it high enough to climb on! When he tried, he fell to the ground!

Grandmaster E hurried out and told him to leave the bicycle with him and helped him out to the main street to flag down a beza, an Indonesian rickshaw.

The next morning, Four a.m. - the time he had to get up for his morning martial arts class - came all too early for Sin, who could still barely move.

With legs still quivering, Sin met Grandmaster E for his morning lesson. As if reading Sin's mind, Grandmaster E went easy on him. For two hours or so he took his pupil through sections one and two of Classical Pakua.

Sin started to loosen up and soon, began to feel much better. At the end of the class, E told Sin that in the afternoon class they are going to do something different. Sin was very happy to hear that, because he had been dreading doing any more squats and bench jumps.

When Sin got to his afternoon class, Sin saw a giant Tai Chi medicine ball and a basketball lying on the floor.

The master inclined his head toward the balls, "I promised you we'd do something different, didn't I?"

Sin scratched his head and couldn't guess what was in the old man's bag of tricks this time. Grandmaster E asked Sin to lie down on the huge Tai Chi ball, facing up. Then the Grandmaster placed a thirty-kilogram barbell on Sin's chest and told him to push the weight off with an *explosive* force, then lower it slowly back down to his chest. Then repeat, and repeat and repeat, until he couldn't do it any more.

It was quite a difficult task, because the Tai Chi ball was constantly wobbling around under him, making it hard to keep his balance.

"This exercise with the wobbling ball will force you to learn how to use your *entire body* to balance and push the weight up. The power you attain from this training can be readily applied to other fighting situations."

Twelve repetitions later, Sin couldn't do any more on his own and E had to help him force out a few more reps.

Then he asked Sin to do some one-handed pushups on the basketball. At the end of each push up, Sin had to hop his body up as high as he could and switch to the other hand in mid air. Sin was going to quit on the fourteen counts, but E urged him on until he reached eighteen counts.

Sin could never remember how many sets of both exercises he did that day, but he knew he was on the brink of throwing up and passing out when E finally switched to doing Classical Pakua, section three.

All through the Pa Kua form, Sin's legs kept quivering from yesterday's endless squats and frog jumps and his hands and chest were aching and subject to cramps from today's endless sets of bench presses and pushups.

At the end of the class, Grandmaster E gave Sin two bananas and a cool glass of water.

The Master told Sin to leave his bicycle at his place again and walked him out to the main street for another beza ride home.

As the beza pulled away, Grandmaster E shouted, "Don't forget to have a big bowl of turtle stew for dinner! See you tomorrow morning bright and early!"

COMMUNICATING WITH THE DEAD

One day, when Sin visited his grandfather Mui Mui and grandmother Ah Ma, he could not find his pet lamb anywhere. It was not kippering around the house as it usually was. When he asked his grandfather where it was, Mui Mui paused, then told Sin that the little lamb had rapidly grown into an adult sheep and become too big to be kept in the house any longer. He reluctantly admitted that he had sold it back to the vendor.

Sin freaked out! What right did his grandfather have to sell *his* pet lamb without even asking him? He loved the darling little creature and missed it dearly. Sin left his grandparent's house upset and angry.

But matters got much worse when, a week later, Sin happened to speak with his grandparent's cook, who accidentally let it slip that his grandparents had not sold the lamb, they had eaten it!

Sin was horrified and outraged! *How could* they have eaten his innocent little friend? How could his grandfather do this to *him*? He had never felt so hurt and betrayed in his life!

Boiling with outrage, for months Sin refused to go near his grandparents. In his eyes, what they had done was unforgivable and he could not bear to look them in the eye.

Mui Mui and Ah Ma loved their grandson dearly and missed him terribly when they didn't see him for a while. So when he suddenly stopped coming to visit them, Ah Ma called Sin's mother to ask why they hadn't seen Sin for a while. When his mother prompted Sin about it, he made an excuse of heavy schoolwork and longer Kung Fu training.

But, when weeks turned into months and his avoidance continued, his grandparents knew something was wrong and came to visit him at his own house.

During the visit, Mui Mui sensed that Sin's attitude had changed toward him and it didn't take him long to realize that Sin had found out what really happened to his pet. Mui Mui had been raised by a practical Chinese family, and like others his age, had survived the hardship of two grueling World Wars that had taught him that farm animals were valuable resources meant to be used to feed their hungry family. This was part of the great cycle of life. He did not believe they should be kept as pets, but had indulged his grandson until the lamb had grown too large and impractical to keep in the house.

Though Mui Mui did not share Sin's ideas about pets, he clearly saw how devastated his beloved grandson was by his thoughtless act, and he felt terrible that he had unwittingly hurt him so badly. Though he tried to apologize, he was at a loss for how to win Sin's forgiveness or make him feel better.

When Sin continued to give them the silent treatment, Mui Mui and Ah Ma grew dispirited and went home soon afterwards, their sorrow and guilt weighing heavily on their minds. In the fullness of time, Sin would have learned to see things from his grandfather's perspective and perhaps come to understand why he had done what he'd done. But time was the one thing they did not have…

Tragically, Sin never was never to see his grandfather again.

Before Sin had had a chance to work through his grief and find a way to forgive his grandfather for eating his pet, Mui Mui died of a heart attack.

Wracked with guilt, Sin was convinced that *he* was responsible for his grandfather's death. He was certain that if he had not shunned him or refused to forgive him, Mui Mui would not have sickened and died. And more tragedy was yet to come…

Mui Mui's death had a profound impact on his elderly wife, Ah Ma. They had been married for over sixty years and she did not wish to face life without him. She cried every day and refused to eat.

Sui Chin visited her mother every day in an effort to console her and brought her tasty dishes she tried to coax her to eat, but to no avail. So, just a few months after her husband passed away, Ah Ma withered away and died of a broken heart.

Sin was even more consumed with guilt. "I have killed them both!" he cried, inconsolable with grief.

It did not matter that everyone said Mui Mui had had a weak heart and his time had come. Or that Ah Ma has chosen to be reunited with her beloved husband. Sin gathered all the blame to himself and wrapped tightly it around his heart like a dark, cutting shroud.
He brooded for months. One day, he broke down and confided his crushing guilt to his Kung Fu master. Grandmaster E listened carefully, drawing thoughtfully on his pipe.

"What would you have me do, My Son?"

"Teach me the Nei Kung technique, Grandmaster, so I can speak to my grandparents one more time and tell them how sorry I am!"
Sin explained he really needed to make peace with his grandparents or he could not go on.

"What you ask is very difficult and even dangerous. This form of Nei Kung is similar to the training that reveals your past lives and deaths. If you get them confused, it could go badly for you…Are you sure you can handle that?"

Sin nodded vigorously, "Please, Grandmaster E! I don't care about me, but I must make peace with my grandparents!"
So, for weeks, Grandmaster E patiently taught Sin the ancient Nei Kung techniques used to communicate with the dead.
Sin burned with purpose and practiced the difficult meditation techniques day and night, driving himself relentlessly. When he finally thought he was ready, he began the exercise and allowed himself to slip into a very deep meditation.

While meditating, he tried to envision Mui Mui and Ah Ma a specific way and invite them into his mind. But, though he tried for hours and hours, all through the night, by dawn, exhausted, he had to admit failure. The next night, he tried again, with no better results. But, on the third night, it happened!

While in his deepest meditation, Sin found himself in a vivid, glowing environment. Everything around him came into supernaturally sharp focus.

Suddenly, Mui Mui and Ah Ma appeared! Sin recoiled, prepared for them to be angry and blame him for their deaths. But instead, they came toward him, their faces wreathed in loving smiles and their arms outstretched to embrace him!

Sin began to stammer out his sorrowful apology, but they raised their hands to quiet him and said in unison, "We know, Dear One. Everything is as it should be. Please don't mourn for us – we are happy together and doing well in the Afterlife."

Then their images began to shimmer and slowly disappeared. Sin roused himself from his meditation and found tears streaming down his cheeks. Released from his guilt, he cried and cried for a very long time.

By the time he finished and dried his tears, the love of his grandparents' benevolent spirits had lifted his crushing load. Sin vowed to move forward with renewed commitment and a more positive outlook on life.

2 8

-

BACK TO HEAVEN

The Grandmaster knew how deeply his grandparent's deaths had affected Sin, weighing down his star pupil's spirit. The boy seemed better now, after speaking with his grandparents in the Afterlife, but he still thought that perhaps a poignant story about how one of Sin's heroes handled this difficult rite of passage might help him handle it better himself.

When Sin came in that day, instead of launching into rigorous training, Grandmaster E sat him down by his tranquil Koi pond.

"Sin I never finished the story of the great Si Gin Kui... Let's pick it up the day Si Gin Kui fell seriously ill..."

Racked with fever, Si Gin Kui's temperature soared so high, he slipped into delirium on the third day and began to hallucinate. Sweat poured from his body, drenching his sheets, as he tossed and turned in agony. Transported to another realm by his fever, on the fourth day he began to hallucinate.

Si Gin Kui saw himself astride his stallion, chasing a fox through a beautiful rain forest, surrounded by towering trees dappled red-gold with the setting sun. In the middle of the chase, Si Gin Kui raised his bow and launched an arrow at the fox.

Strangely, instead of fleeing, the sly fox turned like lightning and suddenly rushed his horse! As the fox flew toward him, Si Gin Kui was stunned to see it morph into a huge, white tiger with razor sharp claws and fangs, roaring straight at him!

Horrified, Si Gin Kui reared back on his horse, trying to escape, but in his dream, his horse disappeared from beneath him and he suddenly found himself sitting atop the tiger, riding it backwards!

Si Gin Kui woke up in his own bed and slowly sat up. But, shockingly, there by the bed sat the White Tiger! Si Gin Kui instinctively knew what it must mean.

"It is time to go, isn't it, My Friend?" he asked the Tiger gently.

The White Tiger regally dipped its head in confirmation and licked Si Gin Kui's hand with its raspy tongue. The man smiled at his celestial companion, at peace with the new path that lay before him. He laid his head back on his pillow and peacefully breathed his last.

His soul rose gently out of his body and settled onto the back of the Tiger. A gust of wind blew over them and swirled them up into the clouds.

Si Gin Kui was an extraordinary man with a *unique, old soul*, so it took a celestial messenger as special as the White Tiger to deliver his soul to the Earth. It required the same celestial White Tiger to transport Si Gin Kui's special soul back to Heaven.

Grandmaster E finished the story and took a long draw from his pipe.

He held the smoke for a long time before blowing it out in elegant rings.

Sin understood what his master was trying to do by telling him this story and he was grateful for it. And it worked. He did find solace in imagining of his beloved grandparents living peacefully together in the same Heaven where the great Si Gin Kui resided!

29
-
FIRST LOVE

As SUMMER PASSED, SIN FOUND HIMSELF back in school for another year of lectures and homework. On the first day, he walked in at the last minute and took his seat. When he turned to say hi to his neighbor, his heart skipped a beat.

Sitting right next to Sin was the beautiful girl he had seen earlier that the summer with his brother splashing in the pool!

Sin stared at her, wanting to say something. But the teacher started class, so he had to stop staring at her and pay attention to the teacher. It was very hard to concentrate, because every second he was acutely aware of her sitting beside him.

Not one to waste time, as soon as the bell rang and the other students started to file out of the classroom, Sin turned to her and offered her his hand to shake.

"Hi, I'm Sin The´. What's your name?"

She blushed and hesitated a moment before shaking Sin's hand.

"My name is Siu Ie."

Sin walked her out and they talked about what funny things they had done over the summer. When he saw that she planned to walk home, Sin offered her a ride home. She accepted.

Afraid of she might think if she knew he came from a well-to-do family, he did not reveal that a driver took him to and from school every day. Instead, he waved over a passing beza instead.

They climbed into the beza and set off. He quietly hoped his driver would forgive him for keeping him waiting in the parking lot!

During the ride, he was acutely aware of Sui Ie sitting next to him. When her arm brushed his, he marveled at how soft and warm it was.

When they arrived at her house, he helped her out and Sui Ie looked at him and giggled. Before he could ask her what was so funny, she asked, "Don't you think your Mercedes is getting lonely waiting for you at school?"

Flustered that she had known about his car and family situation the whole time, Sin wasn't quite sure what to say. He smiled ruefully.

Sui Ie laughed, "I think it's unusual for you to be so modest. Most boys at school would have tried to impress me with their fancy cars and show off their status!"

Sin looked at her thoughtfully, "I suspected you weren't the type of girl who would appreciate such posturing. I'd much rather you liked me for myself than for my family's money."

"My mother would say you should consider both factors," Sui Ie replied, with a smile.

"Oh!" Sin teased her, "So would you still like me if I were poor?"

"Maybe…it's too soon to tell," she teased back, dimpling, and walked inside.

Sin stood at the curb staring after her, his stomach full of butterflies. What a girl!

The next day, he could hardly wait to go to school. And when he got there, he could hardly wait for it to end so he could hang out with Siu Ie! When the final bell rung, Sin asked her if he could walk her home and he was elated when she accepted again. They talked the whole way in an open and pleasant way, and it felt like they had known each other for a long time.

When they got to her house, Sin saw eight bezas parked outside her house.

"What's with all the bezas?" Sin asked.

"My father has a beza rental company," she replied. "It's not a very wealthy business really, but he's a proud man." She cut her eyes at him and joked, "So, do you still like me?"

Sin grinned, "Maybe."

They laughed and she invited him inside. When they walked in, her father greeted them and told Siu Ie that four of the beza tires were punctured and had to be fixed right away. Siu Ie said okay and motioned Sin to wait in the hallway while she went to her room.

A minute later, she came out in her work clothes and asked him to join her in their workshop. There she showed Sin what to do, and together they patched the four tires, talking and laughing the whole time.

Suddenly Sin felt a hard blow on the back of his head! Stunned, when he turned around, he was confronted by a rough-looking young Indonesian beza driver, who was smirking at him provokingly.

Sin got up and was just about to punch him silly, when Siu Ie grabbed his arm to restrain him. Though she said nothing out loud, her eyes pleaded with him not to do it. So, Sin stood motionless, but still filled with anger, and regarded the beza driver with narrowed eyes as the driver laughed again and walked outside.

Turning to Sui Ie, Sin demanded to know who he was and why she had stopped him from hitting him back and teaching him a lesson. Sui Ie told Sin that his name was Akang and that he was a troublemaker who rented one of her father's bezas, but often could not pay his rental fees. He even slept in the beza at night because he had nowhere else to go.

"You would only lose face and have nothing to gain by fighting a loser like him."

Sin understood her point, but the incident still rankled when she walked him out half an hour later. Akang watched them go by and Sin saw his eyes following Siu Ie. They were full of lust and roving all over her body, as he undressed her with his eyes.

There was a troublemaker indeed…

As the months went by, Sin and Sui Ie spent a lot of time together.

Since he was often at her house, he also befriended Hasim, one of her father's other beza renters.

It was usually Hasim who would take Sin to and from her house, and since Sin always tipped him generously, he made it a point to be gracious to Sin. One day Hasim told Sin a disturbing account of Akang.

"It was particularly a cold night and I was wrapping up for the evening. Akang was planning to sleep in his beza outside of Siu Ie's house. I saw him sneak up to the window and peek in while the family was having dinner in their well-lit and comfortable dining room.

Akang saw Siu Ie and her family having a nice time together, eating, talking, and laughing, and he got really angry. He started yelling, 'Why should I have to work so hard just to pay my Besa rent and be cold and hungry, while they live in a warm and cozy house and do nothing? One day, I am going to take everything from that man!' "

Sin listened with growing concern as Hasim continued, "I told him not to do anything crazy or he might end up in jail, but he just scoffed and said that at least in jail he would have a roof over his head and three free meals a day."

Sin climbed out at his destination with a worried expression on his face.

"Please, Sin, be careful of Akang," Hasim warned him before he drove away. "He is a dangerous and unpredictable man with nothing to lose…"

Sin thanked him and felt an unsettling feeling creep over him. He sensed that he was indeed a dangerous man and wished he knew what to do about it.

A few nights later, Sin was teaching a group of advanced black belts some very difficult forms called the *Drunken Immortals*. These forms required a high degree of flexibility, agility, and speed, and were quite hard to grasp.

Soon after he paired up the students for some sparring, he realized they would need to see the forms demonstrated to understand the material better. Sin chose four of the best black-belt students and instructed them to attack him simultaneously. As they made their attacks, Sin used the evasive techniques from the *Drunken Immortal* forms and handily defeated all four at once. The class gasped in awe and applauded Sin's special feat.

Grandmaster E had been watching from the doorway and when Sin was finished, he walked in and said he had a special announcement to make. "Never before in my life have I seen a student as dedicated to the Shaolin Arts as Sin Thé´. I am extremely proud of him. He is the disciple I have waited for my entire life. And on this night, in recognition of his prowess and mastery of the material, I am promoting him to 5th degree black belt."

Sin was touched by Grandmaster E's speech and thrilled by his promotion! He went over and impulsively embraced his revered mentorr.

Grandmaster E was slightly flustered by Sin's show of affection. He chuckled and gently scooted Sin back toward the class, telling them that Sin was the youngest person ever to have achieved this level and that from this day on, he would be addressed as "Master Sin".

The entire class broke out in cheers and congratulations! In unison they shouted, "Hey, Master Sin!"

Sin felt like he was in seventh heaven. In fact, he was so ecstatic, he forgot all about Hasim's warning.

30

-

SEEDS OF MISFORTUNE

IT HAD BEEN A YEAR SINCE Sin and Tze's motorcycle accident. Tze seemed to fully recover and never complained about any continuing problems.

Sin had been dividing most of his time between school, seeing Siu Ie and Kung Fu classes, so he hadn't noticed that Tze had been going through certain changes. One day after school, Sin was supposed to meet him, but his brother never showed up. When Sin went in search of him, he found him still sitting in his classroom staring blankly at the blackboard. Miss Han, his teacher, was at her desk pondering over his report card.

When she saw Sin come in, she motioned for him to come talk to her and quietly explained to him that Tze had failed most of his classes. She was sorry but she could not let him proceed into the next grade. She told Sin that Tze was so worried how his parents would react, he had refused to go home until she agreed to pass him!

Tze began to sob. He begged his brother to tell Miss Han how hard he had studied every day, but that no matter how much he studied, he just simply could not remember the material. He thought something was wrong with him, because this had never happened before.

Remembering the motorcycle accident, Sin told Miss Han about Tze's concussion and explained that this might have something do to with these new problems.

Miss Han was very sympathetic and agreed to talk to the principal about the situation and see what they could do. Sin thanked her and took Tze to see their father at their new textile factory.

Sin's father had established a new textile factory that consisted of several large buildings surrounded by beautiful, sprawling rice paddies in the quiet countryside. But, as their car approached the factory gate, they saw a large crowd of people with picket signs angrily protesting outside.

Rudyat, the driver, signaled to the security guard to let them in, and as the car passed through the angry crowd, the protestors pounded on the side windows, cursing and howling at them.

Suddenly, one of the protesters threw a large rock at the back window with such force, both Tze and Sin jumped at the loud thump it made. After the car made it through the gate, the security guard hastily closed it, locking the protestors outside. They continued to scream and rant.

When they got out of the car at their father's office, they heard the crowd still screaming more obscenities from outside the gate. Tze and Sin were unnerved as they headed into the building. Sin didn't understand why they were protesting, since he was sure his father paid a fair wage.

Inside, they passed a long hallway with enormous windows through which they could see hundreds of workers at their work-stations in front of large textile machines.

They climbed up to their father's office and found him sitting behind his large teak desk working through a mountain of paperwork. Behind him, the wall of windows revealed a panoramic view of the idyllic rice fields, a peaceful scene diametrically opposed to the one that they had just experienced outside the gate.

Sin asked him what was going on. His father looked worried as he explained that a group of agitators from out of town were trying to shut down the factory. They had been out there yelling for hours and had threatened the workers to not come to work anymore.

Sin saw that Tze was nervous and afraid of what his father would say about his failing grades. When he saw that Tze could not muster up the courage to tell their father himself, Sin explained what had happened at school.

When Sin finished, his father was distraught and looked at Tze gravely. Sin hastily volunteered to help Tze with his homework from then on to make sure that he would do better. Then he suggested that his father call the principal, since they had been friends from his father's days as a teacher. Sin thought that if his father could explain the situation and tell the principal that he would help make sure Tze could catch up, the school would let Tze continue on to the next grade along with his age-group and friends. Sin's father sat in thought for a moment, then nodded, found his address book, and dialed the principal.

Sin looked at Tze reassuringly when their father hung up and said that the principal had consented and wished them good luck with the extra studying. Tze and Sin sighed in relief, and Sin's father came over to give Tze a hug to let him know that everything was going to be all right.

Very grateful, but needing a moment to himself, Tze went out to the Koi pond behind the factory to sit and think. After he left, Sin's father's face collapsed into a worried frown. Sin reassured him that Tze would be just fine.

Sin's father looked at him for a moment and said how proud he was that Sin had grown up to be such a competent and good-hearted young man. He said that he would be lucky to have someone like Sin to work for him in the family business. Sin smiled and said that he would be very happy to come work for him as a salesperson, so he could earn more money to support the Kung Fu school.

Heng asked Sin how he was going to go to school, practice Kung Fu, help Tze with his homework, see Siu Ie, and still have time to work for both him and his mother?

Sin said that he would probably have to quit his job at the jewelry shop but not to worry, as mother would be happy for him if he came to work for his father since he would be able to spend more time with him, close bigger deals and make larger commissions.

Sin's father laughed and said he could start anytime. Sin thanked him and went out to find Tze.

At the edge of the pond, Sin found his younger brother gazing at the water lilies and lotus flowers. The sound of children playing reverberated from across the water from the houses their father had built some years earlier for the foremen and their families. Sin looked over there and said that it was wonderful to see that their children looked so happy, despite their relatively modest income.

Tze smiled, "If I could go back to before the accident when my brain was still normal but had to trade my living situation for theirs, I would do it."

Sin's heart lurched in his breast, but he consoled him and said he would feel much better after they got him back on track at school. Tze changed the subject and asked Sin about Kung Fu. He said he often wondered why Sin was so into it. Sin told him about his nightmares and explained how Kung Fu made him feel stronger and more empowered to deal with his demons. He added that since Grandmaster E was the last surviving person who knew almost all aspects of the Shaolin arts, he was determined to learn as much as he possibly could from him.

Tze nodded and started to look sad again. Trying to take his mind off of his troubles, Sin asked him if he knew that their great-great-great grandfather could do Dim Mak, a pressure point technique that could disable or even kill an opponent.

Tze shook his head, clearly intrigued, so Sin said he'd share one of the many stories his mother had told him in the wee hours of the night.

It was a lovely bonding moment, brother to brother.

31
-
AN OLD STORY (PART II)

THE STORY SIN TOLD TZE TOOK place in 1857, long before his great-great-great grandfather Zheng Yen Zi fought the Grandmaster of Shaolin. Zheng Yen Zi had just established himself as the best fighter in Southern China when a man named Hai Lang, reputed as the best fighter in Northern China, came to visit him to challenge him to a friendly duel.

Zheng Yen Zi asked him whether he wanted to fight empty hand or use weapons, and since Northern Chinese martial artists were famous for their weapons training, Hai Lang chose to fight with a spear. Zheng Yen Zi accepted and said that he too would fight with a spear to make it a fair match. He suggested that they put powdered chalk on the spear tips, so that way they could see on their black uniforms just where the spears had hit without anyone getting hurt.

Hai Lang liked this idea and they prepared to fight. After a quick bow, their spears whirled through the air. Both fighters were so fast that it was hard to tell who was superior.

Three rounds later, when there was still no winner, Hai Lang suddenly made a risky move. He spun his spear around his body and neck to display his skill and to distract Zheng Yen Zi, and when he saw an opening, he struck a winning hit. He jumped out of the ring and proudly pointed his finger to Zheng Yen Zi's Stomach Meridian #18, a death point located two inches below the nipple. There was a very clear chalk mark to signify his victory.

Zheng Yen Zi smiled, then pointed to Hai Lang's uniform - there were eleven clear chalk marks, all positioned on either the Stomach Meridian and Ren Meridian!

He smiled and said, "My friend, I got you while you were dancing around."

After this encounter, Zheng Yen Zi became known as the best fighter in ALL of China.

32
-
SIXTH SENSE TRAINING

After Sin had worked several months for his father, Heng started to trust him with bigger clients.

Sin was pleased he was being given more responsibility and was excited that it would mean he could earn bigger commissions. He gave most of his earnings to Grandmaster E to support the school, so more earnings meant good fortune for the school.

In turn, Grandmaster E showed his gratitude by teaching Sin some of his most special techniques. One afternoon, he taught Sin a very special meditation technique, called, *Liu Fu Tao,* or the *Sixth Sense Training.*

Grandmaster E blindfolded Sin and led Sin into a special room he had never been in before. He told Sin there were many hard, heavy rubber balls hanging down from the ceiling and that he was going to swing them at Sin. Sin must concentrate and try to sense them coming and avoid them.

Sin tried hard to concentrate as he'd been told, but he wasn't able to sense the balls coming, nor evade the hard blows coming in at him from every direction.

One by one, the heavy balls hurtled at him, striking him all over his face and body! The pain was excruciating and he gritted his teeth so as not to make a sound. He didn't want to complain, and wasn't going to risk stopping the training.

Sin let the balls continue to pummel him, until he felt dizzy and lost consciousness.

The next thing he knew, he came to in a cot in Grandmaster E's guest bedroom. His head was throbbing and his entire body was screaming in pain. Easing himself up, he staggered out of the room and into the garden.

As usual, Grandmaster E was sitting quietly on his bench puffing on his pipe. He smiled up at Sin and asked how he liked his first Sixth Sense lesson.

"I am frustrated, Master, I can't seem to sense the balls, so how can I dodge them! A-are you planning on swinging those things at me for the next few weeks?" he asked anxiously.

Grandmaster E eyed him, "How else will you learn?"

Disheartened, Sin bid him farewell and went home.

The following morning, Sin looked at himself in the mirror and was horrified to see how many bruises he had on his face! In fact, he was black and blue over his entire body. He looked like he'd been in a car accident!

He went into his mother's bathroom and found some ointments and skin powder and tried desperately to cover up the marks. Needless to say, it didn't work very well.

He put on a long-sleeved shirt and sunglasses and hurried out the door. He figured that if he skipped breakfast he could at least postpone the inevitable fuss his family would make over this reckless treatment of his body.

At school, he tried to avoid everyone and at the end of the day he told Siu Ie that he might not be able to see her for a little while, because he had committed to doing special training with the Grandmaster.

Siu Ie probably knew that he felt embarrassed to have her see him like that, because he continued to hide behind his sunglasses while he talked to her, so she didn't press the issue. He was grateful for her insight and his feelings for her grew even stronger.

As Sin headed over to the Kung Fu school that afternoon, he felt the knot in his stomach grow bigger. He was truly dreading the *Liu Fu Tao* lessons and feared that this was one challenge he wouldn't be able to overcome.

He met Grandmaster E in the garden and when the Grandmaster saw Sin's face, he shook his head and bid Sin follow him to one of the trees with dried up branches. He struck one of the stiff branches with his cane and it immediately cracked off and fell to the ground.

Then he turned to another tree with healthy branches and did the same. Upon impact, the healthy branch just shifted back and forth but was otherwise fine.

Grandmaster E looked at Sin and said, "Trees that don't bend with the wind won't last the storm." Then he ushered Sin into the training room with the awful balls, blindfolded him, and started the balls swinging!

Unfortunately, Sin's sensing abilities had not miraculously transformed since the day before and the pain was even worse as the balls were now hitting his pre-existing bruises. Sin was initially overwhelmed with frustration, but it suddenly dawned on him what Grandmaster E had tried to teach him.

He stopped panicking and forced his body to relax. Then, when the hits came, he yielded to the incoming force of each ball. He tested this method out for a while and the blows seemed to hurt less.

Still, he couldn't wait till the training was over.

The first week of Sixth Sense Training was by far the worst. Sin even had nightmares of hard rubber balls attacking him and he was helpless to stop them. He was getting tired of waking up in a cold sweat when the nightmares suddenly stopped.

By the time he'd had his twelfth lesson, Sin was feeling pretty confident and more aware of his surrounding, and got hit less and less. He had also become more resistant to bruising, which encouraged him to start seeing Siu Ie again.

He stopped by her house after training one day, and her father let him into the workshop. He saw her hovering over a bright light with sparks flying around everywhere. She was welding! He watched her for a while, astonished, as she stood there in her work clothes and goggles, welding a piece of metal on one of the bezas.

She looked so skillful and capable. As he stood there, he realized how much he had missed her. He called out to her and she stopped the machine, came over and gave him a big hug. She was so happy to see him!

Then, since she was still at work, she handed him a beza cover with a tear in it, fetched a needle and thread and asked him to fix the tear while she did some scenery painting on one of the new bezas. When Sin had finished, he went over to admire her artwork.

Suddenly, from out of the corner of his eye, he thought he saw a rubber ball flying at him! He jerked back and looked around wide-eyed, but soon realized his intensive training was making him jumpy.

Startled by Sin's sudden movement, Siu Ie looked at him curiously and asked if something was wrong. He told her he had been dodging rubber balls for the past two weeks and was seeing them everywhere!

She burst out laughing, and, seeing the humor in the whole situation, Sin joined in.

Siu Ie leaned in close and inspected his face. "So that's why you've been acting so silly for the past two weeks. You've been spending quality time with a bunch of deadly rubber balls instead of me!"

Sin blushed and didn't quite know what to say.

Then she teased, "That's ok, you can make it up to me by introducing me to your mother."

Sin was delighted and told her he'd love to. She was overjoyed.

As they were leaving the workshop, Akang walked past Sin and bumped his shoulder into Sin's on purpose. He stared at Sin provokingly, trying to stir up a fight. Sin could hardly contain himself, but Siu Ie pulled him away.

Sin heard Akang yelling after him, "Who the fuck do you think you are? This is my country, not yours!"

In the car, Siu Ie and Sin had a heated discussion. Sin argued that they needed to stand up for themselves and not let such an obvious bully think they were intimidated by his ridiculous, aggressive behavior. She agreed that, in general, everyone should stand up for themselves and fight for their rights, but she saw nothing good that could come out of confronting a loser like Akang. She didn't want them to waste their time and energy getting riled up over him.

When they pulled up to Sin's mother's shop, she changed the subject and told him how excited she was to meet his mother.

Since they would be meeting his mother shortly, Sin tried to put aside his concern about her reluctance to confront Akang, and ushered her inside. Sin's mother was thrilled to finally meet the girl her eldest son had been talking about for so long.

Sin was so pleased to see how well they got along. When a customer came in to talk to his mother, Sin whisked Siu Ie into the workshop in the back. Four goldsmiths were in the process of cleaning, repairing, and creating pieces of jewelry.

Eager to show her his skills in the workshop, Sin picked up a piece of gold wire and hammered it into a die. When it came out, it had a delicate snake design on it, and he bent the piece to form a ring in the shape of a snake grabbing his own tail.

Siu Ie looked at it in amazement and Sin proudly put his new creation on her finger. Sin told her that he had wanted to make her something for a while and hoped she liked it.

She gasped in excitement and said how beautiful it was! And added that she couldn't possibly accept such a lovely gift.

Sin smiled and told her it would make him very happy to see her wear it, so she finally gave in.

Siu Ie thanked him went to give him a grateful hug, when suddenly Sin jerked back and looked wildly around.

"You and your training," she joked.

Sin shook his head to clear it and joked that if she didn't mind putting up with her spastic boyfriend for a little while longer, he would be happy to introduce her to his father at the new textile factory.

On the way to the factory, Sin told Siu Ie the story of how his parents met and what they went through to save up enough money to start their own jewelry shop. She was moved when he told her how he had lost his beloved dog, and laughed when he talked about his first chicken drumstick.

Endeared by her attentiveness and willingness to listen, Sin put his arms around her and gave her a kiss. Comfortable with their modest intimacy, she held his hand the whole way and they kissed several times as he told her about the happy moments and less happy moments in his life. Sin had asked Rudiyat to take the longer scenic route so they had plenty of time to savor this special moment.

They caught Sin's father just as he finished work for the day. He was happy to meet Siu Ie and excited to show her around in the factory.

She paid close attention as he explained in detail what each of the different machines did and how the fabrics were made. He was thrilled to reveal that he was in the process of making some innovative fabrics that would help him compete against the big distributors.

Siu Ie showed great interest and asked several intelligent questions about the business. At one point, when she was talking to one of the foremen, Sin's father whispered to Sin that he was delighted to see that he had found such a smart, delightful girl. Sin's heart filled with pride and happiness.

Sin's father walked them out and as they were getting into the car, he invited Siu Ie to come for dinner the next evening. She happily accepted and gave Sin's father a big hug before jumping into the car.

Surprised by her show of affection, Sin's father blushed and stood there speechless for a second. Sin smiled at him and said, "I know, Dad. She has the same effect on me."

As the car rolled out of the driveway and out of the gate, another mob of protesters rushed to the car and started to attack it, yelling anti-Chinese slogans. Siu Ie looked frightened as Rudiyat maneuvered his way carefully through the angry crowd.

Sin told her that the protesters were against their factory because it was Chinese-owned and that they had been trying to intimidate them into shutting it down. This didn't make sense to Sui Ie, because all the Indonesians who worked there would be out of a job and destitute.

Sin expressed his concern that Indonesia was becoming a dangerous place for the Chinese and his father concurred. They all sat pensively for the rest of the ride home.

The next day, Sin picked up Siu Ie in the afternoon so he could spend some time with her on their own before the big family dinner. Her father always needed her to come straight home after school to help out with the family beza business, so they had never been able to take time off and just hang out at Sin's house. In fact, this was the first time she had come to visit Sin at home.

It was a beautiful day, so they took a stroll in the garden. Sin took great pleasure in showing her their aviary with its many colorful birds. She was stunned when she saw how large the backyard was, with an infinity pool, a koi pond bobbing with ducks and geese, and even tennis court!

Sui Ie admitted that this was all so different from what she was used to. But Sin hastened to reassure her that they hadn't always been so fortunate and that material things were not what his life was about. He guided her towards a small building near the house and said that he wanted to show her something special.

They walked inside. When Sin turned on the lights, she burst out laughing when she saw that the room was full of small rubber balls hanging from the ceiling!

Sin started to describe his routine, but before he could finish, she grinned and hurled one of the balls at him!

He dodged it, laughing, but soon she had engaged twenty more balls! They had a blast running around trying to hit each other with the balls! It turned out to be one of the most fun nights Sin had ever had.

Despite being busy with schoolwork, tutoring Tze, handling major business deals for his father, and spending quality time with Siu Ie,

Sin continued to dedicate himself to the Shaolin arts.

Then xix months passed in a blur and before Sin knew it, he had developed a new kind of awareness. He started to be able to hear the 'shush' sounds as the rubber balls approached him. As time went by, the sounds somehow became louder and louder, until, to his amazement, he was eventually able to avoid getting hit at all!

Today's students would call this a Jedi Master trick, but Nei Kung Masters had learned it centuries before…

Sin told Grandmaster E how pleased he was to have finally mastered this difficult and painful exercise!

Grandmaster E smiled enigmatically and said, "We'll see about that."

He invited Sin to come stay in his guest room the next weekend and said that it would be interesting to see how much he had learned.

Knowing him, Sin suspected that he had some ulterior motive in mind, but not one to pass up a challenge, he accepted his invitation.

For the next few nights leading up to the weekend, Sin had a hard time sleeping, worried about what Grandmaster E might have planned for him. When the day finally came, Sin packed a small bag and presented himself at the Grandmaster's door.

Grandmaster E instructed Sin to go over some of his old material to warm up, then he blindfolded Sin. Sin felt his heart rate speed up as he prepared for the worst.

Sensing how anxious he was, Grandmaster E put his hand on his shoulder and told him to relax.

Sin took a big breath, and in a state of heightened focus and awareness, he heard the first ball come at him loud and clear and he dodged it easily. Then, more and more balls came and again, he was able to avoid them. But as they started to come in faster than what he was used to, he started to worry he might not be able to sustain the level of concentration required for much longer.

Grandmaster E instructed him to do some deep breathing. He did and it helped tremendously. Sin was able to keep up with him for the duration of their usual one-hour training, but then almost passed out from exhaustion when the grandmaster pushed him to continue training for a whole other hour!

When they were finally done, Sin could barely walk and his clothes and even his shoes were drenched in sweat. Sin mustered the energy to ask him how well he had done, but E just smiled his enigmatic smile again and said they would talk about it in the morning.

Sin changed into his sleepwear, lay down, and instantly passed out. Suddenly, his cot shot up in the air and he fell facedown on the ground! He leapt up and looked around, but no one was there! He straightened up the cot and lay there for a while, watching the door. He had almost fallen back asleep when he saw the door handle starting to turn. Fast as lightning, he leapt to the door and threw it open. To his great surprise, there was no one there!

Sin closed the door again and stood behind it for quite a while, when finally he heard footsteps approaching. The footsteps stopped right outside his door, and he immediately yanked it open. Again, no one was there!

Sin was dumbfounded, when all of a sudden, he heard a loud laughter coming out of Grandmaster E's room. Afraid of E pulling another stunt on him, Sin stayed awake the rest of the night.

The next morning, he was exhausted when he joined Grandmaster E for breakfast. The Grandmaster, however, was high-spirited and had cooked eggs and porridge for them. When they sat down to eat, he asked if Sin had slept well, like he had.

Sin told him that he wasn't able to sleep because someone had been playing jokes on him all night long. The Grandmaster asked him, why, with his new mastery of the *Liu Fu Tao* training, could he not just catch the guy?

Sin blushed and wasn't able to give him a satisfactory answer.

Grandmaster peered at him from under his brows and said perhaps he hadn't quite mastered it yet. He should train harder to improve his hearing sense through meditation.

Sin hung his head low and agreed.

His *Liu Fu Tao* training was a blessing both inside and outside the training hall. Sin's Kung Fu sparring improved immensely when he was able to sense people and their movements around him with his eyes closed. And on the rare occasions when he was hit, his ability to yield to their force prevented him from being seriously injured.

Sin accepted that it had become an integral part of him when he realized that he never fell victim to pick pockets anymore, like some of his friends did. In Indonesia, pickpockets were common and tended to work in teams of three. One would bump into you, the second would take your wallet and the third would take it and run away with it.

Now, with his exceptional training, Sin could always sense their presence and recognize their unique demeanor before they could relieve him of his wallet.

He never got robbed again.

33

-

ROSES AND THORNS

As Sin's feelings for Siu Ie grew stronger each day, he wanted to give her something very special that she could cherish always. One month, he received a handsome commission and decided to make her a gold bracelet with precious stones. It took him several weeks to decide on the design for the sentimental piece, and he ended up combining their names and writing out "SIN" in small rubies and "IE" in small diamonds. It was exquisite.

When the bracelet was done, Sin could hardly wait to give it to her! The following weekend, he brought her to a beautiful lake surrounded by a lush green park. They went on a scenic boat ride in the morning and in the afternoon Siu Ie flew a kite and Sin chased her around in the park, laughing merrily.

When Sin finally tackled her, they fell into the soft grass and laughed and laughed together. They lay there in each other's arms for a while and when Sin felt the moment was right, he told her that he had something for her.

He made her close her eyes and slipped the bracelet onto her wrist. She shrieked in excitement when she opened her eyes and saw it!

Sin explained that he had flipped the "U" in her first name so it looked like an "N". That way it would spell "SIU IE" if you looked at it in one way and "SIN IE" if you looked at it in another way, so she and he could be together forever.

She was so touched and tears spring into in her eyes. She vowed to never take it off. She told Sin that she had something for him too, but that she was afraid it was nothing compared to what he had just given her.

She pulled a tiny gourd out of her purse and asked Sin if he knew what the gourd symbolized.

Remembering something his mother had told him when he was little, Sin answered that since the gourd was a container for water and water was the source of life, the gourd must be a symbol of the Source of Life.

She was impressed by his answer and handed Sin the gourd. It had a beautiful picture of her and Sin delicately painted on it. She said that it represented the two of them joined forever by the Source of Life.

Now it was Sin's turn to be moved and they held each other tight as they watched the sun slowly set.

When they arrived back at Siu Ie's house, Sin's heart started to race as he saw Akang sitting out front on his beza.

Siu Ie gave Sin a look to remind him not to get riled up. As they walked up to the house, Akang stepped out and blocked their way.

"What have we here?" he sneered. Then he caught a glimpse of Siu

Ie's new bracelet and had to restrain himself from grabbing her wrist.

Siu Ie tucked her arm against her body and ignored him while Sin's eyes pierced into Akang's, hoping he would make a physical move and give him an excuse to teach him a lesson.

But Akang saw Sin's boiling anger and realized that Sin was ready and able to take him down, so he just scoffed and moved aside to let them pass.

When they almost reached the door, he turned around and shouted, "You stupid rich kid! You have no idea what it's like to have nothing!"

Though Sin had great sympathy for the plight of the Indonesian poor, he had no sympathy at all for a thug like Akang who had no interest in working hard to better himself and no desire to help others.

When Sin got home that evening, he spent some time tutoring Tze. Since the day his father had called the principal, Sin felt it was his responsibility to make sure something like that wouldn't happen again. But, no matter how hard they drilled Tze on his homework, his retention ability didn't seem to be improving. In fact, it seemed to be getting worse.

Sin tried all kinds of approaches, but everything led to the same result. Tze just couldn't retain the material. It was as if his memory had just evaporated. Sin's other brothers and sisters would frequently tell him how hard Tze worked when Sin wasn't there, pacing around in the house reciting information over and over. But by the time Sin came home and quizzed him, Tze's mind was a blank. He would get teary-eyed in frustration and Sin felt helpless to give him any lasting comfort.

Then one day, things escalated. Sin had let Tze drive his motorcycle around town, with Sin in the back, as a way to get Tze's mind off his continuing failure at school. As they were passing a row of street vendors, Tze suddenly veered straight into a cluster of fruit and vegetable stands! They rammed into several booths before he regained control and then he sped away while the vendors ran after them, shouting obscenities!

When they were a safe distance away, Sin made him pull over and tell him what had just happened.

Tze looked disoriented, "I don't know. I don't know, Sin," he mumbled.

Speechless, Sin looked him over to see if he'd been injured. Luckily, Tze had come out of it with only a few scratches and some torn clothes. Sin could see that he was shaken up and distraught, so he consoled him, changed places with him, and drove them both home.

When they parked the motorcycle, Sin told him that he thought they needed to tell their parents about his worsening condition, but Tze made Sin promise not to say anything yet.

A few days later, Sin let Tze come with him to a sales meeting at one of Bandung's largest departments stores. Right before going in to see the company president, Sin asked Tze to putter around inside the store while he met with the President, and he would find him when he was done.

After 20 minutes, the meeting was over and Sin went looking for his brother. But Tze was nowhere to be found inside the store.

Panicked that he might have suffered another episode and might be injured or even killed, Sin ran out to look for him, praying that he hadn't been run over by a car! When Sin finally found him down the street, Tze was beside himself and had no idea how he had gotten there!

Perturbed, Sin asked him why he had left when they had agreed that he would stay and wait for him inside the store. He looked at Sin confused and said he thought he was still in the store. Horrified by this statement, Sin brought him home and decided to talk to his parents immediately. The family was very concerned and started bringing Tze to different doctors to see what could be done for him.

3 4
-
TRAGEDY

A SHORT TIME LATER, SIN WAS having a quiet dinner with his family when one of the servants rushed in to tell him that someone was outside with an urgent message.

Sin hurried out and saw one of his young Kung Fu students, doubled over, gasping for breath.

"It's Sui Ie!" he gasped, "There's a riot at her house!"

Sin took off running and arrived at her house in record time. When he got there, a dense crowd was gathered out front. Stretching above people's heads, Sin saw Akang being led away by the police. What was that nut job doing here? And why was he in police custody?

Suddenly a horrified SCREAM echoed from the house. Sin's hair went up on the back of his neck – something was terribly wrong! He had to get to Sui Ie!

He frantically pushed and shoved his way through the crowd and ran inside. Sin found Siu Ie's mother crumpled up on the floor, sobbing and wailing, while Siu Ie's father held her and sobbed as well.

Sin saw the door to Sui Ie's workshop was open and he raced in, calling her name. Halfway through the door, he saw a policeman bending over a body in the corner.

Terror and grief tore through his body as the policeman moved aside and he saw it was his beloved Siu Ie!

She was lying lifeless on the floor!

Her eyes were still open, reflecting the horrors she had gone through during her last moments. Her beautiful face was bruised and slack, and someone had placed a towel over her hips to cover up where her clothes had been torn off.

Oh my God! Sin recoiled in horror, his knees going weak. Then went into a frenzy, throwing himself down beside her and frantically giving her CPR, trying to bring her back to him!

The police protested and tried to stop him, but he kept going, and going, and going, telling himself that if he just tried hard enough, he could bring her back. His world shrank down to just this moment, just this task, just this miracle…

But, no miracle happened… and it took two policemen to finally pull him away.

When they carried Sui Ie's away in a body bag, Sin screamed as if the gates of hell had opened beneath his feet. Feeling like his life had ended, he ran out of the workshop into the night.

She was gone. Gone. Sui Ie, the light of his life, was gone forever! His legs buckled and he sank to his knees and vomited in the grass.

He fell to the ground, blinded with grief and curled into a ball of all-consuming misery and spiraled down, into the darkness…

A long time later, he dully heard people talking around as if they were at the end of a long tube. He suddenly realized that they were asking a little girl who had witnessed the murder what had happened. Her voice was too soft for him to hear.

He had to know! Sin staggered up and went over to the child's father, Hasim, and begged him to tell him what she had said.

The man knew Sin was Sui Ie's boyfriend, so he gazed at him anxiously and said that it might be better if he didn't know.

Uncharacteristically for him, Sin screamed at him, demanding that he tell him!

Earlier that evening, Hasim said, he had been standing with the other beza drivers to pay the rental fee. At the front of the line, Siu Ie's father was yelling at Akang for not paying his rent as usual. Her father said that he was fed up with Akang's late payments and his harassment of his daughter, so from now on he would have to rent his beza elsewhere.

Furious by this public humiliation, Akang stormed off in a towering rage. Some of the other beza drivers, who were friends with him, went with him.

After paying his own rent, Hasim saw that Akang had been joined by a group of anti-Chinese protesters, and he was egging them on to retailiate against Siu Ie's father.

All riled up and itching for blood, the angry mob marched on Siu Ie's house. Hasim rushed after them, trying to calm them down – to no avail. They burst into the house and threatened Siu Ie's father that if he didn't give them their money back, they would beat him and his wife then and there.

Amidst all the commotion, no one noticed that Akang slipped away to find Siu Ie in the workshop.

Hasim's 10-year-old daughter sometimes helped Sui Ie's mother and she was in their kitchen when the mob broke into the house.

Terrified by the loud, angry voices coming from the hallway, she hid in the kitchen closet. The back wall of the closet had a long crack running straight through it and she could see everything that went on in the workshop.

She saw Siu Ie backing away from Akang as he threatened her! Akang blamed her for losing him his job. He loomed over her, screaming that she had ruined his life!

Siu Ie protested that she hadn't said anything to her father, but Akang refused to believe her.

"You cost me my job, you bitch! So give me your bracelet!" he demanded. Sui Ie looked stricken – it was Sin's loving gift to her and she couldn't bear to give it to this violent pig. She shook her head, and tried to back away, but he grabbed her to yank it off her wrist.

She fought back and he clutched her to him to force her to do his bidding. Her struggles and cries of pain excited Akang and he forced a kiss on her. She recoiled and spit in his face!

Enraged, he slapped her and threw her to the floor and started to tear off her clothes! Sui Ie fought him with every ounce of strength she had, but it was not enough. He was much stronger than her. She screamed and screamed, but no one heard her, except the child who was too terrified to move. She clawed at his face, but he lashed out and slammed her head into the concrete floor to stop her.

Her head hit with a horrifying *CRACK* and blood oozed out of her head. She writhed on the floor, weak and helpless. Akang crowed in triumph that he had her at his mercy and pulled down his pants and raped her, jamming his hand over her mouth to keep her from screaming.

Sui Ie went ominously still as her vicious attacker defiled her limp body.

When he had finished his heinous deed, the rapist got up and sneered at her to keep her mouth shut if she knew what was good for her.

But she did not stir.

She would never stir again…

Realizing he had killed her, her murderer stumbled back in a blind panic. He tried to weasel out the back window of the workshop, but the police caught him before he could get away.

Sin listened to this horrifying account in a miasma of guilt. Why hadn't he been there to stop the brutal scum from defiling and murdering his love? And, why was he alive and his beloved now dead?

These questions were to haunt him for years to come…

35
-
SIU IE AFTERMATH

CONSUMED BY GRIEF, SIN COULDN'T EAT or sleep. All he could think about was Siu Ie and everything they had been to each other. Every happy thought of her that filled his mind tore him apart further.

He sank into a deep depression and wanted only to be left alone. Sin didn't go to school or Kung Fu classes, Tze didn't ask him to tutor him, and his father, despite his busy schedule, took on Sin's clients and never said a word about it. In fact, the whole house seemed to be in the morning.

Everyone had gotten to know Siu Ie over the past several months and already saw her as part of the family. Her lively personality had brought a lot of joy to the household, so they all felt her loss.

Some nights at the dinner table, Sin's father would try to talk to the rest of the family and console them with tales of other Chinese people who had faced tragic events yet managed to transcend their torment. Sin's mother looked at Sin with stricken, worried eyes as he just picked at his food, lost in a dark well of grief.

On the day of Siu Ie's funeral, Sin tried to pull himself together to get ready. He kept procrastinating and changing his mind about going or not going. By the time he finally made up his mind, dressed, and came out of his room, the whole family was waiting for him in the hallway, deep concern in their eyes.

As they approached the funeral parlor, they saw hundreds of people standing outside waiting to go in and pay their respects to Sui Ie. People were sobbing quietly and saying about how tragic it was that such a beautiful young girl should die under such horrible circumstances.

Sin felt a powerful rage welling up inside him at this senseless tragedy that had taken such a good, lovely person from her loved ones. When people saw who he was, they stepped aside to let him through. As he slowly moved down the aisle, he could hear them whispering to each other that he was Siu Ie's boyfriend and how awful it must be for him. His heart kept breaking and breaking, over and over again. And his rage gradually turned to numbness. He felt the emotions drain out of him until he felt like a moving automation. As he walked to the coffin, all he could think was how strange and unreal it all seemed. None of this was actually happening…

But, then when he looked down into the coffin, suddenly, with blinding clarity, he remembered that he had dreamt this exact scene many years ago! Except, back then, the people had been enshrouded in mist and unrecognizable, and he hadn't recognized who the girl in the casket was.

Sadly, this time he knew exactly who she was. His beloved Siu Ie.

She looked strangely peaceful in repose, but Sin had seen her face the night she'd died and knew she had been anything but peaceful as the life had been beaten out of her. All his emotions came flooding back and, incandescent with rage, he swore he would avenge her death!

After the funeral, Sin distracted himself from the pain by obsessing over what he would do to Akang if he ever got his hands on him. Thoughts of castrating him and beating him to death flooded through his mind constantly, torturing him with their intensity!

Since the fact that Akang was in prison had been the only thing that kept Sin from exacting his revenge on him, Sin was almost pleased when he heard rumors that Akang had been released early.

Sin began to look for him in Siu Ie's neighborhood at night, sure that the unrepentant murderer would go back to his old haunts when he got out. One evening, Sin saw him from a distance, sitting on a curb, joking with a group of his friends, like nothing had ever happened!

Sin stepped back around a corner and looked out to make sure that it was really Akang. His stomach twisted when he heard his laugh, a repulsive, evil sound that Sin would recognize anywhere. He slipped around the block to an alley that had a better view, so he could reconnoiter.

Enraged that a convicted rapist and cold-blooded murderer could sit there so carefree after what he had done, Sin made up his mind to follow him and exact his own justice.

After an hour or so of endless waiting, Akang said goodbye to his friends and walked straight towards the alley where Sin stood.

For a moment, Sin thought Akang had seen him standing there and had dared to come and confront him! But then the man turned towards the wall and opened his pants to urinate on the wall.
Sin couldn't believe his luck. He calmly stepped up behind the

murderer.

"Time to meet your maker, Scum."

Akang whipped around at the sound of his voice and when he saw Sin, he peed all over his shoes, terrified!

In rapid succession, Sin punched him in the face and kicked him in the groin. Akang screamed and doubled over in pain! Sin grabbed his head and kneed him in the face, over and over again. When he had collapsed on the ground, acting on an atavistic impulse, Sin grimly reached for his knife to finish the job.

But, some of his buddies heard Akang's screams and rushed to the alley to see what was wrong. Knowing he would have to fight them all, and not wanting to punish others for Akang's crime, Sin reluctantly left his quarry huddled, weeping on the ground in a pool of his own piss like the pathetic coward he was. Sin melted into the darkness.

He thought he would feel a sense of closure the next day, but he was wrong. Instead, he felt more obsessed than ever. He couldn't seem to get Akang out of his mind and thought up scenario after scenario of the pain and suffering he intended to inflict upon him before he finished him off!

Strangely, he felt no guilt about planning to take the law into his own hands. He headed out to the garden to get some fresh air, but saw Tze packing when he walked by his room.

"Where are you going?" he asked his brother.

Tze explained that he had been getting worse lately and that the whole family was really concerned. They had consulted several doctors, but none had been able to help him. Now they had found a specialist, who had requested that he stay at his clinic for 48 hours for observation.

Sin's stomach dropped as he realized how much he had missed out on in the past few months, as absorbed as he had been with his own grief and loss. Sin told his brother how sorry he was that he hadn't been there for him. Tze kindly understood.

As Sin walked back into his room, his rage resurfaced. This was all Akang's fault! If the scum had just kept to himself, none of this would have happened! His dear Sui Ie would still be alive, he wouldn't be wallowing in grief for her loss, and he would have been there to help Tze in his hour of need!

Then a terrifying thought occurred to him: What if this was all *his* own fault? After all, if he hadn't given Siu Ie that bracelet, Akang might not have gone after her in the first place. If he had just been with her that night, she would have been safe.

His heart started racing, as guilt and regret overpowered him. He missed Siu Ie desperately and ached to tell her how much he loved and missed her.

Laying in bed, Sin suddenly realized he could see her again! Why couldn't he use the same Nei Kung technique that he had used to speak with his grandparents when they passed away?

He could speak to Siu Ie this very night!

Feeling more hopeful than he had in months, he sat on his bed and began to meditate.

Hours later, deep into his trance, Sin saw himself back at the funeral, walking past a long line of people. They parted to let Sin pass through.

Sin reached the end of the line and saw Siu Ie lying in the open casket. His heart lurched in his chest, stricken. Silent tears rolled down his face as he reached out and stroked her still hand.

Suddenly, from out of nowhere, a young man dressed in an antique style of Chinese clothing, appeared in the casket next to Siu Ie!

He was also dead. Sin realized it was Hua's fiancé, Li Bai! What was *he* doing there?

Sin heard a woman sobbing beside him and turned to find Hua standing next to him! She was inconsolable with grief and gazed at the young man's body with a look of desolation and love.

She turned and saw Sin.

Startled, they spoke simultaneously, "You!"

Sin was surprised to be able to speak and hear the woman his Grandmaster had said was his Spirit Guardian.

"I-it is an honor to meet you, Lady Hua. Thank you for sharing your life story with me. I have learned so much from you."

She looked at him sadly. "You have looked, but you have not learned…"

He looked startled, taken aback at the disappointed tone in her voice.

She continued in a gently reproving tone, "You choose despair, not hope. You mourn the death of your loved one, instead of embracing the miraculous lesson my own life holds. Is this how you choose to honor the memory of your beloved? Is your misery what she would want your life to be reduced to?"

Sin stared at her, dumbfounded. "What do you mean? What lesson?" *What had he missed?*

Hua sighed deeply, then gave him a kindly smile, "Watch and learn, My Son…"

Suddenly, they were both transported to a lovely Chinese garden. It was so real, it was like watching a spectacular 4D IMAX movie where one could actually smell the fragrance of the grass and flowers!

Hua's mother walked out into the garden and stood watching Hua's father feeding Si'An. Hua left Sin's side and walked over to her mother, leaving Sin to watch the scenes unfold like magic before him.

"Father seems to have formed a male bond with Si'An, "Hua said fondly.

Her mother chuckled, then said gravely, "Ever since your father was in his crippled state, he became a changed person. I think he did a lot of soul-searching during that time and vowed to become a better person."

Hua was saddened by her mother's remark and said quietly, "Mother, I cannot express how deeply sorry I am and will always be for causing you, my beloved parents, so much pain and suffering."

Her mother patted her hand and replied, "We were all deceived, My Child. It's not your fault."

They were quiet for a time, enjoying the beautiful Spring day, and companionably watching Si'An and Hua's father play in the pagoda. He moved with the ease of a much younger man, no longer tormented or crippled.

Eventually, Hua stirred and turned to gaze at her mother, her eyes full of emotion.

Hesitantly, she said, "Dearest Mother, it has been wonderful for me to spend these last few months at home with you and dear Father. But, now that you are both so well and healthy, it is time to continue my work for the poor of China. I must depart to take up the cause again. We will go to Xinjiang, where we haven't been yet."

Hua's mother valiantly tried to hold back her tears. She gave Hua a hug, "I understand, Child. We knew it was only a matter of time, Dear One, and want you to continue your great work. Its feels like we have spent a lifetime together and started anew while you were here. And traveling will help you take off your mind off of grieving for Li Bai."

Hua hugged her mother back fiercely and planted a soft devoted daughter's kiss on her pale cheek and went to see her father.

Her father stood beside Si'An, scratching him behind his ears like a treasured pet. Si'An sensed something in the air as Hua approached and her father did too.

"You are leaving, aren't you?" he asked, swallowing his sadness.

Hua nodded, "We shall go to explore Xinjiang, a place that I heard a lot about. Dearest Father, my heart is with you always, and the honorable deeds I do shall be in your name."

She bowed to him and kissed his cheek, "Take care of Mother and I'll be back before you know it."

Her father touched her cheek tenderly, "I will, Child. Go with my blessing. We will be here waiting when you come home."

The servants lined up in a row to see them off and wished them good journey. Hua gave each of them a handsome gift of money, and they bowed and thanked her profusely.

Her parents walked her down the garden path to the front gate to see her and the tiger off and they waved to each other until Hua and the tiger disappeared in the distance.

URUMQI , XINJIANG UYGUR

Urumqi, the Capital of Uygur, situated next to Tian Shan or the Heaven Mountain, one of the most famous mountains in China. Its beauty is legendary, with high cliffs soaring up to heaven.

To avoid alarming the inhabitants, Hua had left Si'An at the outskirts of the city in a nice wooded area to rest while she strolled into the main marketplace to buy food and supplies. A throng of people in colorful Muslim costumes crowded the marketplace. Vendors of all kinds displayed their goods on long tables and shoppers browsed from table to table, making their purchases.

Hua munched on an apple and threaded her way through the tables to see what wares she wanted to buy. She stood out from the other folk, as she was the only one wearing a Han warrior costume while everyone else wore Muslim garb.

One of the young Uygur vendors noticed the beautiful stranger and plucked up his courage to speak to her.

"Miss, have you heard the rumor that an army of wolves will be descending upon us to devour everyone in its path?

Hua shot him a skeptical look, "I've never heard anything that crazy before. Who said so and when is this supposed to happen?"

"A strange shaman passed through the market yesterday. He warned us all of this apocalyptic prophecy. Now, the market is packed with people from all over, eager to hear more about the prophecy. What a mess!"

A little girl, smudged with dirt and dressed in rags who had been sitting under the table, clambered up and put her hand on Hua's," I know where *he* is. I can take you to him."

Before Hua could reply, the child had tugged her into a small alley. Hua was amused by her forcefulness. It reminded her of herself at that age.

True to her word, the little girl led Hua to a ragged old man sleeping on a bale of rope in the alley. Hua handed her little guide some coins and the little girl bowed and happily skidded away.

Hua prodded the man with her boot, "Old man, I bring you some food. Wake up and have a decent meal."

The old man smelled the delicious food and woke up, instantly alert. We see that he is the mystery man of Sin's dreams, who had frozen time before. Hua did not recognize him. She watched impassively as he devoured everything she put in front of him as if he hadn't eaten for a week.

"What is this I hear about a horde of wolves...?

The Mystery Man replied, "Miss, according to Astrological projections, once every 500 years the wolf population spirals out of control in this region. Naturally, there won't be enough food for all of them and they will descend from the hills in search of food. Nothing can stop them and they'll devour everything in sight, including their own if they are wounded. They will be out for *blood*!"

Hua scoffed and turned to go. He seized her arm, anxiously. "Look at the mountain! They are already here!" He pointed a gnarled finger at the blue mountain across the valley.

Hua recoiled in horror to see a massive wave of grey, furry bodies seething down the mountain, many miles distant.

The Mystery Man got up and started to limp away. "If you value your life you better run now!"

"Wait!" Hua called after him, "Have we ever met before? You look so *familiar.*"

"Perhaps all *beggars* look alike to *you!*"

Hua's eyes narrowed as she watched him disappear. "You don't look like *any* beggar I ever met!"

She put all her questions aside and, after shouting a warning to all the citizens to barricade themselves into their houses, she raced back to where she had left Si'An.

Bursting upon him, she cried, "There you are! Millions of wolves are descending on the village any minute now and they will eat everyone alive unless we stop them!"

Hua and Si'An raced to the top of the mountain. Her mouth dropped open when she took in the scene below: the entire mountain and valley was carpeted with an army of giant wolves - approaching at a terrifying speed!

Hua shook her head and whispered, aghast, "We must try to head them off or all is lost!"

They took off at a run.

Hua and Si'An ran directly into their path of the ferocious pack and within minutes, they were beset by wolves!

Hua grasped her two deadly swords in her hands, and flashed and whirled to cut down dozens of wolves with each swing! As they collapsed, the wolves behind them fell upon them to devour their own wounded with squeals of delight.

This gave Hua a fighting chance to stay ahead of the seething pack. Beside her, the valiant Si'An was ripping and gouging and sinking his fierce fangs into any wolves foolish enough to come within striking distance. But he too was getting mauled by sneak attacks from wolves that attacked from behind.

Thousands of wolves were slaughtered, yet they never stopped coming. Hua was soaked in blood - the blood of the wolves mixed with her own blood as more and more wolves got through to take a bite out of her. Si'An was no better off, bleeding from multiple welts and gouges all over his bettered body.

The wolves were gaining on them... There were just too many of them. Sunset began to creep in. Hua knew they couldn't hold out much longer!

Hua spotted a tall tree in front of her and motioned Si'An to make a run for it. Using her leg as a fulcrum, she kicked the trunk and used the momentum to bounce toward a branch, high above the ground. She clambered to safety as Si'An effortlessly flowed up the trunk and into the branches beside her.

The wolves couldn't climb the tree, but the pack cleverly began to form a mound of bodies around the trunk of the tree that enabled them to mount higher and higher, closer and closer to their prey, trapped in the branches above.

Too tired to remain precariously balanced on a think branch, Hua tied her waist sash around a branch and let her body hang freely, so she could concentrate on slashing with her swords. Beside her, Si'An mauled wolf after brazen wolf as they scrambled ever higher up the pile of twisted and blood-soaked bodies.

Night was descending, but still the wolves relentlessly came on...!

Knowing she could not hold out much longer as night descended, and the wolves would have the advantage of being able to see in the dark, Hua yelled at her beloved tiger, "I wish I could have spared you this, Darling Si'An! Just wipe out as many as you can before they take us down!"

Si'An looked up at Hua and seemed to understand what she was saying. It gave her a mighty roar and suddenly leapt down from the tree into the writhing sea of wolves below! When it hit the ground, Si'An took off at sharp angle, racing away from the path of the wolves. The brave tiger kept turning back as it ran, mauling the wolves in pursuit and roaring his mighty challenge as he ran!

Smelling the blood of the wounded wolves, the pack followed Si'An's path, veering away from the tree. Soon more and more wolves went haring off after Si'An and the fresh blood he left in his wake, until the entire pack had abandoned their attack on the tree to follow the mighty tiger!

After fighting off the last wolf attacking the tree, Hua came out of her killing frenzy and realized what Si'An had done: the noble beast had sacrificed it's life for her!

A sob escaped her throat! No, she loved the courageous and selfless animal and would not allow it to give its life for hers!

With one swift stroke of her sword, she sliced through the sash that tied her to the tree branch and dropped down from the tree. She stumbled with exhaustion, but righted herself and followed the wolves' trail in search of her friend.

The trail led Hua to the edge of a mountain cliff that fell away to a massive drop. She looked down and saw, 500 feet below, as vast mound of wolf bodies that had fallen off the cliff in pursuit of her beloved tiger!

Another sob tore from her mouth at she looked at the carnage below. Just when she was turning to stagger away, she spotted a thin ledge, twenty feet below. Peering through the dusk, Hua saw Si'An lying on the ledge, surrounded by with a dozen of dead wolves!

Sheathing her swords, she quickly climbed down to the ledge and rushed to her tiger's side.

"Si'An, Dear Si'An, are you okay?"

Hearing her voice, the brave tiger struggled back to consciousness. He tried to raise his head, but was too weak to raise it.

Hua dropped down beside him and pulled his mighty head onto her lap. She gently stroked his face with a trembling hand.

"My dearest, brave and mighty Si'An, I could not hope for a better, more loyal friend. Please don't leave me!"

The beautiful white tiger whined in answer and thumped his tail, once, twice, then lay still.

"NOOOOOOOOOOO!" Hua roared out a thunderous denial! The whole valley reverberated with her sorrowful cry.

She staggered to her feet and pawed through the little bag at her waist, mumbling, "This isn't fair! You have saved my life too many times to count, and I have never once saved yours! What have I done for you but always lead you into danger? Now, where is my medicine bag? I *must* have *something* that can help..."

As she fumbled for her bag, the little gourd she'd slung on her belt fell off and hit the ground with a clatter! The magical spell that had cloaked its presence broke and she stood rooted to the spot as she saw, in her mind's eye, the time the Mysterious Man who had stopped time, praised her for being the champion of the poor, and left her the magic gourd.

Hua immediately recognized him as beggar she'd met in Uramqi alley!

She listened incredulously as he said to her: "Lady, your heart is pure and so I bestow upon you a mighty gift- some day you will need it." He placed the tiny gourd in her hand.

"Inside the gourd is the most *potent* medicine known to man. No wound, however serious, cannot be cured by this potion. Even the recently *deceased* can be brought back to life, if it is administered quickly enough. But, be forewarned, to bring back life, your own life force Chi must be sacrificed to replenish his. A life for a life. The decision is yours, Great Lady..."

The vision in her mind's eye disappeared. When she snapped out of her trance, Hua did not hesitate. She seized the gourd and poured the entire contents into Si'An's mouth and rubbed his throat until the potion flowed down throughout his motionless body.

Then, resolutely, she crossed her legs to make herself comfortable, and cradled his mighty head in her lap.

"Now is the hour of my death. A life for a life. So be it!"

With one hand on her tiger's still head and the other on his chest, she began to slip into her deepest meditation. Sweat began to roll down her face. Her entire body began to tremble and convulse! Slowly, a golden aurora of light began to glow from the crown of her head.

She started to vibrate faster and faster, at inhuman speed! The golden light around her glowed brighter and brighter. Soon it engulfed her entire body.

VROOOOM! With a mighty BOOM, she was thrown ten feet away and landed in a motionless heap.

For a second, nothing moved. Then, with a gasp, Si'An drew a new breath, reborn! He stretched his aching body and slowly stood up. He padded unsteadily to where Hua lay. He nudged her body with his huge head and whined plaintively.

Attracted by the light, a group of savage-looking dwarves appeared on the cliff's edge, armed with menacing spears. They saw Hua lying still on the ground and were mesmerized by her beauty. They did not realize she was dead and wanted to take her prisoner for their own diabolical purposes.

They slid down to the ledge and inched closer. Determined to protect his beloved lady even in death, Si'An moved to place his battered body between the dwarves and her prone form.

Without warning, the dwarves attacked! Si'An was wounded and every movement was a torment to him. Yet he guarded Hua's body with his life. Surrounded by the vicious dwarves, he kept them at bay with lethal swipes with his giant, razor-sharp claws. But he still took jab after jab from of their sharpened spears until his flanks were coated red with blood.

Just when the dwarves closed in for a final push, a Thunderous shout shook the air and sent the dwarves fleeing for safety!

A strange half-man, half-ape creature appeared in front of Si'An. "Don't be afraid, Noble Beast, I have come to save you."

Si'An seemed to understand. He trusted the unusual creature to approach Hua to check her for signs of life. It put his hand on Hua's neck, but found no pulse.

Cocking its head at the tiger, it shook it sadly, " I am too late. She is gone. A life for a life... she gave her life for yours, my friend. There is nothing I can do for her now."

As the creature prepared to withdraw, suddenly, from nowhere, they heard someone shout "Si'An, don't leave me!"

Si'An and the Creature leapt back in shock! It was the voice of Hua – but how was this possible?

The creature knuckled its head in perplexity. "Perhaps she is trapped between Heaven and Earth. Then her Chi must be very strong – perhaps it's not too late!"

He settled himself down beside her on one side and Si'An took her other side.

"I will try to use my own magical Chi power to lead her back to the world of the living."

It put both of his hands on Hua's abdomen and began to meditate.

Tremendous energy coursed through him and fed into her body.

Hua was trapped in an interim state of near death. She felt her body spinning in a fierce whirlwind down a dark tunnel. Strange and colorful lights flashed by her as she was sucked down toward the other end of the tunnel, where a warm yellow light pulsed.

At the end of the tunnel, she was suddenly spewed out into the clouds. Hua was amazed to find herself walking on clouds! They rippled and flowed around her feet. Everything was so vivid and beautiful – more beautiful than anything she had ever seen on Earth.

Hua was surprised to see Si'An on the other side of the cloud.

"Si'An! I am so glad to see you! Where are we?"

The giant white tiger loped over to her, and reared up o his hind legs to lick her face. They played on the clouds for a long time, running and tumbling and laughing. They felt completely free and safer than they ever had before.

Suddenly, before her eyes, the tiger began to morph! As the wispy clouds cleared away, she was stunned to see her beloved Li Bai standing before her! His eyes were shining with love...

When Little Li Bai had been murdered, Hua's heart had shattered into a thousand pieces and she had never been able to put them back together again. So, seeing him standing there before her again opened a floodgate of emotions that completely overwhelmed her!

She threw herself at him and began to cry uncontrollably, sobbing, " Oh, Li Bai, how I've missed you!"

Li Pai hugged her tightly, crushing her too him. He lifted her face and kissed her gently, whispering, "I would have missed you too, My Love, if I had ever left you."

She raised her inquiring eyes to his, "What do you mean?"

Li Bai took her hands in his and looked her lovingly in the eyes, "When my soul went to Heaven when I died, my heart remained on earth with you. When I was met in Heaven by the Immortal Beings, I told them that I would rather *walk through hell beside you for eternity than live in Heaven without you.* The Immortal Beings told me that according to the Laws of Heaven, it was not yet my time to be reincarnated. I would have to wait for several generations to come back again as another person. But I begged them with my whole heart and soul to find a way to reunite us now. One of the Beings stroked his beard and mused, "Even if you were an animal?"

"When I cried, 'Yes! Yes, with all my heart, yes!, the Immortal Being kept his word. And lo and behold, I was reincarnated as a white tiger in time to save your life!"

Hua was deeply moved by Li Bai's story. Her eyes welled up with tears.

Li Bai continued, "So, please don't die on me now! Not after moving Heaven and Earth to come back to you!"

Hua's eyes widened in shock and she gasped for breath as convulsions began to wrack her body!

Li Bai's crushed her in his arms and thrust his face into hers, "WAKE UP!" he roared!

Compelled by a love stronger than death, Hua's body, lying still in death on the mountain ledge, suddenly twitched!

Si'An crouched closer as her eyes flew open.

She smiled as he bathed her face in rough kisses with his raspy tongue! The half-ape creature smiled at her and said, "Welcome Back To Life, My Lady."

Hua recognized subconsciously that the half-man half-ape creature had something to do with the Immortal Beings and bringing her back to life. She gave him a kind smile, "Thank You, Friend," she said gratefully.

Throughout this entire adventure, Sin had been watching. Now, Hua turned to face him, drawing SIN back into the dream with her.

36
-
REINCARNATION

HUA LOOKED AT SIN EXPECTANTLY.

"Do you see, My Son? Do you see what I've been trying to tell you?"

Sin wasn't entirely sure. "That love...that true love conquers all?"

She beamed at him. "That is part of it. True love can cross *all* boundries. Death itself cannot tear such love apart. And that love in all its forms must be treasured..."

"You mean...your Si'An?"

She nodded and looked out into the field where her great white tiger was frolicking around chasing crickets, like a little kitten! He looked majestic - and absurd!

When her gaze fell on Si'An, a wistful look of infinite longing crossed her face. She turned back to Sin and gave him a kind smile, "Love and life are precious. Don't waste either of them."

With that, she ran off to rejoin her beloved Si'An.

3 7

-

REINCARNATION

Sin awoke in his own bed. His mind was reeling at what he just learned. Si'An - Hua's beloved Li Bai, reincarnated!

Sin suddenly remembered a long talk he had had one day with Grandmaster E about reincarnation. He had asked the Master if he believed in it.

Grandmaster E had told him that of course he did and that there was a powerful Nei Kung technique that could help induce a meditative state that could enable him to recall his past lives. Using this Nei Kung technique, Grandmaster E had experienced several of his past lives himself.

The Grandmaster had explained that when you died and your soul passed on after, during the reincarnation process, your soul would pass through a "Heavenly Waterfall" designed to wipe out the memory of your past life so you could begin anew with no old issues and baggage.

However, he also said that there were cases in which the memory-wiping process had not been complete, so there had been people throughout history who had been reborn with the full memories from her or his past life.

As Sin thought back to that conversation with Grandmaster E now, he realized that perhaps the original Li Bai had been reincarnated into Little Li Bai, because the boy had retained the full memory of his past life. Even as a toddler, he had been able to quote Li Bai's poems from the time he could first speak.

And, according to what Hua had just told him, Li Bai had been reincarnated again as Si'An, her great white tiger, whose devotion to Hua was absolute!

Hua and Li Bai's love had been so strong and so loyal, that they kept being reincarnated into each other's lives time after time! How many lives had they spent together, Sin wondered? And how magnificent was that!

He suddenly felt hopeful and elated. The depression that had dogged him for months evaporated as quickly as it had come.

Just talking about reincarnation with Grandmaster E hadn't been enough to truly convince Sin that reincarnation existed. It had taken Hua and her willingness to share her own private joys and sorrows to do that. Now he was a believer!

He had been so devastated by the loss of his beloved Siu Ie, he had not been able to get through the grieving process or move on with his life, as everyone kept urging him to do.

In the depths of despair, Sin had been in danger of losing his bright future. But Hua had visited him again and again until finally he understood her message!

Through her intervention, she had shown him that there is a chance that Siu Ie, too, might be reincarnated, just like Li Bai had been.

That gave him a whole new reason to hope!

Hua's words opened a mystical doorway for Sin into a whole new realm of possibility. Where might it lead him? And would he be reconnected with Sui Ie again one day?

Grandmaster E had said that a good Spiritual Guardian could change your path and even your destiny at a critical juncture in your life when you needed their insight the most.

Sin felt like Hua had shifted his path from a dark and despairing one back to the bright and promising one he had been born with, and for that, he would always be deeply grateful.

38

-

AN ENLIGHTENING EVENING

SIN HAD NOT BEEN TO KUNG Fu school since Siu Ie's death, so, to avoid the painful questions and condolences of the other students, he waited until they had all left before he went in to see Grandmaster E.

When he knocked on the Grandmaster's door, Sin felt nervous and unsure this had been a good idea. He dreaded that his master would blame him for being derelict in his studies. But, when Grandmaster E opened the door, he was happy and relieved to see his favorite pupil. Without waiting for Sin to speak, he asked if he would like to take a stroll in the garden.

After strolling silently around for several minutes, they sat down on a bench and Sin started telling his mentor everything that had happened. This was the first time Sin had talked to anyone about what he had seen and felt, and his emotions were still raw and chaotic. It was painful to talk about it, but somehow, his mentor's quiet and sympathetic manner made him feel better.

Grandmaster E listened attentively as Sin divulged his hate for Akang and confessed what he had done to him. Sin admitted that he still felt an irresistible urge to hunt him down and finish the job.

Without judgment, Grandmaster E said that he wanted to share his own troubling story with him. He told Sin the tale of his gruesome encounter with the eleven Chinese soldiers in the forest who had tried to kill him, and how he had killed them all in order to save his life and escape to Indonesia. He confessed that he had already been an expert in Dim Mak techniques by then and could have paralyzed his opponents rather than killing them. But after so many years witnessing the despair caused by the Bei Yang army as it raped and murdered innocent people without a second thought, he had allowed himself be carried away by rage and hatred and succumbed to vengeance.

He quietly shared with Sin how the ghosts of those eleven soldiers, though all evil men, had followed him all the way to Indonesia and had tormented him day and night. It had gotten so bad, he had started to smoke opium to escape them and had wasted ten years of his life enslaved by the filthy drug.

One night after smoking, he had had a frightening dream about his own reincarnation. He understood that in his new life, he would be punished for throwing away his present life.

He saw himself, a sickly, underweight baby, reborn prematurely to a heroin-addicted mother. She was weak and cried out in agony as she strained for hours to push the baby out.

When he finally came into the world, the newborn began to convulse and had trouble breathing. It couldn't eat or sleep and seemed unlikely to survive the night. The newborn had grown addicted to his mother's drugs while in the womb, but, he was a fighter and by a miracle of strength and will to live, the tiny newborn pulled through.

Grandmaster E said that the dream had frightened him tremendously, but it had also motivated him to straighten out his life. The baby's will and spirit inspired and encouraged him to fight to live his own life, but it was a long and difficult process. He had to face his fears and the faces of the ghosts and learn to come to terms with what he had done.

Then he had to learn to forgive himself and learn to accept his dark side, rather than try to deny or run away from it.

After a long pause, Grandmaster E turned to Sin and said that all people have darkness within them, but it is the path they choose that will define them. Whether they will fight to stay in the light or succumb to the darkness is entirely up to them.

"Violence only feeds more violence, but, I know you, Sin. You have the strength to avoid my mistakes and find a better path, one that will not lead you down the same road I took when I let anger and vengeance consume me.

Master and pupil sat quietly side by side in companionable silence. Something made them look up at the night sky simultaneously – just in time to see a shooting star streaking across the Heavens.

"Ah, a soul has just left the Heavens to visit one of us on Earth," Grandmaster E said.

Sin knew in his heart that his master was right about not succumbing to a life of hate and vengeance, but understanding and accepting this evolved lesson did not come easily to him. A great feeling of sadness overwhelmed Sin, as he tried to shed his hardness and anger and find his way to acceptance. He felt so empty and the pain just kept coming back. He realized how he had sought to avoid his pain by focusing on a lust for revenge. It was going to be much harder to find his way down the more evolved path that Grandmaster E had just described.

But, he wondered, what about justice? Was he doing Siu Ie a great injustice if he let Akang's atrocity go unpunished? He had no answer yet and knew it would take him time to puzzle out the right thing to do.

39
-
RESOLUTION & PREMONITION

The morning Tze was going to stay for two days at the local hospital, Sin asked Tze if he would mind if he took him to the clinic himself. Sensing that Sin had resurfaced a tiny bit, his brother was very happy to take Sin's offer.

When they pulled up to the clinic, Tze started to get really nervous. Sin reassured him that he would be all right and that this was necessary so they could get him better. Sin's heart felt heavy as the nurse walked Tze down the hall. When his brother turned to look back at him, Sin waved and said that he'd be back to pick him up in 48 hours.

Two days later when he went to pick Tze up from the clinic, his brother looked like he had had a rough couple of days, so Sin asked if he wanted to go to the pool and relax in the sun instead of going straight home.

Tze seemed relieved at the idea. As they sat next to each other with their feet in the water, Sin asked him questions about his stay at the clinic. But Tze seemed preoccupied, so after a few listless 'yes' and 'no' answers, Sin decided to not press the issue.

After sitting there quietly for a while just watching the ripples in the water, Sin suddenly saw Siu Ie's reflection behind him. He whipped his head around and spotted a silhouette moving through the trees. It disappeared behind a giant ficus tree.

Sin leapt up and ran to check behind the tree, but no one was there. Bemused by his foolish fantasies, he was turning to go when a soft wind blew some leaves off the tree and they fell to the ground at his feet.

Sin picked up a firm, healthy-looking leaf and suddenly heard Siu Ie's voice, "Make the leaf sing for me, Sin!" Her voice was as clear as a bell!

Sin walked back to Tze looking so dazed that Tze asked him if everything was okay. Sin didn't want to overexcite his brother, so he just shrugged and pretended he'd just been stretching his legs.

He sat back down and examined the leaf.

"What's up with the leaf, Sin?" his brother asked.

Sin grinned, put it up to his lips and made a sweet, pleasant sound with it.

"Where'd you learn to do that?" Tze asked, enchanted.

Sin explained that one day, he had been spending time in the garden with Sui Ie and she had picked up a strand of grass and made funny noises with it. He'd followed suit with a ficus leaf and she been impressed by the melodious sounds he produced with the leaf. She'd made him promise to create a song and serenade her with it one day.

When Sin talked about Siu Ie in the past tense, he started to get heavy and depressed. Tze immediately picked up on his state of mind and said that it wasn't too late for him to serenade her.

Sin's eyes widened at this notion. What a brilliant idea! He could channel his sorrow into something positive - and bid her farewell with a beautiful song worthy of her memory!

But, he knew he would have to practice until he was good enough for the final song. But for now, he raised the leaf back to his lips, and as if divinely inspired, a lovely sound wafted from the little leaf.

Several months went by, and as Sin slowly got back into his school work and Kung Fu classes, he also got better at blowing the leaf.

Tze would often keep him company as Sin practiced, emitting strange, off-key notes, but eventually as he learned some control over the leaf and a started to emit melodies. They were both thrilled every time Sin made progress.

Unfortunately, there was not any similar progress with Tze's medical condition. To their great distress, they were running out of doctors and specialists to consult.

They had learned that Tze did not have problems with episodic memory of people and events, but he had major problems with semantic memory for language and academics, which eventually made it impossible for him to return to school.

On top of that, his blackouts were happening more frequently now, which made it increasingly difficult for him to leave the house unattended.

Desperate to help their second-born son, Sin's parents turned to alternative medicine and set him up with weekly acupuncture treatments. He never got used to the needles but went through it anyway so that the family would not feel that he had given up hope.

One day, when Sin thought the time was right, he took Tze with him back to visit the swimming pool where he had met Siu Ie. He had first seen her on a Thursday, years ago, so since Sui Ie's death, Sin had gotten in the habit of stopping by the pool every Thursday to honor her memory.

But today was going to be special.

Sitting by the pool edge with Tze, Sin relived his first memory of Siu Ie, and envisioned her laughing and splashing in the water with her friend, happy and carefree.

He took his leaf from his pocket and held it in his hands. "To you, my lovely Sui Ie," he said quietly. And began to play a lovely, *haunting* melody.

The sound reverberated across the swimming pool and swept over the terraced rice paddies and up the mountainside beyond. It echoed back to the swimming pool, surrounding him and his brother with its lovely, heartbreaking melody. His music has a mystical feel to it that mesmerized the other bathers.

By the time Sin had finished blowing his eerie, haunting music, everyone at the swimming pool felt like they had experienced a poignant, surrealistic experience.

Tze finally broke the silence, "Wow! Sin, you *did* it! That was the most beautiful memorial that any one has ever dedicated to their loved one that I have ever heard!"

Sin smiled at his brother, "Thank you, Tze, but remember, it was *your* idea to learn how to blow the leaf well enough to use it to say *goodbye* to Siu Ie. You've encouraged me from the beginning." Sin chuckled, "Remember how awful it sounded at first?"

Tze giggled, remembering Sin's terrible squeaky sounds.

Then Tze got a strange look on his face, "Sin, will you promise me something? Someday when I die, would you say goodbye to me with a beautiful song on your leaf too?"

Sin scowled, uncomfortable with this topic, "Why are you always talking about dying, Tze? You'll be fine."

But, even as he said that, Sin was overcome by a tidal-wave of grief that swept through him as he got a clear premonition of Tze's future. He knew then that the time would come - soon - when Tze would no longer be at his side.

Tze refused to be put off. He asked again, persistent, "Will you, Sin?"

Sin looked at his younger brother and saw his eager, guileless face raised to his, his kind eyes pleading.

Sin got all choked up. Afraid to speak, he managed to nod his head. "Promise?"

Sin found his voice. "I promise."

Tze clapped his hands and laughed happily. "Thank you, Sin! And I promise I will come down from Heaven and listen."

Sin turned his brimming eyes to the mountains and sat cherishing this special moment with his brother and vowed to cherish every moment he had with him thereafter.

40
—

DIM MAK | THE DEATH TOUCH
(PART 1)

HIS RECENT EXPERIENCES HAD MADE HIM feel more appreciative of the important people in his life, so Sin asked Grandmaster E if he could invite him out for some turtle stew for dinner. Understanding that Sin's struggle with all the tragedies in his short life must have left him feeling very lonely, he graciously consented.

As usual, Grandmaster E had his pipe clamped between his teeth while he walked. He loved his tobacco.

The way to the restaurant took them through a poorer section of the town with a bad reputation. As they rounded a corner, four thugs armed with knives suddenly appeared out of nowhere and blocked their way!

Akang was one of them! Feeling strength in numbers, he leered at Sin, ready to bash his face in! He ignored the Grandmaster, thinking he was a harmless old man.

Sin turned and shot a quick glance behind them. He saw four more thugs stepping into view, blocking their retreat. A grotesque little ambush with eight against two!

Akang barked out an order and the gang moved in on them, confident of their ability to subdue and rob an old man and young Sin.

Sin dropped into a fighting position, his gaze never leaving Akang's smug face. He sensed Grandmaster E beside him, as unperturbed as ever, still calmly smoking his pipe.

The thugs struck all at once in a vicious, coordinated attack. Sin raised hands to deflect the first blow and counterattack, when Grandmaster E leapt into action, whirling his long pipe in a blinding blur of motion too swift to follow!

As suddenly as it all began, it was over.

All eight thugs slowly collapsed to the ground. And without even pausing to admire his handiwork, Grandmaster E walked on toward the restaurant.

Sin was stunned, rooted to the spot. He gazed down at Akang's still form and heard Grandmaster E's voice in the distance.

"Coming?"

Sin assumed they were just unconscious, but he couldn't bring himself to check or even care if they were dead. With a wide-eyed look at the eight motionless bodies, he ran to catch up with Grandmaster E.

While the Grandmaster enjoyed his stew, Sin blurted out, "I never knew a human being could move so fast! You were amazing!"

Grandmaster E waved away his pupil's compliments, "Your stew is getting cold."

"That was *Dim Mak, the Death Touch*, you just hit them with, wasn't it? My Great-great-great Grandfather knew Dim Mak and I have always dreamt that one day I would know it too."

He looked at the Grandmaster, his eyes round with hope. "One day, Grandmaster... would you be willing to teach it to me?"

Grandmaster E pierced him with an assessing look. "Maybe... But, let me ask you something... That wasn't a random attack, was it? That mob leader *recognized* you."

"That pig's name is Akang. He was the one who raped and murdered my girlfriend, Siu Ie! And he is already out of prison! What kind of crazy, unjust system do we live in anyway?"

Grandmaster E sat quietly for a moment, then replied, "Be careful, Son. I saw blood in his eyes. And yours. He is the type who will stop at nothing to end you. Make sure you never sink to his level..."

Sin looked grim and finished his meal in silence.

41

-

LOSING GROUND

One evening, it was pouring down outside as Sin and his family gathered in the dining room for dinner. Sin's father looked worried and told them about his ride to the textile factory earlier that morning.

He had been passing Bandung Institute of Technology when traffic slowed, and he saw a big, angry crowd carrying picket signs with rude and racist signs against the Chinese. The nicest one was "Chinese go home!"

They were bunched up on the front lawn to hear anti-Chinese speeches by the group leaders. As Heng's car rolled by, a group of people went straight for it and started banging on the windows screaming that he should go back to China where he belonged!

Sin and the rest of the family listened anxiously as he told them how he was afraid that things would only get worse.

Sin's mother noticed that Tze hadn't come down to dinner and asked one of the servants to go fetch him from his room. When the servant came back a few minutes later and said that he wasn't in his room or anywhere in the house, everyone panicked and split up to find him.

Most of the family went to look for him in the garden areas, so Sin decided to take his motorcycle and check the streets nearby, in case he had wandered out the front door.

Sin had been riding around in the rain for half an hour before he finally spotted Tze curled up on the sidewalk with his back against a storefront huddling out of the rain.

When Sin got to him, he was shivering badly, so Sin quickly put his raincoat on him and got him on the bike behind him. He seemed terribly disoriented and kept mumbling incoherently. Sin carefully drove him home.

Everyone was so relieved that Tze had been found, but seeing him in such a state revived the family's anxiety about his future. After they cleaned him up and put him in bed, they all went back to the dining room to discuss what to do about Tze.

Sin's father was terribly frustrated that none of the treatments had worked and that they were running out of options. Western medicine had failed altogether and so had traditional Chinese medicine.

They sat there feeling helpless, trying to come up with ideas, when suddenly Sin's father said that they could send him to a Dukun, an Indonesian shaman with supposed healing powers. They discussed it for a long time, and several of the family members worried it wouldn't be a good idea. No one was really familiar with their methods and they didn't know one they could trust.

Sin's sister, Cheng, was especially against it because she had heard a horror story about a Dukun that had taken advantage of a twelve-year-old girl after her parents had let him perform an overnight blessing ceremony. He had raped her and gotten her pregnant. Anyone who could do that to a twelve year old child, was a monster!

Their father argued that the story might just be a rumor, but if it was true, it must be an isolated incident, otherwise no one would use Dukun anymore. He asked Sin what he thought.

Sin replied that he was not comfortable with the idea either and that he didn't really believe it would help. Sin's father was disappointed for a moment, but then he grew stern and said that he wasn't going to just give up on the idea. As long as there were possibilities out there, he was going to explore them. He got up, walked into his bedroom and closed the door. The whole family could tell what a tremendous strain he was under, not to be able to find a way to help his son.

When Sin got home from school the following day, Tze was just getting out of bed. He looked dazed and his skin was pale, so Sin suggested they get out of the house, have lunch at the pool, and just hang out and do some 'people watching'. After they sat in the sun for a while, Tze started looking a little better. Sin asked him if he remembered how he got out of the house the night before.

Tze looked down and said he had snuck out because he needed some space. He had been cooped up in the house for so long and hated being restricted from going anywhere without someone with him. He just wanted to feel normal for a while and didn't think anything would happen if he just took a short walk around the block.

Sin nodded understandingly and imagined how insane he would have beome if he had been confined in the house like that and could not go anywhere without a chaperone. Tze said he had overheard them talking in the dining room and asked if Sin really thought their father was going to send him to a Dukun.

Sin said he didn't know but that they were all trying to come up with better alternatives for him to consider, but so far no one had thought of anything they hadn't already tried. Sin saw the dread in his brother's face and told him not to be afraid, as it might not happen.

Tze confessed that, lately, he felt afraid all the time and wished he could be as fearless as Sin.

Sin was surprised that Tze saw him like that and told him that when he was little, he often didn't want to fall asleep because he was afraid of an imaginary madman. Tze looked at Sin incredulously, so Sin finally told him the whole story about how he used to wake up screaming all the time and how their mother had to sit with him for hours at a time in the middle of the night. Sin also told him that the madman was the initial reason that he started Kung Fu.

Tze was amazed and said he had had no idea, but that it made so much sense. Then Sin told him not to worry about the Dukun. Sin said that knowing him; he would probably just be bored and slip a cockroach up the shaman's sleeve during those lengthy monotonous chants.

Tze laughed, his face lighting up. Sin stared at him, dumbfounded, suddenly realizing how long it had been since anyone had seen his brother smile, let alone laugh.

42

-

WHAT GOES AROUND COMES
AROUND

SIN UNDERSTOOD THE DESPERATION THAT HAD prompted Tze to sneak out of the house that night, so he decided to start taking him to his Kung Fu classes with him to get him out of the house and give him a sense of accomplishment. Sin hoped it would make him feel less lonely and left out.

Tze was excited to meet Grandmaster E and impressed by the classes Sin taught. When Grandmaster E saw Tze's eagerness, he kindly asked Tze if he would like to join the beginner class. Tze nodded happily and looked eagerly over at Sin, thrilled to part of something special.

Grandmaster E gave Tze a brandnew uniform and, with a hidden wink at Sin, asked Sin to show his brother how put it on correctly. Sin nodded gratefully and hoped his master could see just how much this gesture had meant to him. No student had ever been accepted to the school without an extensive screening process first.

Tze loved his uniform and stood up straight and proud in it. From that day on, because he had Tze among his students, Sin taught the beginner class with heightened interest and excitement. And Tze did really well in the class. Sin was so proud of him.

Grandmaster E always made it a point to talk to Tze after each class and Sin could see how his brother's face lit up from all this special attention and encouragement.

Several weeks later, Tze and Sin were on their way home from Kung Fu on Sin's motorcycle, when four men surrounded them in the dark street. One stepped forward into the light and leered.

It was Akang!

He and his burly friends caught the brothers by surprise and pulled them off the motorcycle. Two of them ganged up on Tze while Sin held Akang and the other one off with a series of high kicks that forced them to keep their distance.

Enraged to be denied easy prey, Akang snarled and pulled out a *kris* – a lethal Indonesian dagger with a wavy blade that often had a poisonous tip. As Akang circled to the left wielding the knife, his friend came at Sin from the right with a pair of long, sharpened grass clippers. He lunged at Sin and tried to lop his ear off! Sin dodged at the last second and the would-be maimer was left with just a chunk of Sin's hair.

Akang sprang at Sin from the other side with his deadly *kris*, but Sin's years of training allowed him to deftly sidestep him and dance lightly out of reach. Then Sin lashed out with his fist and clocked Akang in the face, snapping his head back. Akang staggered and bleated in pain!

Sin's other attacker chopped at his fingers, but only succeeded in slicing off a piece of Sin's sleeve. Sin centered himself and prepared to take them both down, when he heard Tze scream! He whipped his head around and saw his brother being savagely beaten.

He raced over to protect his brother and used his advanced skills to quickly disable his attackers. But, his distraction gave Akang time to scuttle back on his feet and sneak up behind him.

The thug stabbed at Sin's neck with his gleaming blade, murder in his eyes! But Sin, alerted by his heightened perception, sensed him behind him and hurled himself aside in the nick of time.

But, he felt sharp pain as the knife grazed his neck, drawing blood.

His neck burned! He knew in that instant he'd been poisoned! He had to act fast, before he succumbed to the poison. Outraged at his own careless inattentiveness, Sin deftly turned on Akang, grabbed his knife hand and twisted it, hard, until it *snapped*! Akang shrieked and dropped the knife, cradling his broken arm.

Akang's friend roared and lunged at Sin with his sharpened clippers, trying to slice open his stomach! Sin sidestepped, twisting out of the way, and the thug's brutal thrust missed its mark, carrying him stumbling past Sin into the darkness.

There was an ominous *squelch* and a horrific *scream*!

Hyper-vigilant, Sin tensed, ready for anything. He peered into the darkness and saw Akang doubled over, his hands clutched between his legs as blood gushed from his privates! The clippers that missed disemboweling Sin had ended up embedded in Akang's groin, slicing right through his genitals!

The stricken murderer emitted a high-pitched, piercing yowl and collapsed to the ground. Mortified at what he'd accidentally done, Akang's friend ran off. The other two thugs stumbled back to their feet and staggered away. Akang, the rapist, would never be able to rape anyone else ever again.

Sin rushed to his brother, fearing the worst. But, other than a bloody nose and some painful bruises, Tze seemed ok. But Sin, on the other hand, was sinking fast. Tze exclaimed in shock as Sin told him that the knife had been poisoned and insisted that he get him to Grandmaster E as fast as he could.

Weaker by the second, Sin let Tze load him onto the motorcycle. He passed out against Tze's back as they sped away.

Sin woke up tangled in sweaty sheets in Grandmaster E's guestroom. Tze and Grandmaster E were sitting by the bed talking quietly. Tze was worried and demanding to know if Sin was going to be all right.

"Only time will tell, Son," Grandmaster E replied gravely.

Just then Sin coughed. They both turned to him anxiously.

Sin mustered some strength. "G-good job getting me to the G-Grandmaster, Brother," he said weakly.

Tze smiled proudly, "You should have seen the Grandmaster suck the poison out of your blood! It was all black and weird. He gave you special medicine and saved your life!"

Sin turned gratefully to Grandmaster E. He could barely speak, "T-hank you, Sir, for saving my life."

Grandmaster E looked at him gravely, and with uncharacteristic gesture of affection, patted Sin's hand.

"Tze told me what happened. It is the Law of *Karma* at work. And because you did not instigate this fight out of a need for revenge on your girlfriend's murderer, I know that I can now trust you with the secrets of Dim Mak. It will enable you to protect yourself and your family against future attacks.

Sin was speechless, but Tze exclaimed in excitement knowing how badly Sin wanted to learn this secret art.

And so was how a good came out of an evil.

43
-
DIM MAK (Part 2)

ONCE HE HAD RECOVERED FROM THE poison and riding high on excitement, Sin arrived at Grandmaster E's for his first Dim Mak lesson. The Grandmaster was waiting for Sin in the garden, standing beside a life-size, wooden acupuncture figure. Master E invited Sin to sit on a nearby bench and began to explain the philosophy behind the *Dim Mak* technique.

He started with a quick review of the basics - the twelve meridians running through the human body and the seven hundred and twenty acupressure points located along those meridians, which Sin knew quite well. Then he moved on to the eighteen points that could be used for injuring or crippling an opponent and the other fifty-four points that were also vulnerable sites, but only during certain times of the day.

But then, the Grandmaster finally taught Sin about the thirty-six secret pressure points known to the rare few as the "death points," that could kill an opponent with a touch. These were completely new to him and his heart pounded to be so honored.

Sin listened avidly, drinking in this rare and fascinating knowledge.

Presently, the Grandmaster led Sin to the acupuncture figure and for the next several hours, pointed out the death points located in the head, neck and upper chest area. Next, he showed Sin how to strike these points using his fingers, knuckles, or side-hand chops.

After Grandmaster E demonstrated the strikes several times, he had Sin practice them on his own. Half an hour later, Sin felt he had learned how to hit the points with good accuracy and speed. Grandmaster E, wanting to temper Sin's newfound confidence, cocked an eyebrow and asked Sin to step aside. Suddenly, the grandmaster let loose with a blizzard of powerful, accurate, and lightning fast strikes that all hit their targets!

Sin was completely in awe and tried his best to imitate him, but it was impossible for a novice to do what the master had done without much more training. When Sin finished his round of strikes, his fingertips were in agony!

Grandmaster E brought him over to two cauldrons he had prepared. One was filled with a thick, brown substance smoldering over an open fire and the other was filled with smoking hot sand on a burning fire. He dipped his hands in the brown substance and told Sin to do the same. It was very hot, but Sin was determined to not show any weakness and forced himself to keep his hands in the brown liquid until the Grandmaster removed his. After that, the Grandmaster put his hands in the smoking hot sand and directed Sin to follow suit. Sin hesitated for a split second, but then put his hands in. The sand was burning hot, but Grandmaster E told Sin to keep his hands in for as long as possible and concentrate on controlling the pain.

Sin gritted his teeth and tried to block out the pain as the heat burned his skin and sweat rolled down his face. E explained how the brown liquid, combined with the heat from the sand, would toughen and harden his hands and fingers. Sin started huffing and puffing, fighting the pain. Finally Grandmaster E removed his hands and Sin immediately pulled his out too.

He was shocked to see his hands were actually smoking! Sin shook them vigorously and blew on them to cool them off.

Grandmaster E chuckled and asked if Sin was ready for another round.

They repeated this new routine over and over for the next several weeks, and despite all the pain, dread, and nightmares about fire ants eating his fingers, Sin was determined to continue the training until he finished it.

After a while, he started to feel how much stronger and more resilient his hands had become. The Grandmaster gradually increased the amount of time he had Sin submerge his hands in the burning sand.

One day, Grandmaster E said he was going to teach Sin the *Liu Sing, or Meteor Fist.* He demonstrated the form and Sin was spellbound by how fast he moved and how powerful his hits were. In what seemed like a blink of an eye, he had executed dozens of deadly attacks.

Sin started to learn the form, section-by-section, and practiced conscientiously. But he didn't feel he had reached his optimum power and speed. Grandmaster E told Sin to keep practicing, while the Master went into the house. Sin practiced over and over again until the sun set. When it was too dark to see, he went inside the house and found the Grandmaster in the living room looking at a picture of a half-man, half-ape looking creature.

"Who's that?" Sin demanded anxiously. "I saw *him* in my dream!"

Grandmaster E looked up, "He was my teacher, Su. He taught me everything I know. What did he do in your dream?"

Sin told Grandmaster E that one night he was dreaming about the crazy madman who was chasing him down the street. Usually the dream would end when the madman caught up to him, grabbed him by his collar and beat him, then he would wake up screaming!

But, this time, it had a completely different ending. This time, a half-man, half-ape looking creature appeared out of nowhere, and the creature beat up the madman, and saved Sin!

Grandmaster E listened intently to Sin's story, nodding sagely. They sat silently together for quite a while, then Grandmaster E offered to enhance Sin's *Meteor Fist* training that weekend with a special *Nei Kung* training to make him stronger and faster.

Sin eagerly accepted.

When the weekend came, Sin told his mother that Grandmaster E had invited him to stay over for the weekend for a very special Nei Kung class and his mother agreed to let him to go.

At Grandmaster E's house, Sin stopped by the acupuncture model in the garden and pointed to a pressure point on the back near the kidney. "You said this one was called *Ming Men* or *Gate of the Soul.* Is there any significance to that name?"

Grandmaster E nodded, "Yes. It was the point used to exorcise evil spirits."

Sin had no idea the special meditation training he was learning that weekend was what he had seen Grandmaster E doing when he went to return his bowl with the 800 grains of rice so many years ago.

His training for the weekend was to keep himself suspended between two benches – one under his head and the other under his feet – with nothing in between. But it was much more difficult than what Sin could imagine.

He kept collapsing to the ground and hurting his back and wrists. When Sin was ready to give up, Grandmaster E picked up a chopstick and a wooden hammer and told Sin to hammer the chopstick into the Grandmaster's neck with all his might!

Sin looked at him in alarm, hesitating. He was reluctant to do it, afraid he would seriously hurt his Master. But the Grandmaster yelled at Sin, *ordering* him to do it. Frightened but used to obeying his Master, Sin put the chopstick against E's neck and slammed the hammer on it. To his great amazement, the chopstick smashed to pieces and there was barely a mark on his neck!

Grandmaster E took off his shirt and Sin saw he had well-developed muscles bulging all over his body. The Master assured Sin that the bench meditation could make one's muscles become like impenetrable rocks.

Impressed, Sin regained his motivation and went back to his exercises on the benches.

44

-

MASTER WU (PART 2)

SIN KEPT UP HIS EXERCISES ON the benches until he could stay stretched out for a very long time. One day toward the end of his exercise lying stretched between the benches, his concentration faltered and he fell from the benches and hit the floor with a hard thump.

"Oomph!"

Grandmaster E looked over his newspaper at Sin curiously. "You have been stretched there for a very long time, my Son."

Sin burst out, "I was in another world again. It made it easier to concentrate."

Grandmaster E chuckled. His prodigy was really coming along. That night he had instructed eight of his senior students to attack Sin simultaneously. They thought that, all together, they would easily defeat him. But using the *Nei Kung Internal Power* techniques he had recently learned, Sin defeated them all.

"Now that you've mastered another Internal System, why not see how you would stack up against Master Wu?" Grandmaster E suggested.

"Go and have a friendly match with him, my Son."

Sin thanked Grandmaster E for the confidence he had in him and promised to do it soon. But, first he asked Grandmaster E if he could review the *Nei Kung* technique he had taught him some years ago that had enabled Sin to talk to his departed Grandparents?

Grandmaster E gazed at him thoughtfully and asked if this request had anything to do with Hua's recent story?

Sin nodded sadly and told Grandmaster E that Hua's story made him miss Siu Ie tremendously. He desperately wanted to see her one more time.

Grandmaster E grew grave. He knew how hard it was to let go of a departed loved one, but he also respected Sin's judgment, so he began to review the *Nei Kung* technique.

Sin paid close attention and carefully memorized the entire acupuncture process in the exact right order. He wanted to make sure he did not mix up the order and risk sending him into the realm of reincarnation instead by accident!

On his way home that night, Sin stopped by a fruit vendor to buy some durian, his favorite fruit. Friction between the local Indonesians and the wealthy Chinese had been heating up, and at the shop, Sin witnessed an Indonesian man berating a Chinaman, "Look at you Chinese! Buying so much fruit, while we Indonesians hardly have enough to live on!"

Sin paid for his own fruit and left, wondering what was going on in his country lately. He had never been interested in politics, but he was concerned that there seemed to be so much hostility and anger between the Indonesians and the Chinese lately. He didn't know who was to blame, but his training had taught him to deal honorably with everyone involved in a conflict and not give in to racist views or entrenched prejudices.

On the way home, Sin passed a group of Indonesian youths gathered around a street corner. As Sin passed by, they spotted him and started chasing after him, "Get outta here, Chinaman, if you know what's good for you!"

Sin didn't like the look of the angry gang. He gunned his motorcycle and sped away.

Later that week, Sin finally convinced himself to go to Master Wu's house. Wu's servant answered the door and led him to the living room, then went to get Master Wu. Master Wu entered the living room and shook Sin's hand and invited him to take a seat.

"What brings you here, Young Man?"

Sin noticed Master Wu looked ill and his eyes were strangely red.

"Master Wu, your eyes are all red. Are you all right?"

Master Wu shifted uncomfortably. "My *Chi* is not flowing properly through my body. It's stuck somehow and I'm having a hard time getting it to budge."

Sin listened, concerned.

"It just happened recently. But, never mind about my problems, to what did I owe this visit?"

"I came to ask you if you would be willing to have another friendly sparring match with me someday?"

Wu eagerly replied, "Sure. But why wait? Let's do it now."

Sin was surprised by this answer, "Oh no, not now. You are not at your best. I'll come back when you have rested and feel better."

Master Wu shook his head. "I would rather do it now. I'll tell you why. You know as well as I do that in a match, the adrenaline spikes and your *Chi* flows freely. A good match might be just what I need to unclog my stagnant Chi. You would be doing me a favor."

Sin appreciated Wu's logic and agreed to fight him. They bowed to each other. Sin was fully alert, as he still had the bad taste of defeat from the last time they had fought. His initial strategy was to move defensively for a while.

Sin remembered in the last fight how Master Wu had gone on the offensive the moment his hand had touched Sin's, and been able to push him into the wall and pin him there. So Sin was anticipating another aggressive offensive from Wu. But, he waited and waited as they circled each other and the onslaught never came.

He knew then, Wu must be *very* sick indeed for his fighting style to be so radically altered.

So Sin went for the kill. As fast as lightning, he executed several powerful attacks toward Wu. Sure enough, Wu was not able to block Sin's attacks and all the missiles Sin launched hit their targets. Sin was stunned how easily he had hit Wu. He began to feel much more confident that he could beat him this time and launched another barrage of attacks. Like the last round, all of his punches landed squarely on target.

Master Wu, on the other hand, seemed almost oblivious to the blows Sin was landing. He almost seemed to *enjoy* the beating! In fact, the more Sin hit him, the higher his spirits rose!

Wu cried out enthusiastically, "Yes! *This* is exactly what the doctor ordered!"

Sin thought this was a bizarre reaction and got goose bumps all over his body. He wanted to end the fight.

But, just then, Master Wu executed a fierce retaliatory attack on Sin, forcing him to keep fighting. Sin blocked all the incoming missiles, then suddenly saw an opening when Wu left his groin undefended.

Sin took the shot and kicked Wu square in the groin. His kick landed right on target with a loud 'thump! Sin stepped back, happy with his maneuver and expecting Wu to buckle over and capitulate. He was totally shocked when Wu just breathed deeply for a few seconds, then showered Sin with a virtual blizzard of attacks!

Only Sin's vigorous training enabled Sin to evade Wu's incoming cruise missiles. When Sin saw another opening, he kicked Master Wu in the groin again with all his might!

'BOOOM!" A loud popping sound cracked through the air as Sin's kick landed on Wu's groin. This time Sin knew Wu couldn't possibly shake such a blow off – he'd be on the floor in seconds!

Yet, to Sin's astonishment, for the second time, Wu was only momentarily stunned and quickly recovered enough to execute another blazing round of attacks against his opponent.

Sin was exhausted and getting worried. *How was this even possible?*

Suddenly Wu turned to look at Sin and his eyes glowed *blood red*! His hair looked shaggy and wild and his face was contorted into a monstrous visage!

Sin gaped at him in horror - Master Wu had turned into the *crazy madman* who had plagued Sin's dreams since childhood!

The Monster Wu fixed his glowing red eyes on Sin and his face slit into an evil smile.

A chill rippled through Sin reaching all the way to the bone!

Without thinking, Sin gasped, "*You* are the crazy madman my nightmares have been preparing me for!"

Wu's eyes glowed redder and he leered evilly at Sin, "Yes!" he roared! "I *am* the crazy madman of your nightmares. And now I'm going to *finish you!*"

He bombarded Sin with a vicious series of attacks that came from everywhere and nowhere at once! Sin felt beaten to a pulp and tried to regain his senses. Too late!

Wu laughed and launched another barrage of attacks that struck Sin like meteors striking the earth! One after another, the hits struck home. Sin was just about to lose consciousness, when Hua appeared in the air before them, her hand outstretched, ordering Wu to stop!

Monster Wu staggered back, stunned and distracted by this strange apparition! He turned his back on Sin to stare at Hua.

Sin saw his chance and struck Wu sharply in his *Gate Of The Soul Point or Ming Men.*

Wu crumbled to the floor!

Sin watched in relief as Wu's appearance slowly changed back to normal. When he no longer looked like the crazy madman who had tortured his unconscious mind for years, Sin stepped forward, helped him up and settled him into a chair.

Wu shook his head groggily to regain his senses.

"What happened?' he asked Sin, still dazed.

"I-I don't know. Did you see the woman?"

Master Wu shook his head. "What woman?"

"Never mind. How do you feel?'

Wu grinned, "The best I've felt in a long time! Thank you, Sin, you really helped me unblock my *Chi*!"

Sin smiled, bowed, and bid Wu goodbye. He felt euphoric as he stepped out into the cool night air. He'd just beaten the "Best Fighter in the World!"

By right and tradition, what did that make him…?

4 5

-

RECONCILIATION

SIN WAS SO EXHAUSTED FROM HIS grueling encounter with Master Wu, he wanted nothing more than to fall into his bed.

But, he wanted so desperately to *see* Siu Ie again, so he sat down on his bed and made himself perform the special Nei Kung training that Grandmaster E reviewed with him, hoping that would open the door for her to crossover long enough to see him.

But, though he meditated all night, nothing happened. Sin blamed it on the exhausting ordeal he had had with Master Wu and vowed to try it again the next night.

The next night, he fared not better, nor any night for the whole following week.

But on the 7th day, everything changed!

Siu Ie came to him!

She was just as beautiful as Sin remembered. She was wearing a lovely silk dress covered in delicate flower patterns. She walked over to him, her face wreathed in a stunning smile and bent down and kissed him.

"Hello, My Love," she said tenderly.

Sin broke down in tears. He told her how much he missed her and how hard it was to go on without her.

She sat down next to him and hugged him gently, murmuring, "I know, Sin, I know." She wiped away his tears and said that she understood just what he had been going through and that was why she had come back to see him.

She told him she was happy and safe and that she needed him to find a way to move past his pain and get on with his life.

Sin told her that he couldn't possibly be happy without her and instead of smiling at him, as she used to, she got cross with him!

"Sin, if you throw your life away on depression and obsessing about vengeance on Akang, I will never forgive you! We have always disagreed on how to deal with that pathetic creature, but given the circumstances, you must agree to do it my way!"

Trying his best to smile, Sin told her that she was as stubborn as always.

Siu Ie laughed and told him that she refused to be the reason for his life-long misery. He had his whole life ahead of him!

Sin seized her hands tightly and gazed into her eyes, "Remember how we used to ponder the question of reincarnation when we just started dating? All this time I have been thinking of you and missing you so deeply, I kept seeing a girl named Hua whose fiancé was murdered and he was able to be reincarnated back into her life as her tiger companion so that he can be with her always!"

He looked at her, not sure how she would react to his next question, "Would you like to be reincarnated, so that we'd be together again?"

A worried look crossed her face, "Oh, Sin, of course! But we are not allowed to discuss that."

She suddenly whipped her head around as if someone he could not hear was talking to her. "Yes…Oh, Dear. OK. Sin, I must go - Now!"

She squeezed his hand lovingly, "Please, Sin, you must move on with your life. You have a bright future – I can see it all from here - but only if you choose to live it! Whether or not you and I meet again in this life or another, only Fate can decide…"

Then… she was gone.

Sin came to in bed, soaked with sweat.

He replayed his encounter with Siu Ie in his mind. He had hoped seeing her again would give him some kind of closure, yet all he felt lonely and sad.

But, to honor her memory and wishes, he would try to do as she asked, though how he could ever move on with his life without her was beyond him.

Into his tear-stained pillow, he whispered, " Goodbye, My Darling Siu Ie. Rest in Peace…"

46
-
DUKUN

Sɪɴ ᴡᴀs sᴏ ᴀʙsᴏʀʙᴇᴅ ɪɴ ʜɪs quest to see Siu Ie again that a whole week passed before he realized he hadn't seen Tze all week.

He went to his mother first and asked, "Mom, how has Tze been this week? I haven't seen him."

His mother looked at him a little anxiously. "Sin, your father and I decided to take him to a *Dukun* for some treatment. The Dukun said it would take him a week to exorcise the demon that possessed Tze."

Sin could not believe what he was hearing! He was shocked and stunned.

"Since *when* did you all believe in the occult and possession?" he demanded angrily, afraid for his brother.

"Since *nothing* in Western or Chinese science or medicine has been able to help Tze!" She answered defensively, then burst into tears.

Sin felt bad that he had made his mother cry. He gave her a hug, "I'm so sorry Mom, I didn't mean to be so harsh on you. I'm just worried for Tze's sake…"

She broke away from Sin's hug, "Today is the day we're supposed to pick him up. Why don't you pick him up on your motorcycle? He'll be so glad to see you."

Sin jumped at the chance and set out to pick him up. He arrived at the Dukun's place and, strangely, found it looking deserted. The Dukun was nowhere to be found, nor could he find anyone else who could show him where Tze was, though he called and called around the compound. So he walked through the place on his own in hopes of finding his brother's room. The place was spooky and seriously creeped him out.

Finally, he heard a moaning sound coming from one of the rooms. It sounded familiar. He hesitantly opened the door and found Tze crouching on the floor, sobbing his heart out! Sin ran to him and Tze's face lit up when he saw his older brother. He threw himself into Sin's arms and clung to him like his life depended on it!

"Oh Sin, I am so glad to see you! I thought I was going to die in this place. You won't believe what they did to me!"

Tze burst into hysterical sobs and shook his head over and over again. Still sobbing, he showed Sin the burn marks and livid bruises covering his torso and legs!

"The *Dukun* said he had to exorcize the Demon from my body so that I could return to normal. And then he had his guys torture me while he chanted mantra's over me! They said it would force the Demon out of me and into a less hostile place, so I agreed to it at first. But, then they started putting their cigarettes out on my skin just for fun, until I screamed and screamed! When they stopped that and

I thought it was over, his assistants started beating my legs with big sticks! I screamed and screamed and begged them to stop! But they just kept beating me and beating until I could not stand up anymore! I fell down and curled up to get away from them, but they grabbed my legs and pulled them out straight and beat me and beat me until I finally passed out, Sin. And I thought it was over...I thought I had made it through..."

Sin listened in growing horror to this litany of abuse and torture!

Tze continued, still clinging to him, "But, when I came to, the beatings continued!" Tze cutched at Sin's hand, squeezing it tight enough to hurt. "Every day, Sin! Every single day they tortured me until I wished I was dead!"

Sin was mortified! How could such monstrous cruelty have been allowed to happen to his beloved little brother? Guilt overwhelmed him. And how come he had not been there to protect him?

His brothers legs were so bruised they looked deformed and his young body was covered in burn marks that would leave scars all his life. He had to get Tze out of this torture chamber this instant!

Just then, the door opened and three very large men with huge sticks in their hands entered the room.

Sin got a killer's look in his eyes and was ready to burst into action to take them down. But his brother clutched his arm, terrified and begged him, "Please, Sin, no, no. Listen to me. I'll die in this place if you fight them! While you are fighting two of them, the other one will kill me! Please, please just take me home!" Tze sobbed.

Sin knew his brother was right. He might fantasize about the vengeance he should exact on these mindless brutes with his deadly Dim Mak training, but he couldn't risk putting his brother's life in jeopardy to do it.

Giving the men a murderous glare that had them nervously stepping back out of the room, Sin gathered his brother up in his arms and carried him away from that evil place, out into the pure, clean air.

47
-
THE RIOT

SIN GOT TZE SAFELY OUT OF the evil Dukun's place and onto his motorcycle. He gently settled Tze on the back, then jumped on and took off for their house. He had to get him home to safety!

As Sin cruised the streets, Tze felt asleep on the back of the motorcycle, leaning against his warm back. He felt safe with his big, fearless brother, Sin. Sin turned onto a street in the downtown shopping area, but when he rounded the corner, he saw an angry mob up ahead shouting and waving anti-Chinese and anti-capitalism signs! He could hear their enraged, racist shouts, ranting against the predominantly Chinese shopkeepers of the area.

The mob was throwing rocks at the shop windows, sending shattered glass flying everywhere. The shops in Bandung were built European style where the owners of the shops lived upstairs above their shops, so the owners were cowering inside, trying to escape the flying glass!

Most shops had iron-grills in front of the windows to prevent theft and home invasion. But these grills were no match for the angry mob that stormed the shops that day. Not content with damaging or looting property, the angry rioters hurled jagged rocks and thrust long bamboo poles in through the windows trying to spear the terrified occupants, hoping to wound or even kill them.

The raging mob were ransacking every shop along the street!

Sin stopped, aghast, and hastily turned his motorcycle around. He had to get his brother to safety!

But several of the rioters realized they were Chinese and started to chase them, sending a shower of rocks raining down on them.

The screams woke Tze up, "Whaat? What is happening, Sin?" he cried.

Sin gunned his motorcycle, desperate to get them out of there. But before they had reached a safe distance, a big piece of rock smashed Tze on the back of his head. He screamed and clutched his head in pain!

The motorcycle wobbled almost out of control as Tze lost his balance and almost fell off the bike. Sin grabbed his arm with his one free hand and yelled, "Hold on, Tze, HOLD ON!"

Tze grabbed Sin's waist, but his grip was weak. His head wound was bleeding profusely. Sin roared down the empty side streets, trying to get home to his mother's jewelry shop as fast as he could.

Luckily, the riot had not reached the street where they lived above the shop. Sin sped to the alley behind the shop and carried his brother hurriedly inside. He screamed for the shop attendants to close up and lock the iron gates!

Their mother rushed to meet them and was horrified to see Tze bleeding profusely and his shirt soaked with blood. She started to rush to his aid, but Sin told her he would take care of Tze, while she helped the shopkeepers close and secure the shop. "A riot is coming! Hurry, hurry! There is no time to lose!

Sin and the servants helped get Tze upstairs to his bed. Their mother saw her husband running toward the shop and quickly ordered her assistant to open the gate just wide enough for him to slip in. They slammed and bolted it just as they heard yells and the sound of breaking glass approaching from down the street!

"The rioters are everywhere! I barely missed them!" Heng cried. "Everyone, get upstairs and hide!" They all fled upstairs in terror!

Their parents raced in to check on Tze. He was lying on the bed, incoherent. The servants had given Sin a clean, wet towel that he had used to clean Tze's head wound, but it was still bleeding.

Sin's mother took a good look at the wound and burst into crying when she saw what a huge, gaping gash it was! Heng ran to fetch some first aid bandages and he tightly wrapped Tze's head with them, trying to stem the bloodflow.

But blood kept soaking through the cloth. Tze had lost a dangerous amount of blood! Then their father took a large piece of cotton, placed it on Tze's head wound and applied pressure.

Finally, that seemed to do the trick. They rewrapped his head and lay him down to rest. Their mother covered him with a warm blanket and sat down by the bed next to him, trying unsuccessfully not to sob.

Heng stood beside her, trying to comfort her. He looked around to take stock and make sure his whole family was safe. He got a terrible shock when he realized his 2nd to youngest son, Seng, had not made it home!

Just then an angry commotion broke out in the street downstairs as the rioters reached their shop!

Suddenly, rocks the size of oranges smashed through the windows, shattering them all and spraying razor-sharp shards of glass everywhere! Screams and slurs and curses from the vicious mob splashed over them like poison and Mirah, a faithful family retainer who had been with the family for twenty years, shrieked in terror and lost control of her bladder, pissing all over the floor.

Heng barked out, "Everyone, down! And cover your head with both hands!"

Everyone hit the floor and curled into defensive balls, covering their heads with their hands.

Besides rocks, the rioters had armed themselves with long, sharpened, bamboo poles, like spears, that they used as weapons, thrusting them through the shattered windows and into the rooms beyond. They stabbed them into ceilings and walls with loud, frightening 'thumping' sounds, trying to panic and flush out the people hiding inside so they could stab them!

Even though they hid, the sharpened spears found their soft targets! The room was not very deep, so soon the rioters were able to beat and stab them without mercy.

Old Mirah screamed more gibberish, while her entire body trembled uncontrollably. The family huddled on the floor, terrified that they were all going to be murdered in minutes! Debris of all kind – rocks, glass, metal shards, showered down on their helpless bodies.

The *ordeal* seemed to last an *eternity*. Miraculously, out for fresh blood, the wave of rioters moved on, destroying anything in its path. After they had moved on, an almost eerie, but blessed silence fell.

Cautiously, the family uncurled from the floor. Heng took a quick reckoning to see if everyone was ok. One had a gash from a sharpened spear, and all of them had cuts and bruises from the glass and falling debris. Thankfully, none but Tze were badly hurt.

Seeing that they were okay, Heng began to seriously worry about his 2nd to youngest youngest son, Seng. Just then the phone rang, Heng rushed to answer it and his face light up.

When he hung up, he told the worried family that that had been Seng calling to say he was safe - at the police station! He had seen the rioters running toward his car, and had pulled into the police station and run into their office for sanctuary. That had saved his life! If he had been caught out in the open like other unfortunate Chinese citizens were, he could have been beaten to death.

Knowing Seng and the rest of the family were safe, Heng and Sui Chin cautiously picked through the rubble to view the devastation. The shop was completely destroyed – and much of the merchandize had been looted or crushed. How in the world would they survive?

48
-
THE RIOT AFTERMATH

THE RIOT SHOOK THE ENTIRE CHINESE community. For two days and two nights Indonesian marauders roamed the streets on a vicious witchhunt, brutally attacking and even killing any Chinese person they came across.

The The´ family stayed hiding in their house, behind barricaded doors, terrified their house would be broken into and they would be dragged out into the street and murdered. They listened in terror to the radio, seeking any scrap of news that might tell them how badly the riot had escalated.

The news reported that the authorities had finally flooded the streets with an army of police who had stormed and quelled the rioters. They had clamped down on the worse offenders and by the second day, had managed to clear the streets.

The news agencies finally reported that order had been restored and it was safe to go out again. Government officials urged citizens to work together to clean up the mess in the streets, reopen their shops, and go about their business as if nothing had happened. There was little chance of that happening...

Sin and his family were shaken by the whole experience and, since their lives might still be danger, they didn't know whether to trust the news reports and go out or not.

They called all their Chinese friends, mostly other shopkeepers to hear firsthand news, and by the third day, they finally decided to chance it.

They surveyed the wreckage around them with heavy hearts, distraught at the devastation. With all their recent misfortunes, they did not know how they would find the will to carry on… But, they were a strong and resilient family and knew that, together, they would somehow find the strength and courage to rebuild… Without a complaint, they bent their backs to clean up and began to set things to rights.

At one point Heng turned to Sin and said, "Son, you must leave this place. You must go and study abroad, away from such terrors and calamities…"

Sin looked at his father and saw the pain in them, made worse by his fears for his family. "I don't think I should go, Father. There is too much to be done here."

His father shook his head. "We will talk about this later, Son."

The entire time they had been trapped inside, Sin had feared for Grandmaster E's safety, knowing he lived alone with no iron gates to protect him. The moment curfew was lifted, Sin rushed across town to make sure that he was all right. On the way to the Grandmaster's place, Sin could not believe the carnage the rioters had left in their wake.

The streets were littered with torched cars and iced with mounds of broken glass from smashed shop windows. People huddled together in frightened clumps, sobbing before shops that had been sprayed with gasoline and burnt to the ground. In some areas, only the strong iron gates bolted across the entrances had saved the residents inside from being dragged out and beaten to death in the streets.

These disturbing scenes of rage, hatred and devastation devastated Sin. What caused one race to hate another so much? We were all human, after all… How had it come to this? What were the injustices that had caused such hatred to fester and what could be done to prevent this from happening again?

An intense feeling welled up in him and he suddenly felt isolated and alone, as if he did not belong here in his own homeland – the place where he had been born and lived all his life. It was a desolate and hollow feeling. He realized he no longer wanted to live in a country filled with so much hate. He sadly feared that people here were too set in their ways and their hatred and divisiveness too entrenched to change… He realized that his father was right - he should leave to study abroad as soon as his family didn't need him anymore.

When he reached Grandmaster E's home, he pounded on the door and called his name, terrified he might find him dead inside. He breathed a huge sigh of relief when the Master himself opened the door and pulled him quickly inside.

He immediately saw Sin had a piece blood-stained cloth wrapped around his head.

"Were you attacked?" Grandmaster E asked, concerned.

"Oh, this is nothing" Sin replied, gingerly touching his head, "Just a flesh wound, outside. But inside, I am... devastated. I cannot comprehend such violence - such hatred! My father wishes me to go abroad to study and I see now that he is right... But don't worry about me, Master, were you attacked?"

Grandmaster E shook his head, a deep sadness settling on his shoulders like a shroud. He was saddened by the senseless violence and by the realization that his star pupil would soon be lost to him...

The Grandmaster said, "I, too, am devastated, as is the whole Chinese community... I'm afraid life in our small country is more fragile and unpredictable than I had thought. I am sad to say I have not properly prepared you for the struggle ahead. I must correct that oversight this very day. Who knows if there will be a tomorrow?" he pondered soberly and gestured Sin to follow him into his garden.

He stopped under a shady tree, "I have concentrated on teaching you mostly fighting skills to make you faster and more powerful. But life can be too fleeting. Too many friends have died and you, My Son, must live a long, healthy life to pass on the wisdom and training you have learned..."

Sin bowed, honored by his teacher's concern for him and only too willing to do whatever it took to pass on his special training.

"Today I will teach you something special – a secret technique passed down for centuries but known to few - that will *extend* your life by *decades*. It is a *Nei Kung* technique called the Golden Embryo or *Eternal Youth* and it will keep you feeling youthful and full of energy."

Sin was humbly grateful and eager to learn, as always.

Grandmaster E began the lesson by explaining that in ancient China, the Taoists, who historians sometimes referred to as 'Scientists of the Human Body', were preoccupied with finding the *secret* to living a long and healthy life or even achieving *immortality*. They observed *all* forms of life around them, including plant life, searching for clues to longevity. They stumbled across certain Gingko trees in China that lived to be over two thousands years old, while ordinary Ginkos had a life span of just 80 to 120 years.

The Taoists discovered that the trees with extremely long life spans had survived a severe climate change by no longer putting any energy or resources into producing flowers, seeds, or fruits, all of which required huge amounts of life energy to produce.

The Taoists extrapolated that it might be possible to use a similar technique to prolong human life.

The Nei Kung techniques they developed used advanced meditation techniques to focus their awareness on their testes or ovaries and convert the massive cache of *sexual* energy stored there into a form of *mental or physiological* energy that could be used by the entire body to live longer.

The abundance of energy that resulted from this practice could be utilized for whatever one needed to do in life and could enable practitioners to live a very long, cheerful, and healthy life of 120 years - or more!

Sin was fascinated by Grandmaster E's story. Imagine being able to live for 120 years – practically double the average lifespan!

Grandmaster E puffed his long pipe and noted Sin's excitement with satisfaction.

"Imagine how much benefit this Nei Kung Eternal Youth technique could bring to Humanity, Sin? Most Masters regarded this as a very special secret that they would rather carry to their graves than share with their students. And so, over time, it became almost a lost art. But I was extremely fortunate. I was honored to be entrusted by my teacher, Grandmaster Su Kong Tai Gin, to inherit the invaluable art of longevity."

Grandmaster E fixed his bright eyes on his star pupil and beamed, "Now I shall pass on this sacred art to you. And though you may not live as long as Li Ching Yuan, who was purported to live over 200 years, you could strive to live a life of 120 healthy and productive years."

With that, Grandmaster E began teaching Sin the Nei Kung Eternal Youth training.

Sin was considerably cheered by the story and felt honored to be deemed worthy of being taught such a rare and secret technique. He prepared to be his most attentive, realizing his Grandmaster's gift to him today would literally be the 'Gift of Life'!

The boy who had grown to a young man and his martial arts Master, threw themselves with extra vigor into the study of the art that had ruled both their lives, perhaps prolonging the lesson that day, because they somehow instinctively realized it might be the last time they ever saw each other...

After hours of study, when Sin had absorbed the lesson to Grandmaster E's satisfaction, he thanked his master for the great honor he had bestowed on him. He felt a lump in his throat as they walked companionably to the front door together.

Sin found himself at a loss for words now that the hour of farewell was upon them.

Grandmaster E seemed to feel the same. He hesitated, then asked Sin what his plans were, now that the future for the Chinese community in Indonesia was dangerously uncertain.

Sin told him that his father wanted him to go to university abroad to study Nuclear Physics, perhaps even to the United States.

Grandmaster E nodded, pleased. "I took Shaolin Arts from China to Indonesia many years ago. Now, it will be your turn to take Shaolin Arts from Indonesia to the United States of America – that is the New World, Son."

Astonishingly, Grandmaster E suddenly choked up. Tears welled in his eyes. It was clear he had something important to say.

"Son," he began, "You may not have heard that the Indonesian Government has just banned the teaching and expression of *all* Chinese culture. I was crushed to learn that this will include *Kung Fu*. I am forbidden from teaching it any more." His face collapsed in grief and he struggled to control his emotions, "All I have left to me now is broken dreams…"

Sin was crushed. He revered his master and knew how much teaching meant to him – it was his whole reason for being - he lived, breathed and slept *Kung Fu!* What would become of him if he could *never* teach again?

It was horribly racist and unfair that the Government could take a man's dreams and livelihood away from him and randomly outlaw an entire culture with the snap of their fingers!

"Grandmaster, I am so sorry! Shaolin is your *Life*. No one should have the right to take that away from you. If it is any consolation, I vow to preserve the Shaolin Arts and take it with me wherever I go!"

Grandmaster E nodded gravely, "That is my greatest wish, Sin! These long years together, I have taught you nearly everything I know. You have done well, my Son, very, very well. And it is time for a new beginning."

Grandmaster E surprised Sin by standing up very straight and proudly, and gravely giving his pupil a low, formal bow. Before Sin knew what was happening, his Master had removed his red Grandmaster belt from his uniform and held it reverently in his hands.

"I have been wearing this belt for a long time, My Son… too long,. According to Shaolin tradition, only one person at a time can wear the red belt and that is the reining Grandmaster. Today, we have a new Grandmaster: Grandmaster Sin Kwang Thé!"

Sin's mouth dropped open and he stared at his mentor speechlessly. Again, Grandmaster E bowed to him formally and held the belt out for Sin to take in his own shaking hands!

As if in a dream, the young man hesitantly took the belt. He suddenly broke down and hugged his old tutor. This was the culmination of his entire lifetime of training and he was overcome with emotion and pride. Yet, he knew at what great cost to his old master this tremendous honor had come.

He could not hold back his tears as he choked out, "I-I won't let you down, Grandmaster. I know with this honor comes great responsibility.

It will be my honor and mission to take Shaolin to the New Land and spread it across the entire continent. This I vow to do!"

Grandmaster E nodded gravely and unbent his reserve to hug Sin in a warm farewell.

With tears in his eyes, Sin left to return to help his family.

Grandmaster E stood looking after him for a long time, tears coursing unashamedly down his face. The young man's life was just beginning, while his was nearing its end… He saw such promise in that brave young man – the kind of promise he had once seen in himself, but that cruel circumstances beyond his control had extinguished.

Now that the mantle had passed from one generation to the next, the future of Shaolin in America rested on his young pupil's shoulders… What Sin would do with it, how successful he might be, only time would tell…

But Grandmaster E dearly wished he could be there to see it all unfold…!

Before turning to enter his home, he said softly, " Goodbye, My Son. 星星之火，可以燎原." ("A single spark can start a prairie fire").
星星之火，可以燎原

49
-
TZE'S GRAVE

ALREADY WEAKENED BY THE DUKUN'S CRUEL tortures, after the devastating head wound he sustained from the rock the rioter smashed into his head, Tze steadily declined.

His mother took him to the hospital where the best doctors took care of him, but even they could do nothing. Sin came to the hospital everyday to sit with Tze and tried his best to cheer him up.

But even Sin's efforts and the support of the entire family was not enough to change his fate. On the last day, Tze opened his eyes wide, seeing something the others could not see, and breathed his last.

It was a devastating blow to the entire family. Shaken with grief, they prepared for a traditional Chinese funeral.

A funeral in the Chinese tradition is entirely different from that of the West. The family members formally mourned the departed one for a three-day period. During these three days, at the funeral home, the deceased was placed in an open casket or a closed casket through which their face could be seen in a small glass window. The family hired two or three nuns to sing special songs, starting at 6am in the morning until 2 am at night. It was said that their strange, high-pitched songs were performed to ease the soul of the departed into the Kingdom of Heaven.

The family members would wear traditional white funeral outfits and kneel on the hard floor in bare feet while the nuns wailed all day and most of the night. Periodically the nuns would motion the family to stand up and walk to the casket.

At the casket, they would light incense sticks and pray to *Tien Wang*, the Heavenly God, for mercy so that the departed's soul would be allowed to enter the Kingdom of Heaven. After the family had finished praying, they would walk around the coffin seven times and then kneel down on their knees again for hours while the nuns continued their eerie, high-pitch wailing.

This was repeated over and over again until noon, when the family was permitted an hour break for lunch. Then they would repeat the entire elaborate process until 6 pm when the visiting guests arrived and the family was permitted to rise from their knees and greet them. Their ankles and knees were always throbbing from the long hours of kneeling and they could barely walk without hobbling.

In between greeting the guests, the family would snatch a hasty supper, then, after the last guest left around 9 pm, the family would kneel on the hard floor until 2 am, their ears barraged by the nuns' unrelenting funeral songs.

By the time 2am rolled around, most of the family would be wracked with leg cramps and spasms. They would drag themselves out to their cars and head home for the best sleep of their lives, albeit a very short one. A few hours later, they would be back in the funeral home to do it all again for two more days!

This kind of devotion and ordeal is seen by the Chinese as not just a way to send their loved ones to Heaven. It was also a way of purifying and cleansing the souls of the surviving family members as well. Those three grueling days enabled Sin and his family to come to terms with their loved ones death and to accept the fact that the departed one was truly gone from their lives forever, never to return.

And they made peace with themselves.

In the olden days, a Chinese funeral procession involved walking from the funeral home to the graveyard. However, nowadays the family drove to the gravesite. The hearse containing the coffin led the funeral procession.

The Indonesian style of hearse was a truck that resembled an army truck with benches along the sides of the flatbed. The coffin was placed in the middle and the entire family sat around the coffin, as if guarding it on its way to its eternal resting place.

Sin and his family sat around Tze's coffin and their mother cried all the way to the cemetery. Their father's eyes were red and swollen too. The rest of the family sat stoically, staring mournfully at the coffin.

A table was placed in front of the tombstone with Tze's picture in the middle and Heng, as the head of the family, lit incense in front of his picture as Tze's coffin was lowered into the cold, dark ground.

His mother followed suit, then Sin and the rest of the family. Once they had all finished lighting incense and praying, they formed a line beside the table to greet and thank each of the solemn guests who came to pay their respects and pray with them.

After the incense ceremony, their father took the incense burner filled with ashes to the coffin and prayed silently for a few minutes. Then he sprinkled its contents on top of the coffin and placed a red rose on it too.

Their mother couldn't stop crying, but everyone waited patiently for her to pick up another rose and place it on her son's coffin beside her husband's. Sin and the rest of the family added their own beautiful roses on his coffin, then all the guests did too.

After the internment, the family shook all the guests hands one more time and accepted their well-intentioned condolences.

The funeral reception dinner was given at a nice, local restaurant, and was an elegant ten-course meal served in Tze's honor to celebrate his wonderful, all too short life.

After the meal, Heng assembled the family into one last reception line by the door, and the last ritual handshake and words of kindness, gratitude and remembrance were exchanged with the guests. When the last guest had left, Sin and his family wearily headed home at last.

But, when Sin got home, he had an uneasy feeling about his brother. He realized he wanted to say farewell to Tze in a more private and intimate way than in front of so many people. Despite his exhaustion, he told his mother he needed to return to the grave. Reluctantly, his mother let him go.

Sin meditated in front of Tze's grave until the sun set in a slow fade from rose to purple to black. Exhausted from the heavy weight of grief and from days of kneeling and praying, Sin fell asleep on Tze's grave while meditating.

He dreamt he was standing in the middle of a beautiful tropical garden surrounded by bubbling waterfalls and elegant lagoons. The colors are vibrant and alive, every flower and plant seemed aglow, and lovely, unearthly music filled the air and soothed his soul. He looked everywhere for the source of such exquisite music and finally realized it was coming from a beautiful white peony. The flower's lovely petals were vibrating, causing it to sing!

Sin was astounded. "What a beautiful song!" he exclaimed aloud.

He was surprised when the flower answered, "Thank you, Young Man. I can sing a different song if you like."

Sin demurred, "Oh, no. Please go on. I like it."

As the flower continued to sing, Sin wandered the garden paths toward a lovely blue Lagoon with a delightful waterfall. He was amazed by the sheer beauty around him - it was the most stunning place he had ever seen.

"What sort of a place is this, I wonder?" he mused.

A voice behind him answered, " It's Heaven, of course."

Sin turned and was overjoyed to see Tze standing there looking well and happy.

"Tze!" he burst out, joyously.

" Welcome to Heaven, Sin."

"Wow! So this is what Heaven looks like?" Sin said in a rush of excitement. "I should have known, everything is so vivid and colorful.

They say there are only seven true colors on Earth, but there must be ten thousand colors *here*! And did you see that magic flower over there? She talked and sang to me!"

Tze smiled, touched by his brother's excitement, but then turned serious, "Sin, listen. I brought you here to tell you something important. Remember when we had the motorcycle accident and I told you my soul went to Heaven and the Gods in Heaven kept saying I had chosen my own Fate?"

Sin frowned, "I remember…"

Tze said : "We were best friends you and I--"

Sin interrupted, " 'Best friends'? What are you talking about? We are brothers, man!"

Tze shook his head, "Yes, in *this life*. But in our past life, we were best friends! When you were reborn in *this* lifetime, I wanted so much to be with you, that I agreed to the fate that awaited me if I was to be reborn in this life too: that meant the accident, losing my mind, the torture, the riot, and dying young. Everything. I accepted it all just so that I could be with you, Sin."

Sin was flabbergasted, "I-I do not understand, Tze! How can you say such things? You are talking Greek!"

"The Gods wanted to teach you the lessons of Patience, Humility, and Humbleness. They knew the only way you would understand and eventually accept these important lessons was through the death of someone close to you."

Tze reached out and touched Sin's hand. "I accepted that role –

willingly. But, now, *my* Journey ends here, Sin. But yours has a long way to go yet."

Sin looked at him in confusion - and love.

Tze continued, "The road ahead for you will be full of joys and sadness. There will be a time when your heart will sing with elation and a time it will be crushed with despair. When you are at your lowest point, Sin, come back here to my grave. I'll come down from Heaven and comfort you..."

Tze kissed his forehead, "Goodbye my brother."

"Tze, wait...!"

Sin shot awake, shocked to his core. What had just happened? Could it all be true? It felt right and resonated inside him with the force and clarity of Inner Truth.

He sat by Tze's grave, breathing in the poignant scent of freshly turned dirt, letting the years of fond memories of his beloved brother wash over him. He broke down and wept for a long, long time.

When he had no more tears to give, the memory of the time he'd spent with Tze in the swimming pool swam into his mind: Tze had earnestly asked him, "Sin, when I die, would you sing me a farewell song with your leaf? If you do, I promise you, I will come down from Heaven to listen."

The memory was so strong and Sin's heart warmed at the thought of fulfilling his brother's wish. He picked up a leaf, put it to his lips and played a haunting, heart-breaking, lovely melody to bid his brother farewell.

Midway through the song, a shooting star blazed across the horizon, just as a different shooting star had shone once before in Grandmaster E's garden when Sui Ie had died. Sin had known then it was Sui Ie saying goodbye, and this time, he knew it was his beloved brother, Tze, giving him one last luminous farewell!

He watched the shooting star for a long, long time as it flew across the sky, leaving a brilliant trail of light that dazzled his eye and made him smile at Tze's exuberance.

When the star finally vanished over the distant horizon, Sin, ever so gently, said, "Goodbye, my Dear Brother, Tze."

5 0
-
COMING TO AMERICA

FOR THE FIRST TIME IN A long time, Sin felt at peace. With Hua's help and the reassuring words of his beloved Sui Ie and brother, Tze, he prepared to embrace his future…

When Grandmaster E ceremonially passed the venerable title of Grandmaster to him, Sin felt a little overwhelmed by the responsibility he was shouldering. It both inspired and weighed on him. These great teachings had been passed down from generation to generation for more than 1,000 years. And here he was, the youngest Grandmaster in history. Would he be up to this noble task?
The riots had thrown his life in Indonesia into chaos. And the government's edict banning Chinese culture had finally closed his own adopted country against him. Sin knew that in order to carry on the great teachings he was heir to, he must leave his homeland and immigrate to a country where he would have the freedom to teach openly, without censorship.

Should he go to Europe? Sin considered moving to Germany to study Nuclear Physics at the famed University of Heidelberg. He had even studied German to prepare for it. But the increasing tensions between East and West and the dangerous face off between the Americans and the Russians across the Berlin Wall made him hesitate. He realized after all that he and his family had endured in Indonesia, he wanted go to a country at peace where the threat of war would not be hanging over his head.

It was his father who had suggested America and Sin's heart leapt at the idea.

Now he just had to learn the language! Sin had a gift for languages, and though he hadn't studied English yet, at the time he had mastered Indonesian, Sudanese, Malaysian, Mandarin, Fujianese, and six German dialects. He was confident he could pick up English as well. One day when he was out cycling, he saw an American woman in her front yard having tea and cookies with her two young daughters. Sin was intrigued and realized this could be the opportunity he had been waiting for to learn English. There was no better way to learn a language than from a native-born speaker who knew all the idioms and speech patterns of his country.

Sin overcame his reserve and politely approached the mother and introduced himself. He told her that he planned to go to United States and study at one of their great Universities. He asked if he might join them to practice his English? The family was a little surprised by Sin's frank approach. The mother hesitated, then asked Sin to please wait a minute, then she disappeared into the house.

Sin started to get nervous. He was worried that maybe he had made a mistake and she was calling the police on him! With anti-Chinese sentiment running so high, he could get in a lot of trouble for bothering American visitors. Much to his relief, the woman quickly reappeared carrying a chair and a cup of tea for him! She politely invited him to join the family for tea. Her little girls smiled shyly at him and giggled.

While they had tea, Sin learned that they were the Wesners from Lexington, Kentucky, one of the southern states in America. The mother was Edna, the eldest daughter, Debby, was 13, and Denise, the youngest, was 10, whom they nicknamed 'Nisee'. Edna's husband, Bill, had been accepted into an exchange program between the University of Kentucky in Lexington with Institute Technology of Bandung, Indonesia, and had brought his family with him.

They were new to the area and eager to learn all they could about Indonesia, including the language. They all had a lovely conversation that lasted over an hour, during which they taught Sin English phrases and he taught them Indonesian. At the end of the visit, Edna invited Sin to come back every Thursday afternoon to meet Bill and have tea, cookies and educational conversation in English and Indonesian with the whole family.

On Sin's next visit, since Bill was a scientist like Sin, they hit it off immediately and for the next several months, Sin enjoyed cycling to their place for their weekly language sessions.
Sin was grateful for the Wesners' generosity and kindness and wanted to return the favor. So, he invited them to his home above the jewelry shop for a traditional Chinese dinner with Sin's own family. When the Wesners arrived at Sin's house for dinner, Debby and Nisee's eyes lit up when they saw a bowl of Red Delicious apples. Imported apples from the U.S. were very hard to find and the girls had not had an apple for over a year. Needless to say, the apples were the first food they enjoyed together that evening!

Sin and the Wesners became fast friends and continued to meet once a week for the next six months until Bill's contract was up with the Institute of Technology of Bandung. Before they left for the States, they introduced Sin to another American couple that was moving into their house, who had also come to Bandung through the exchange program.

The new couple was Mr. and Mrs. Nick Rice, who were also from Lexington, Kentucky. They had three children, Larry, the eldest, was 8, Kathy was 5 and the youngest was a mischievous 2 year-old named Robby. After Sin got to know them, he also invited them to have dinner at his home and, when the soup was served to each of them with a traditional Chinese porcelain spoon, everyone chuckled when little Robby spooned the soup from the handle end of the spoon by mistake!

Sin had done his homework on US Universities and had planned to attend the University of California, Berkeley, which was like Heidelberg University of Germany. It had an outstanding Science and Physics program, attracting some of the finest minds in the world to its campus. The plan he had worked out with his parents was for Sin to study Engineering, focusing on automotive manufacturing in particular. His father had a longterm plan to build the first Asian-owned, auto manufacturing factory in Indonesia.

But, rather than go to U.C. Berkeley, the Rice's suggested that Sin first go for a year or two to a college in Lexington, Kentucky near them that had an excellent curriculum and was three times more affordable then the high rates in California. A smaller college would also enable Sin to get more specialized attention from his professors than a big school like Berkley would. That way, Sin could learn the language fluently and save up money to attend the University of his choice later on.

In order to come to the U.S. universities as a foreign student, Sin needed an American citizen to sponsor him. This policy was the U.S. government's way of ensuring that foreign students would always be able to pay for their tuition while in the U.S. If he or she fell short of money, their sponsor was required to pay the balance of their expenses.

Sin knew no one in California and Mr. Rice was kind enough to volunteer to be Sin's sponsor in Kentucky, so Kentucky it would be! His parents were elated! If all went well with Sin's U.S. Visa application, their eldest son would be off to America – the land of opportunity where dreams could come true!

Sin always felt extremely grateful for Nick Rice's help and for generously sponsoring him to come to U.S. For this, the Rice's would always occupy a warm spot in Sin's heart.

Sin was nervous when he went to Jakarta for his Visa application and interview. He had never been in an air-conditioned building in his life, and he was freezing! He was used to the hot, balmy air of South East Asia and waiting in the American Embassy for hours with the air conditioning on full blast, made him sick and shivering.

He realized that he must prepare his body for the adjustment it would have to make in the new environment of Kentucky, where so many things were different than he was used to. It paid to be prepared – something his Grandmaster had taught him all his life.

So, he began eating an American diet of steak, baked potatoes, and salad every day, knowing that he would not be able to obtain Indonesian food in Lexington. And, he started taking cold showers with ice water in order to prepare for Kentucky's cold winter months of ice and snow.

A few weeks later, the family learned that Sin's Visa application had been approved! He was beside himself with excitement and nervous as he prepared to go on the Adventure of His Life!

For three whole days before he left, his mother, Sui Chin, cried every day and couldn't bring herself to leave her room. It broke Sin's heart to hear her crying day and night, and he knew there was nothing he could do to console her. He wondered if he was doing the right thing and even started to reconsider his decision to go to America.

But the day before he was supposed to leave, he heard a faint knock at his door. When Sin opened it, he saw his mother standing outside with red, tear-stained eyes. Sin quickly ushered her in.

When she saw his suitcases she said, "My Son, I see that all of your dreams are coming true – your lifetime of discipline and study of Shaolin and becoming Grandmaster, and now going to America for your continuing education… I am so proud of you! But, you will be on your own now, in a strange new world all by yourself, and a mother cannot help but worry!"

Sin nodded kindly, "Oh, Mom, I have you to thank for it all! Remember it all started when *you* told me the story of my great-great-great-grandfather. Ever since then, I was inspired to learn Kung Fu and become one of the best fighters in the world. Now that Grandmaster E has passed his title to me, I have a great responsibility to spread Shaolin in the New Land so others may learn from its wisdom and amazing techniques."

Sin's mother nodded sadly, "You know, Sin, the other day I found your father in our room, crying. He quickly wiped his tears and pretended as if nothing happened, but I knew. For twenty-one years I have been married to your father and never once did I see him cry – until now. Though it is hard for a father to say to his son, he *loves you dearly*, Sin, and will miss you as much as I will."

Sin bowed his head, fighting back his own tears, "I know, Mother. I will miss you both just as much! You always did so much for me. I love you, Mom."

Overcome with emotion, his mother burst out crying and ran back to her room. Sin hung his head and felt all the emotions he had repressed for so long rise up in him. His entire body began to tremble uncontrollably as tears poured down his face.

Sin's whole family came to the airport to see him off in style. He noticed that even his usually reserved father had eyes red and wet with tears and his mother cried constantly.

The rest of his brothers and sisters were looking sad and blue as well and they prepared to send him off to America. He was the eldest and it was only right that he be the first to leave home to make his own way in the world, but it still hurt to leave his beloved family behind.

His eyes ran over them, lingering on each one, imprinting this special moment and their faces and personalities more deeply on his memory, as if he was afraid he might never see them again:

His father, a strong, hard-working man of integrity and learning, who set a high moral tone for the whole family.
His mother, smart, devoted, loving, who placed her family above all else, who had given them a home full of love and delicious home-cooked meals. His sister Yu, a gifted musician who loved playing the piano and who had been studying for years with a famous Hungarian pianist who had hand-picked her to join his elite students because she had what it took to excel in the art.
His brother Seng, a mathematics prodigy, who would become a genius at business as well. Unlike most other math whizzes, Seng was not a shy, nerdy type. Instead, he was turning into something of a playboy who liked nothing better than to take the family Mercedez out for a spin with several girls in the car with him, always managing to make each one feel she was his favorite!
Hiang, his baby brother, who stubbornly tended to get his own way, even at the times he shouldn't. He was high-spirited and a real daredevil. He'd gotten a motorcycle license when he was only 13 years-

old and loved to challenge the older kids at school to race through town after school. Sadly, one day in the not too distant future, during a race through the crowded streets, he would accidentally run over an Indonesian boy. The family would have to make a large settlement to the victim's family to try to make restitution.

Cheng, the baby sister, who was the apple of her father's eye. She was the youngest and the sweetest of them all. Though beautiful, she was also kind and thoughtful. From an early age, she had loved to sing and had a beautiful voice. Sin would miss her lovely voice, the way she had sung to them all on their family trips.

Only Tze was missing – his dear departed Tze. He had always been a little bit naughty and loved to play practical jokes on the rest of the family. But his smile had been so infectious and charming, he usually got away with it! Sin knew his beloved brother Tze was in a better place and could almost picture him grinning down at him from above...

With a heavy heart, Sin hugged them all one last time, exchanged heart-felt words of endearment and said goodbye before heading through the security gate.

His entire family watched until their Sin's plane had taken off and disappeared over the horizon.

Sin fastened his seatbelt and settled back into his seat. He had thought he might be too excited to nap in flight, but the constant vibration of the engines soon lulled him to sleep.

He woke in a beautiful meadow and saw Hua leisurely walking through the tall grass, picking flowers and humming a happy tune. She called out to Si'An, who had wandered off chasing mice.

Sin looked down at himself and realized he had magically appeared in his 4 year old body!

In the woods nearby, the half-man, half-ape looking character he now knew was his Grandmaster's Grandmaster, sat under a tree rubbing Si'An's belly. Si'An looked like a goofy lap dog, lying on his back with his giant paws dangling in the air!

In the distance, they heard Hua calling, "Si'An, Si'An, where are you?"

The magical ape creature smiled, "Your loved one is calling you, Si'An. Your time together is precious, make the most of it."

Si'An leapt to his feet and raced away.

Hua stopped dead when she saw Sin – looking like a little 4 year-old boy who had appeared out of thin air. He was dressed very strangely and stared at her with big dark eyes.

"Hua, it's me, Sin!"

Hua looked amazed. It was the younger version of the man she had met in her visions before! They had both been mourning the death of a loved one and a strong connection between them had formed. She knew that part of her Karma had been to teach him some of the harder lessons she had learned in her life and how to reclaim his life instead of succumbing to tragedy.

"Sin, it is so lovely to see you looking so happy…"
"Life goes on, and so must I…" he said in his piping, childish voice.

He smiled up at her and offered her his hand. She reached out and their fingers touched. ZAAAPPPP!

An electric spark flew between them. Hua and little Sin felt the power coursing between them, like an electric current connecting them and refueling them through time and space!

The giant tiger bounded out of the woods into the meadow just in time to see Hua and the little boy touch hands.

After the ZAAAAP, the little boy vanished!

Hua turned to Si'An as he padded up to her, "Did you see that? It was my spirit friend from another time…"

The magnificent beast cocked his huge head to one side and regarded his beloved lady with an intelligent gleam in his eye.

She chuckled at him, "Never mind. Ready for another adventure?" Si'An let out a mighty roar in agreement!

Hua threw her arms around her beloved tiger's neck and gave him an affectionate squeeze. Then they ran laughing off to face their own future.

The disembodied voice of a stewardess crackled over the inflight intercom system: "Welcome to Pan Am flight 108 landing shortly in Honolulu, Hawaii. Please put your trays and seat backs in their locked and upright positions for landing…"

Sin, dosing against the window of the plane, began to slowly rouse from his slumber. From the smile on his face, it was clear that he had been somewhere far, far away…

TO BE CONTINUED…

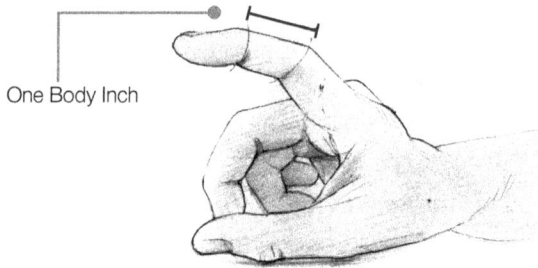

One Body Inch

THE GIFT OF LIFE

I want to give you a special gift, *The Gift of Life*.
I received this gift from Grandmaster E and I am going to pass on
The Eternal Youth Nei Kung technique to you. The *Eternal Youth Nei Kung*
technique is deceptively simple, but has two extraordinary effects:

1. It fills you with an abundance of life energy to enrich your daily life
2. It can significantly prolong your lifespan

Like the fabled Fountain of Youth, this is a gift beyond price.
I wish you the joy of this Gift and a long, happy, and fulfilling life.
Nei Kung Practitioners believe the 720 Acupressure points they have
identified in our bodies each have a very specific function. Just as
your eyes are for *seeing*, your nose is for *smelling*, your tongue for *tasting*,
and your ears for *hearing*, Acupressure Points have specific uses as well.
Some points enable us to discard the foul and sick *Chi* out of your
body and bring in fresh *Chi* that is brimming with an enervating *Life
Force*. This Life Force enables your body to nourish and heal itself.

Other pressure points enable you:
• Quicken your Digestive System and aid in the assimilation of
  nutrients into your cells.
• Stimulate your body's Endocrine System and the production of
  hormones.

- Aid in the production of white and red blood cells.
- Facilitate the flow of *Chi* throughout your body and optimize your overall health and longevity. If your *Chi* flows through your body effortlessly, *Life* can be continued for a very long time.

Likewise, if the flow of Chi is impeded or stops, life itself ends. Acupressure Points have been likened to windows in your home. Awakening various acupressure points through special training is like opening the windows in your house and letting the fresh air flow in. Pressure points represent some of the important mysteries of life. Understanding your own pressure points can reveal the great power and astonishing self-control available to you when you learn to master them.

STEP 1

Stand upright with your feet shoulder-width apart, with your arms hanging down along your body. Allow your entire body to relax. From now on, this will be the position you will be doing all your meditation in unless instructed otherwise.

Begin your training with 'passive breathing'. In passive breathing, you take short shallow breaths in through your nose for a count of two, then lightly breathe out through your nose for another count of two, while you curl your tongue up to touch the root of your upper teeth. This helps you to calm and focus your mind.

Meditate on your Third Eye, the point above your nose where your eyebrows would meet. In India, they refer to this spot as the *Agya Chakra* or the *6th Chakra Center of Spiritual Consciousness.*

Close your eyes and focus them toward the site of your third eye. Let your thoughts, fears and worries fall away. If it helps, slowly count backwards from one hundred.

Do this for about three minutes, then proceed to

STEP 2

For Step two, you will need to locate your *Tan Tien or Chi Hai (Ocean of Chi)* using the following method:

Get a piece of string or a rubber band. Measure it against the bent knuckle of your first finger (see diagram). We refer to this knuckle length as a "body" inch. Now cut a piece of string that is two body inches long. Put one end of the string at the center of your navel and let the other end drop down below the navel along your stomach. Use a marker to mark the point where the string ends.

That point is your *Tan Tien* (or in acupuncture terms, your RN 6). It is located exactly two body inches below your navel.

Now you are ready to continue your Nei Kung training. Shift your meditation point to focus on your *Tan Tien* from now on.

Breath in slowly for a count of five. Then hold your breath for a count of five. Then breathe out for a count of five.

Repeat.

Do this for ten minutes.

For the best results, I recommend that you do this breathing exercise two or three times a day.

Before you proceed to Step Three, practice this Nei Kung exercise for two or three weeks until it becomes effortless.

STEP 3

Begin with passive breathing and focus inward on your third eye for two minutes.

Next, you must apply something called 'mindful meditation' as you breath in. This requires putting your thoughts into the air that you breathe in. You must concentrate hard and visualize each point as you move your energy through it.

As you breathe in:
1) You will focus your attention on a pressure point called *Tanh Chung*

(RN 17). To locate *Tanh Chung*, draw a horizontal line through your nipples, and *Tanh Chung* is the center-point of that line, in the middle of your chest.

2) Next, let your thoughts travel with your Chi down to Tanh Tien (RN 6), the point just below your navel.

3) Next, your focus your concentration on your *Chi* as it continues to travel down to another point between the genitals and your bowel, called *Hui Yin* (RN 1).

4) Hold your breath for a count of three. As you *hold* your breath, imagine using your *Chi* to *absorb* the life essence that is contained in your semen (for men) or your eggs (for women).

Then *breathe out* and:

5) Carry this life essence from *Hui Yin* (RN 1, the point between your genitals and your bowel) up to the lower tip of your spine, *Wei Kung* (DU1, or *Palace of the Tail*).

6) Next, follow it up your spine to your *Sien E* point (DU 4, or *Kidney Point*) in the middle of your kidney.

7) Continue focusing on it as your *Chi* moves up your spine to *Ta Chue* (DU 14). DU 14 is where your vertebrae meet your neckbone, a bulging point the size of a knuckle.

8) Continue focusing on it as you move the Chi up to *A Men* (DU 15), the base of your head.

9) Then pass *Sung Yi* (DU 17), located in the middle of your head.

10) Until finally reaches the crown of your head (DU 20). Here, you release the life essence you have been carrying into your DU20 point. Feel the tingle from the extra energy.

Still on the same *breath out*, go around the perimeter of your head until your Chi's journey ends *Chie Chiao* (Du 26), a point inside your upper lip, right beneath your nose, where your teeth meet the roof of your mouth.

Curl your tongue up to touch it this spot to complete the Chi's journey. Repeat this entire process, from #1 to #10 for ten minutes, two or three times a day.

ACUPRESSURE POINTS:

Let me explain the significant of each of these Acupressure Points, taking them in order, so that you understand the effect of passing your Chi through them:

• *Tanh Chung* RN 17 (*Middle Chest Point*): is the first point you move your Chi through, located in the middle of your chest. It is slightly above the Solar Plexus and close to the vital organs of your heart and lungs. There is a high concentration of neural pathways passing through this area that effect many parts of the body.

This acupressure point is predominately associated with the production of hormones that make you feel more *youthful.* Hence it is important to press this pressure point several times a day for a period of 10 seconds each time to stimulate it.

Passing your Chi through this pressure point during your *Nei Kung* training will *enhance* the function of this pressure point.

•*Tan Tien,* RN 6 (*Chi Hai* or the *Ocean of Chi*): the point just below your navel. It is the site of the residual *Original Birth Chi* that was passed on to you from your mother through her umbilical cord. It is also where *all* our *Chi* is sourced from when we meditate.

• *Hui Yin,* RN 1 (*Gathering Point of Yin*): the point between the genitals and bowel this is where our *life essence is* produced and stored in the body. As in *Nei Kung,* Tantric Yoga practitioners also channel this energy to their brains to invigorate the mind.

When we connect RN 1 to DU 1, we *symbolically* seal the energy leaks that exists through the orifices of our genitalia and bowels, and by sealing these leaks, we return our bodies to the pure embryonic state when these orifices were still sealed and energy was continuously re-circulated throughout the body.

• *Sien E,* DU 4 (*Kidney Point*), which lies in the kidney, is the center that controls all the movements of our lower body. As the "Root" of your original *Chi,* according to traditional Chinese Medicine, it is a very important and powerful pressure point that influences and even controls many bodily functions and internal organs, as itemized below.

The Chi circulating through DU4 influences the production of the *Essence of Life* in our semen and eggs and our bone marrow, amongst others.

When you pass your chi through DU4, it strengthens it and makes you *full of energy and life*. Your thoughts will be clearer and quicker. Your memory will improve. It can also help you to develop better judgment and wisdom.

Physically, it can also help strengthen your bones, enabling you to become quicker and more agile. It helps overcome any strength problems you might have with your teeth, neck, chest, and back areas. It can also help with sleep disorders, calm a troubled mind, incontinence, and semen leakage. It helps with the functioning of your internal organs, including the liver, gall bladder, small and large intestine, prostate and lungs.

Stimulating DU4 also helps your *Chi* to traverse smoothly through all twelve meridians in your body.

• *Ta Chue*, DU14 (*Big Vertebrae*): the vertebrae where your neck meets your body, serves as the center point to control all your *upper* body's movements. By strengthening both DU4 and DU14, you will enhance the body's ability to coordinate your lower body's movements with your upper body's movements.

• *Sung Yi*, DU17 (*Jade Pillow Point*) will help you to have a restful sleep and wake up with a clear mind.

• *Pai Hui*, DU 20 (*One Hundred Revelations*) is located at the crown of your head and is where you will deposit the *life essence* you have carried through your body. It is the source of all your wisdom and intellect. Charging it with your life essence will culminate in increasing your intelligence, saturating you with an abundance of life energy, and sensitizing your mind to the mystical realms.

• *Chie Chiao*, DU26 (*Canary Bridge*), is located inside your upper lip where your upper teeth meet the roof of your mouth. Passing your

Chi through your nose to DU26 and curling your tongue up to touch this point symbolizes the sealing of energy leakage through the orifices of your mouth and nose, also helping to return you to the energetically-balanced embryonic state.

When you breathe in, the meridian Line or "energy channel" that RN17, RN6, and RN1 all lie on is called the *Ren Meridian*. It is considered *Yin* and associated with 'female' force.

When you *breathe out*, the meridian that DU1, DU4, DU14, DU15, DU17, DU20 and DU26 all lie on is called *Tu or Du Meridian*. It is considered *Yang* and associated with 'male' force.

The Eternal *Youth Nei Kung, or The Golden Embryo* technique was discovered thousands of years ago in ancient China by Taoists, refined by the renowned Imperial physician, Hua Tou, the leading medical scholar in Chinese history (the Einstein of the East!) and improved on ever since.

I have shared these rare techniques here, with you, so you, too, could share in the extraordinary benefits they can bring you.

Though the exercises seem deceptively simple, do not be fooled into underestimating their importance and effect. If you faithfully follow the exercises as I have laid them out in this revealing chapter, I promise you, they should reward you with a long, healthy and enjoyable life.

THE GIFT OF HEALTH

-

A RECIPE FOR LIFE

I want to share with you an important understanding of nutrition and my own special raw vegetable and fruit drink, called Grandmaster Sin The's *Eternal Youth Super Green Smoothie Drink*, which will keep you healthy and your body younger for a long, long time.

It may seem hard to believe that pound for pound, kale has more nutrition than steak, but it's a scientific fact. Kale is also loaded with anti-cancer agents that fight off cancer cells. However, to get these benefits, you must eat the kale raw.

But eating a pound of raw Kale everyday is no picnic! To break down all the nutrients in raw kale, you must either chew it until you break down its cell walls or turn it into kale juice.

Kale can be a bit bitter, so chewing a lot of it is not much fun. Kale juice, on the other hand, is easy to drink and can be mixed with all kinds of other vegetables and fruits to make a delicious, healthy power drink!

Fruits are succulent and sweet, but contain too much sugar when taken alone, which can destabilize your blood sugar levels and overwhelm you with too many empty calories of sugar or fructose. No one could eat two pounds of fruit every day for a week without feeling it's adverse effects, much less for a lifetime.

My solution is to combine these two things in a balanced super food drink that gives your body the nutrition and support it needs. I have researched and prepared the perfect recipe for your below, which anyone can make quickly and simply in a high-powered kitchen blender, such as Vitamix or Blendex.

Voila! Problem solved.

The blender rapidly shreds the kale and breaks it down to a cellular level that is easy for your body to digest and absorb. When you add blended fruit, the sweetness in the fruit makes the kale more palatable and the enzymes in kale nullifies some of the sugar in fruit to a point where it shouldn't raise havoc with your blood sugar levels.

Now you can enjoy consuming the pounds of vegetables and fruits a day that your body needs in delicious smoothies. You can have this drink 365 days a year, for the rest of your life, and be amongst the healthiest people on the planet!

Find the Grandmaster Sin The's Eternal Youth Super Green Smoothie formula on the following page - one of the world's most nutritious drinks! A blenderful of this nutritional powerhouse should last you a day or two. Bon a petite!

I hope to see you again in my next book.

Take care, my friend, and "May The Force be with You."

Pai Hui DU 20

Yin ang

Yi Sung DU 17

Hsia Chie Chiao
DU 26

A Men DU15

Ta Chui DU 14

Tu Me

Chug Lou

Tien Chung
RN 17

Breathe In

Ren Me

Breathe Out

Ming Men DU 4

Tan Tien RN 6

Hui Yin RN 1

Wei Kune DU 1

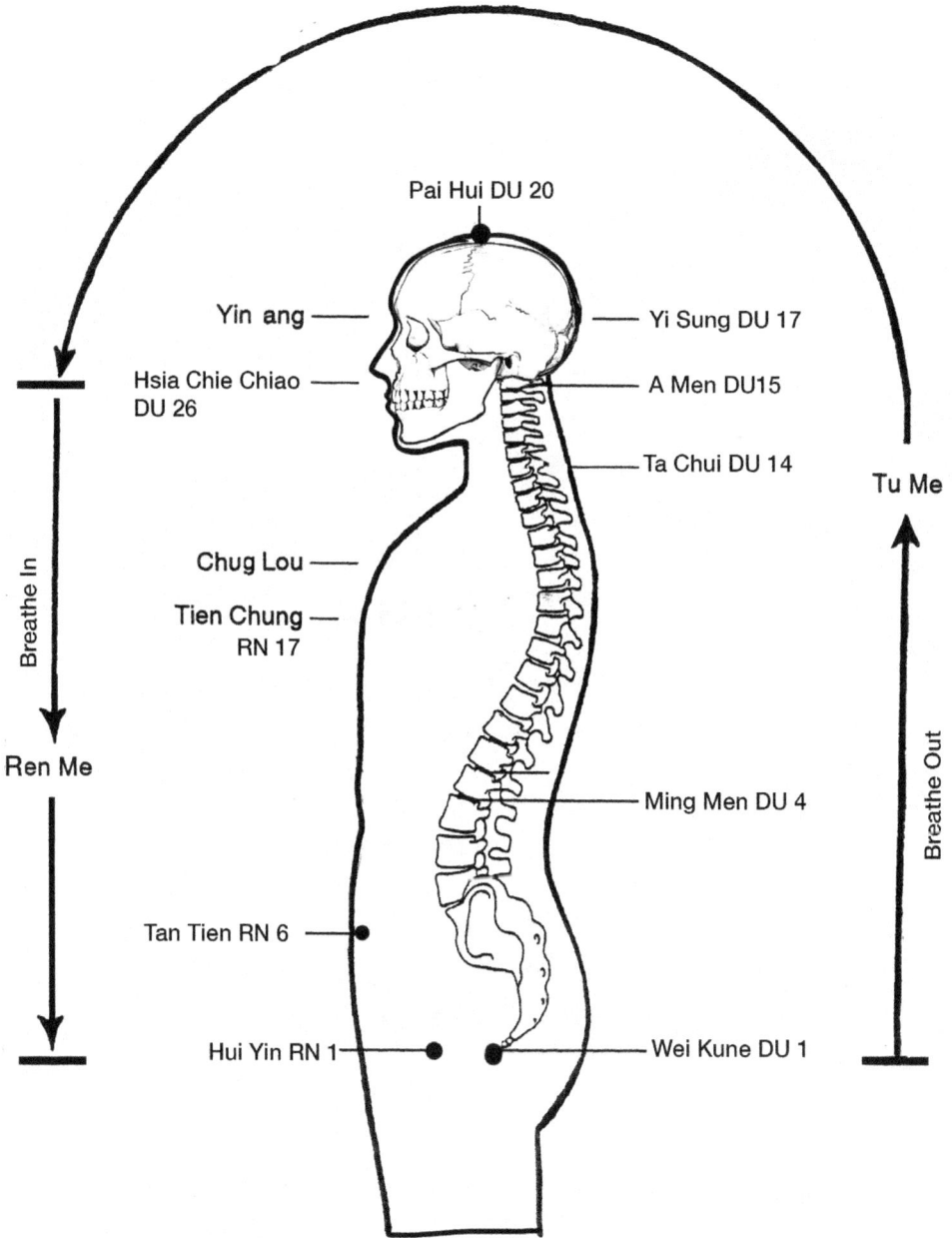

The Breathing Passge of "Eternal Youth" Nei Kung

GRANDMASTER SINTHE'S ETERNAL YOUTH GREEN SMOOTHIE RECIPE

INGREDIENTS

2 cups of water

3 oz of water

Handful of Goji Berries

1 t of Maca powder

1 t of Cacao powder

2 pack frozen Acai puree (no sugar added)

¼ of a fresh pineapple

½ cup of frozen or fresh mixed berries (blueberry, blackberry, raspberry)

¾ cup of frozen or fresh mango

1 fresh banana

½ fresh apple

½ large fresh lemon

3 dried Modjol dates

2 sticks of fresh turmeric

¼ inch of fresh ginger

1/3 lb of fresh red kale

1/3 lb of black kale

1/3 lb of broccoli leaf or collard greens

1 pack of Emergen-C powder

1 scoop (4.5 g) of L-Glutamine powder

3 oz of Kombucha Tea

RECIPE MIXING DIRECTIONS

In an 8-cup blender, add 2 c water, then add all the ingredients from Goji Berries to ginger and blend it thoroughly. When well mixed, add 1/3 lb of Red Kale and mix thoroughly. When well mixed, add 1/3 lb of broccoli leaf of collard greens and mix thoroughly. When well mixed, add 1/3 lb of Black Kale and mix thoroughly.

Take a 16 oz protein shaker or covered container and add 3 oz of water, 1 pack of Emergen-C powder, 1 scoop (4.5 grams) of L-Glutamine powder, and 3 oz of Kombucha tea and shake well.

To this mixture, add 8 oz of the green mixture, above, and shake thoroughly.

Now you have one of the world's most nutritious drinks in your hand. A blenderful of this mixture should last you a day or two. Bon Appetite!

Always consult a doctor for your specific health needs before switching diets.

This photo was taken on June 22, 1992 at Honan Shaolin Temple, as the photo at the book's back cover was taken on February 13, 2016 in Grandmaster Sin's backyard: 24 years age difference and he has hardly changed! This is proof that the "Eternal Youth" Nei Kung and his special formula Green Smoothie WORK!

HUA TOU

-

Scholar, Shoalin Master and Imperial Physician

Over 2000 years ago, a famous martial arts master and scholar named Hua Tou lived during in China during the Three Kingdom Period. He had a unique ability to see the world with unfiltered sight, much like the famous mathmetician and astronomer, Copernicus, who took a scientific leap that the earth revolved around the Sun, not the other way around as all others believed.

Hua Tou intuitively sensed, as no one had before him, that that it was the flow of Chi through an embryo's body while it was developing inside its mother's womb that gave it Life. And Hua Tou discovered he had the ability to sense which of the 720 pressure points the embryo's Chi passed through. Long before the ultrasound devise was invented, Hua Tou envisioned the development of the human fetus from a tiny zygote to the fully formed infant was at birth, all within a few short months. This astonishing rate of growth fascinated him and he devoted long hours to researching his discovery.

And it was an important discovery, because Hua Tou also believed that if the flow of Chi could create the spark of life in an embryo, it could also revitalize and rejuvenate older people.

His unique awareness of the flow of Chi enabled him to see that, as we grew older, our Chi began to deviate from that of the unborn child, taking radically different paths through our bodies. He hypothesized that these deviations were one of the primary reasons we grew old and our health began to decline.

He began experimenting with Chi breathing techniques, directing his Chi through the embryonic pressure points, which he called, The Golden Embryo breathing method.

His age-defying techniques were profoundly successful at promoting good health and longer life. So much so, that a well-known Shaolin nunnery outside the Temple gates that adopted his techniques, became famous for its youthful-looking nuns! Visitors were amazed to learn that nuns who looked in their 30's and 40's were actually in their 60's and 70's! For centuries this nunnery attracted wealthy female patrons who paid a handsome donation to learn Hua Tou's ancient Secret of Eternal Youth.

Happily, Hua Tou passed on his esoteric learning to his advanced students, who in turn, have passed it on for generations to this day.

*

The Great Hua Tou, was also a renowned physician, widely regarded as the greatest medical practitioner in all of China.
And his most famous patient? The Emperor himself!

The Emperor at the time was the same King Ciao Ciao, from northern China who had fled from General Kwan Kung! With his massive army, Ciao Ciao had gone on to conquer all of China. But in his old age, Ciao Ciao had found an adversary he couldn't conquer: Sickness. He developed debilitating migraines that none of his retinue of learned physicians could cure.

One day, in an agony of pain, he sent all his other physicans away and summoned Hua Tou to the Palace to attend him.

Hua Tou examined Ciao Ciao carefully and instantly sensed the disruption of the flow of Chi through the Emperor's body. When he was absolutely sure he knew what was wrong, he regretfully informed the Emperor he had an incurable brain tumor!

The Emperor was appalled. "But surely something can be done?" he protested, used to getting his way. How ironic it would be to conquer all of China from without, only to be conquered himself from within?

"Assuredly, your Grace," Hua Tou reassured him. "But I fear you will not like it, because it has never been done before." He told the Emperor he wanted to saw open his skull and remove the tumor!

"How could that possibly work?" The angry Emperor demanded, torn between hope and scorn.

Hua Tuo bowed low. "Your Grace, I bet my life on it."

But the Emperor refused to consider it and dismissed him angrily. Months later, when the piercing headaches became unbearable, Ciao Ciao took his own dagger and contemplated killing himself! In that desperate moment, he was forced to accept that it would be better to let Hua Tuo try his procedure - and possibly succeed - then to die by his own hand.

Summoned by royal command, Hua Tuo was ordered to operate and assured by the Emperor that he would be handsomely rewarded if he succeeded.

Hua Tuo gave him a strange, sad smile and said nothing. Using long, thin acupuncture needles placed along the Chi meridians to block all pain, Hua Tuo anesthetized the Emperor, then gently sawed opened his skull. He found the enormous tumor just where he said it would be and deftly removed it all. Closing up, he replaced the skull segment and delicately stitched the scalp back together with strong silk fibers.

When Emperor awoke, he was stunned that he had survived and thrilled to find his excruciating headache was gone! He had tears in his eyes when he thanked Hua Tuo for his unparralleled service to the crown and again told him he would be handsomely rewarded.

Hua Tuo bowed respectfully, then rose to face the Emperor, man to man. Quietly he replied, "I know that is not to be, Your Grace, as tomorrow you will have me beheaded."

The Emperor was shocked that his physician knew the unfortunate truth.

"Why did you agree to heal me, knowing your life would be forfeit either way?" the puzzled Emperor asked.

"Because I am a good and loyal citizen," His physican replied. "And like all good citizens of China, I am willing to sacrifice my life for the welfare of our noble leader."

Ciao Ciao was deeply moved. "If I could do otherwise…", he faltered, for the first time feeling a sense of kinship with another human being.

Hua Tuo shook his head gravely. "I understand, Your Grace. You must remain infallible in the eyes of your people. There must be no suspicion a blight was removed from your brain. Otherwise others might question your decisions or fear you were insane or possessed."

Ciao Ciao nodded, his dark eyes pools of sadness. "Beautifully said, Great and Noble Physician."

Without another word, Hua Tuo bowed low and walked bravely to his fate. XXX

These are just a few examples of the wonders that can be achieved by controlling ones Chi and pressure points.

Modern readers may find it hard to believe the extraordinary, almost magical, effects our pressure points can have on our bodies and minds – just as the wonders of modern medicine would have seemed magical to folk of the Middle Ages.

But open your mind up and enjoy the mystical ride!

NEI KUNG FOR STRENGTH

MIAO GIOK, A 16 YEAR-OLD MONK AT THE TEMPLE, WAS A STRONG BOY WHO DREAMT OF BECOMING A STRONG AND POWERFUL WARRIOR MONK. UNLIKE SOME OF THE OTHER BOYS, HE LOVED STRENGTH TRAINING.

To make training more fun for the young initiates, the Shaolin Masters developed an amusing competition - a lamb-lifting contest!

Each boy was assigned a newborn lamb that they had to lift up over their heads repeatedly, until their arms screamed in protest! As the days past and the lambs grew into mature sheep, they become heavier and harder for the boys to lift.

If at any point the sheep became too heavy for the initiate to lift, he would be immediately disqualified. Keen to avoid the humiliation of losing, and determined to win the contest, all the young monks pushed themselves beyond the limits of their strength to train, train and train some more.

None worked harder at it than Miao Giok.

Miao Giok's diligence paid off and he ended up the champion! But, not content with just bench pressing a sheep, Miao yearned to become the strongest man in the world! He was convinced that, with more diligent training, he could learn to press a donkey or horse over his head instead. So every night, he began to sneak out to the barnyard and try with all his might to pick up a new born donkey, but he could not manage it. He became obsessed with achieving this passionate goal.

One afternoon after days of failure, during his meditation practice, his mind veered off the regular meditation pathway into something completely different. As his Chi passed through different pressure points, they heated up, becoming warm to the touch. His entire body began to feel more powerful and strong than it had ever felt before.

Racing out to the barn, he was stunned to discover that he was able to pick up the baby donkey – almost effortlessly! It was the happiest day of his life!

Over his lifetime, Miao Giok went on to explore and refine his special Chi breathing and meditation technique to achieve superhuman strength and lift full grown horses as no man had ever done before.

NEI KUNG FOR KEEN HEARING, SENSE, AND EYESIGHT
-
Ming Liang, Night Dream

MING LIANG WAS AN EAGER, YOUNG MONK, ONLY 15 YEARS. HE LOVED BIRDS OF PREY - THEIR GRACE, THEIR MAJESTY AND THEIR NOBLE POWER. ONE DAY HE FOUND A BABY HAWK UNDER A TREE THAT HAD FALLEN FROM HIS NEST. HE RESCUED IT AND HID IT UNDER HIS BED IN A WARM BOX. HE BECAME LIKE A MOTHER TO THE TINY CHICK, BRINGING IT WORMS AND GRASSHOPPERS AND CRICKETS. EACH DAY HE WOULD BRING THE LITTLE HAWK OUT TO THE GRASSY AREA NEAR HIS QUARTERS TO PLAY AND TEACH IT TO FLY. AS THE MONTHS WENT BY THEY BECAME INSEPARABLE, FORMING A SPECIAL BOND.

Before long, the hawk matured and took to glorious wing, soaring high into the sky, far beyond Ming's reach. But, it loved Ming and would always return to his upstretched hand when he called it, to be rewarded with a tasty mouse or other tidbits. Ming was amazed that his hawk's ears were keen enough to hear his call and its eyes sharp enough to spot the mouse in his hand from miles away.

One night, Ming Liang dreamt his consciousness entered his friend, the hawk's body. He felt the miraculous sensation of extra keen hearing and was able to hear a mouse rustling in the reed matting two rooms away. His eyes too, were suddenly as sharp as razors, and watching a feather drift down to rest on a post a mile away was child's play! He was stunned to see how the world looked through his hawk's eyes. But when he woke up the next day and found the feather where he had dreamt it had fallen, he knew he had stumbled onto something important: a way to heighten our senses beyond normal human capacity.

He began to experiment with channeling his Chi to see if he could achieve the same results when he wasn't dreaming. At night when all his roommates were sleeping, Ming meditated on his bed. He recreated the sensations he experienced when he had entered the hawk body and listened to the winds and surrounding sounds. Deep into his meditation, he began to hear faint noises across the distance from senior monks's quarters as they talked. Months turned into years and Ming Liang developed a keen hearing sense like those of his friend, the hawk.

Ming Liang continued using the Gift of that night dream to develop his eyes sight as well. His teacher had been asking everyone to record the breathing patterns of some unusual events, Ming Liang recorded all these and proudly handed to his head master. It added another colorful dimensions to the archive of Nei Kung.

NEI KUNG FOR "SLOWING TIME"

TE SIU WAS A MONK OF THE SHAOLIN TEMPLE IN THE MIDDLE AGES. HIS PASSION WAS FOR ARCHERY. IN PARTICULAR HE LOVED TO HAVE FELLOW MONKS SHOT ARROWS AT HIM AND HE WOULD BLOCK IT WITH SWORDS. HE WAS SO GOOD AT IT, HE CAN EVEN CATCH ARROWS BY HIS BARE HANDS. HOWEVER HIS DREAM WAS TO BE ABLE TO BLOCK ARROWS SHOT BY A DOZEN OF HIS FELLOW MONKS SIMULTANEOUSLY.

Days and nights his thought was always preoccupied with this feat. One night in the midst of his meditation he fantasized that a dozen of the monks shooting arrows at him and he blocked them all by his swords. He noticed that he was no longer follow his regular breathing and meditation pattern. Instead he was on a quiet different path of meditation's route. He did his best to remember this new pattern while continuing his meditation.

A moment later he woke up from his meditation and went to the out house to relieve his bladder. Midway to the out house a bat flew by him. It took him by surprise as he notice how slow the bat flew by. Then another bat flew by and it was slow as well. Te Siu ended up watching the bats flew by him all night long and forgot about his bladder. He did remember his breathing pattern as he observed the bats flew by.

Early the next morning Te Siu summoned 12 of his fellow monks to shoot arrows at him. At first he asked them to shoot at him successively first. he closed his eyes and went into the breathing pattern that he stumbled on the night before. He then imagined that he was able to block their arrows. When he was ready he opened his eyes and signal the monks to attack. Sure enough he was able to block all the arrows coming at him because suddenly these arrows seem to travel in slow speed. Months later he worked his way up to all 12 of his friends firing their arrows at him simultaneously and Te Siu was able to block all of them.

Somehow, by altering the flow of Chi through different meridians in our bodies, master Kung Fu and Chi Kung practitioners have been able to create a difference between their time perception of the outside world versus their inside world. Much like the difference between time on our world and time in a Black Hole. Everything is relative, everything is One...

In the popular Chinese film, "Hero" Jet Li plays a character who carries on a conversation with a woman warrior when hundreds upon thousands of enemy's arrows were showering down on them.

Yet, they calmly talked as these arrows flew by them, because they could perceive the arrows approaching them in slow motion, giving them plenty of time to twist one way or another to avoid being hit. This too is an example of the Nei Kung art of slowing time

ONE MAN AGAINST 800 MAN

-

Kwan Kung: The Giant

KWAN KUNG WAS A GIANT OF A MAN, TOWERING OVER HIS COUNTRYMEN. HISTORIANS BELIEVE HE STOOD OVER 8 FEET TALL AND WEIGHED IN AT 400 POUNDS WITH A LONG, FU MAN CHU-STYLE MUSTACHE AND A NEATLY TRIMMED LONG BEARD. INTIMIDATING, YET HE HAD A KIND AND GENTLE LOOK.

His weapon was a huge steel blade mounted on an eleven foot steel pole as thick around as a telephone pole. It weighed 200 pounds.

Kwan Kung sworn brother, Liu Pai, was the king of the southern region of China. Wildly out-numbered, he commanded only 20,000 men, while his enemy, Ciao Ciao, marched against them with 800,000!

However, with Kwan Kung's rightiousness and the brilliant strategies of his chief advisor, Chu Ke Liang, they dared hope they could hold out against their such overwhelming odds.

Since it was impossible for Kwan Kung to ride a normal horse, the king had scoured the realm to find him a mount strong enough to carry him. It last, in a distant part of the kingdom, they discovered a giant of a horse, half again as big as a normal horse and black as night. Legend has it could gallop 300 miles in a single night! Kwan Kung was thrilled with his magnificent new steed, who he called 'Jet Black'.

Kwan Kung's most famous heroic feat was the battle of the bridge... He and Chu Ke Liang engaged the enemy in an epic battle, but found themselves needing to retreat cross a bridge over a roaring river to regroup. But the vast enemy army quickly pursued them and Kwan Kung saw that thousands of their men would be slaughtered and all would be lost if the enemy made it across the bridge.

Kwan Kung bravely volunteered to man the bridge alone, to give his comrades time to get across to safety. It was common knowledge that Northerners couldn't swim, so he correctly surmised that if he could hold them off at the bridge, they would have no way to cross the raging river.

Chu Ke Liang gazed at him and bowed low to show his profound respect for Kwan Kung's selfless heroism, before leading his army away across the bridge.

He never expected to see Kwan Kung alive again.

But Kwang Kung had other plans.

He stalked to the bridge and settled himself into a wide, strong stance, his body poised for action, and hefted his massive poleaxe in his mighty hands.

The enemy army laughed and ridiculed him for thinking one man, no matter how big, could oppose an entire army!

But, when they massed and all attacked him at once, he let loose a savage roar and sent his massive poleaxe scything through the crowd in a devastating arc of destruction!

In one fell swoop, he beheaded twenty men! Every single time a group of soldiers stormed the slender bridge he guarded with his life, trying to cross, Kwan Kung would whack their heads off, not letting a single soldier get by him. He repeated this gruesome act over and over and over again, until he had thoroughly demoralized the enemy! His epic feat earned him the name of "He who can slice off a 1000 heads at once!"

When the enemy king, Ciao Ciao, finally arrived in his splendid chariot, he demanded to know why his soldiers had not crossed the bridge to crush his enemies.

One of his generals pointed to the thousand headless corpses floating down the river and shook his head: "Kwan Kung's first title is "He who can slice off a 1000 heads at once!"

"Then let fly your arrows and strike him down!" shrieked the worried King, looking at the hulking giant guarding the bridge.

His general shook his head, "My King, he is a Shaolin Master warrior, and arrows cannot touch him. And beware, My King, his second title is, "He Who Can Pass Through a Million Soldiers to Pick Any Head He Wants!""

Just then, Kwan Kung caught sight of King Ciao Ciao and bellowed his challenge, "Ciao Ciao, I'm coming for YOU!"

Ciao Ciao blanched in fear and whipped his horses to speed away in his chariot. But, Kwang Kung leapt onto Jet Black and took off after him as fast as lighting! As he raced through their ranks, the enemy fired a black rain of deadly arrows at him, but he effortlessly blocked them all!

But, King Ciao Ciao, with his faster chariot, managed to escape leaving Kwan Kung roaring with derisive laughter at the cowardly king - defeated by one man!

When the soldiers saw their leader disappear in a cloud of dust, they all turned tail and ran.

So it was that one mighty warrior, trained in the mysterious Shaolin way, defeated 800,000 men! xx

THE MAN WHO BASKED OPEN THE CITY GATE
-
Li Kui: The Double Axe Warrior

Li Kui was a well-muscled, 250 pound man, who stood over six feet four inches tall. He wore a bristling mustache and a wild, bushy beard and had a sharp, penetrating gaze that gave you a chill when he stared at you.

He was famous for carrying two gigantic axes that weighed 80 pound each. Famed as a powerful warrior, he was often summoned to use his axes to demolish the formidlable gates protecting an enemy fortress.

so the soldiers could breach their defenses and rush inside.

But, on this particular occasion, that was easier said than done, since the enemy had a row of one hundred archers lining the walkway above the gate, poised to defend the gates with lethal force if he dared to approach.

Undeterred, Li Kui hefted his mighty axes and stepped resolutely toward the gates. Instantly, one hundred archers notched their arrows, aimed them at him and let loose a rain of death!

Shiing! Shiing! Siiing!!

Everyone froze, horrified that their hero would die impaled by a hundred arrows in seconds! But little did they know that Li Kui was a Nei Kung master. Summoning his concentration he channeled his Chi and shifted his perception of time into slow motion. Instead of lying dead, riddled with a hundred deadly shafts, Li Kui blocked the first arrow speeding toward him with his mighty axe, then the next, the next, the next, until he had blocked them all and the enemy's arrows lay as shattered kindling around him.

He demolished the gates without suffering a scratch and his army swarmed through the gates!

SU KONG TAI DJIN

THE MOST THRILLING TALE OF A SHAOLIN MASTER USING THE SUPERHUMANLY KEEN SENSES HE HAD DEVELOPED AT THE TEMPLE WAS DEMONSTRATED IN THE LATE 1800S BY SU KONG TAI DJIN, GRANDMASTER E'S TEACHER.

Was his use of superhuman senses, later on in his life, that saved the lives of an entire Imperial delegation.

Rebellion was sweeping the land, threatening the smooth reign of Emperor Quangxu of the Qing Dynasty. Su Kong, by then a master well–respected for his wisdom and sharp understanding, was commissioned by the Emperor to meet a contingent of ranking rebel leaders who had been fomenting rebellion against him in a last-ditch attempt to negotiate a peace with them.

The top secret meeting took place in an out-of-the-way house owned by one of the rebel leaders. When Su Kong entered the Hall, twelve rebel leaders were already waiting for him, arranged around a long table in the middle of the room.

As he approached the table, the twelve rebels stood up and bowed to him to show respect. Su Kong hesitated, as something triggered his awareness sharply, but then bowed back to repay their respect in kind. He seemed strangely preoccupied as he moved to take his place in the only empty chair, where a knife, bowl and chopsticks had been placed in readiness for the meal soon to be served.

He lingered in front of his seat for a brief moment, then, in a blur of motion too fast to follow, snatched up the knife from the table and hurled it up into the ceiling! Everyone gasped as a body tumbled down from above and crashed on to the table! It was a Ninja! An assassin sent by the all-powerful Empress Dowager Cixi, the Emperor's aunt and regent who was secretly plotting to take over the throne.

How had Su Kong instantly noticed the Ninja's lurking presence, when twelve other highly-trained warriors had not?

He had heard thirteen people breathing, when only twelve were in the room! So did his special skills enable a humble priest to save the day.

THE THIRTEEN MING
DYNASTY MONKS

ANOTHER INSPIRING STORY OF EXCEPTIONAL MASTERY IS THE STORY OF THE 13 MING DYNASTY MONKS. THE EMPEROR HAD BEEN TAKEN BY SURPRISE AND IMPRISONED BY HIS ARCHENEMY.

Thirteen Shoalin masters took it upon themselves to risk their lives to save their imperiled monarch. Drawing upon their special powers, they were able to mask themselves with 'concealing energy' - like a cloak of invisibility - that made them blend into the background.

Using this amazing power, they were able penetrate unseen through the ranks of ten thousand enemy soldiers and rescue the emperor before he could be assassinated. What an extraordinary feat!

LADY WARRIOR

The Nei Kung Golden Embryo technique for longevity and sexual pleasure has been used over the centuries to excellent effect.

One of the most magnificent examples is a legendary Lady Warrior in ancient China. The winds of war were rising as two powerful and belligerent generals claimed sovereignty over the same territory. Though one was open to parlay, the other absolutely refused to negotiate.

Wishing to avert a war that would cost thousands of innocent lives, our lady warrior concocted a plan to convince the generals to come to a settlement without bloodshed. She meditated to direct her Chi into a powerful series of meridians. So extensive was her mastery of Chi, our hero succeeded in drawing an unprecedented level of powerful energy into her body.

The energy she had harnessed enabled her to run like the wind, She covered 100 miles in a single night! She reached the enemy camp before dawn and slipped unnoticed past all the sentries. Darting through the darkness, she crept into the tent of the enemy general, where he lay sleeping, resting up for the epic battle he intended to wage the next day.

While the intractable general lay helpless, instead of dishonorably beheading him, she stole his most prized possession from under his pillow - the privy seal given to him by the emperor himself. In its place she left a brief note that cautioned: "Beware: I could have stolen your head instead of your seal!"

Astonished by such powers, the general reconsidered his rash decision to go to battle.

The Lady Warrior's bravery and extraordinary feat averted war. Without her mastery of Chi, none of that would have been possible and thousands of lives would have been lost in a senseless, bloody battle.

YANG KUI FE

Back in the mists of history, during the Tang Dynasty, there lived a beautiful woman named Yang Kui Fe. To maintain their position in Society, her family planned to place her as a royal concubine in the Emperor's household. As a sign of his status and to form political alliances, it was customary at that time for the Emperor to have hundreds, even thousands, of concubines in his Palace.

Yang Kui Fe was beautiful and intelligent and knew, for the sake of her family, she must find favor with the Emperor himself. So, she went out of her way to learn something that would keep her young and beautiful even as she aged – something that no other concubine would know: the Eternal Youth Breathing Method. She had mastered this secret talent by the time she moved to the palace.

Like many Emperors before him, the Tang Emperor overindulged in sexual activity with his concubines and eventually, was so worn out from the constant depletion that he began to lose interest in sex. He felt tired and irritable all the time.

Every day, several concubines would be assigned to tend to him and fulfill whatever chores he might require of them. But he was so out of sorts and short-tempered all the time, the women concubine were frightened to be chosen to be near him.

Except Yang Kui Hui. She had studied the Emperor from a distance and, with her deep understanding of the flow of Chi, she instantly realized what his problem was. At last, here was something she could help him with! She went to her superior and volunteered to attend him that very day.

When Yang Kui Hui entered the Emperor's chamber, she found him surrounded by untidy piles of scrolls and mounds of documents that he was supposed to read and act upon. But he was so out of sorts, he could not work and the business of the kingdom was grinding to a halt.

When he saw her, he threw the documents at her and snarled, "I'm sick of these infernal documents! I command you: read them to me!"

He said this as a trap, believing that she, like most women, had never been taught to read, and that he would have a good excuse to punish her when she couldn't obey his command.

He was astonished when she picked up the scroll nearest her and started reading it out loud! And from the way she read, it was obvious she was highly educated and had a pleasant peaking voice.

Intrigued, The Emperor sat back to listen.

When Yang Kui Fe finished reading the document, she went on to analyze its contents and calmly recommended whether the Emperor should sign it or not!

The Emperor was astonished that this little slip of a woman was not only intelligent and clever, she also seemed to have no fear of him, unlike all his other concubines! What sort of a woman was this, he wondered?

To reward her for the unusual experience she was giving him, he took the document and stamped it with his Imperial Seal - just as she had recommended!

They kept this up until the servants entered with trays of sumptuous food for the Emperor's lunch, laden with varieties of meats, heavy starches and thick sauces.

Yang Kui Fe took one look at these heavy, fatty dishes and gently shook her head, suggesting instead they bring some raw vegetables and ripe fruit. The astonished cooks could not believe their ears, but when the Emperor nodded, they hurried to do as he commanded.

The Emperor had never met anyone like Yang Kui Fe. Not only was she stunningly beautiful, but she was bright and fearless as well! She could easily have been beheaded for speaking out front of the cooks, yet she had done it in such a friendly and innocent way, the Emperor had not taken offence. And her energy was boundless! He felt more alive than he had in years just by being around her!

As he gazed at her nibbling on a healthy piece of fruit, the Emperor was surprised to realize he really liked her.

Naturally, when evening came, he desired her to spend the night with him - a great honor, which no one dared refuse. Yang Kui Fe smiled and bowed her head in acceptance and he led her to his bed chamber.

As she slowly undressed him, the Emperor became wild with excitement and desired possess her immediately.

But, remarkably, at the risk of her own life, Yang Kui Fe gently told him that he must first rebuild his Chi, which he had seriously depleted from having too much empty sex. His current state of depletion was serious, she said and warned him that if they coupled now, tomorrow he would feel exhausted and unwell.

"Instead," she suggested, "May I teach you the Eternal Youth Breathing Method that will enable you to control the flow of Chi through your body and wake up feeling euphoric and full of energy every single day?"

The Emperor frowned, unused to being denied anything, but he instinctively sensed she was speaking truth and he decided to trust her.

"Teach me," he commanded.

For the next few days, Yang Kui Fe happily taught the Emperor the Eternal Youth Breathing Method. After awhile the Emperor learned it to her satisfaction. Then she told the Emperor that she was going to help him " jump start " the healing process by gently caressing his body to make him feel stimulated, causing his body to produce hormones.

While she was doing all this, she instructed him to continue doing the Eternal Youth breathing to "re-absorb " all the hormones or ching into his damaged body to rebuild his Chi. The Emperor loved the idea.

So all night long Yang Kui Fe gently caressed and massaged the Emperor's body while he did his Eternal Youth Breathing exercises, concentrating hard on absorbing his essence into Pai Hui (the "One Hundred Revelations" point on the top of his head). Every time he approached too close to a climax, Yang would instinctively sense it and would stop to enable him to reabsorb his Chi.

The results were miraculous! The Emperor awoke feeling refreshed and more alive than he had in years!

Yang Kui Fe and the Emperor

And so they went on for some time, until the Emperor's strength had been rebuilt sufficiently for them to finally consummate their love. Their love-making was legendary – unlike anything the Emperor had ever experienced – and ripening into genuine love and affection, causing him to refuse all the other women at his disposal.

To this day, Yang Kui Fe is revered in China as the most beautiful woman in Chinese history and her beauty shone on the inside as well as the outside...

Nei Kung Golden Embryo
-
ETERNAL YOUTH METHOD

MANY CENTURIES AGO, THE TAOIST'S FORMULATED A SPECIAL NEI KUNG TECHNIQUE THAT CONSTANTLY CONVERTED OUR SEXUAL ENERGY INTO MENTAL ENERGY.

Just like the Gingko Tree used all its energy for survival instead of wasting on flowering and bear fruits, this Nei Kung technique uses the chi we generated through meditation, to and passes that Chi through our testicles or ovaries and converts the massive energy stored there into mental energy. This mental energy is then stored in our brains, and is available for our use at any time.

As a result, we have an overabundance of energy for whatever we need to do in life. We can live a cheerful, healthy, and long, long life.

The Nei Kung Eternal Youth Method was also used by another famous Emperor: The Yellow Emperor, who ruled China from 2697 to 2598 B.C., almost 5000 years ago.

Over the many years of his reign, the Yellow Emperor had made love with thousands of women, chosen from the many concubines who had been brought to the palace to pleasure him. By the time he was 68 years old, he felt drained and exhausted, and had little energy to carry out his duties.

An astute scholar and eminent physician in his own right, the Yellow Emperor had written several of the most famous Chinese medical books – some still in use today.

It galled him that in spite of his superior education and advanced medical knowledge, he was unable to cure himself and stop this debilitating energy drain that kept him from his scholarly work and the enjoyment of life.

Amongst his retinue were three brilliant lady advisors. They told the Emperor about an ancient and fabled Taoist's teaching called the Nei Kung "Eternal Youth Method," that might be able to rejuvenate him.

According to Taoist teaching, having too much sex is not really the problem. Squandering his sperm was the real issue, as it takes an incredible amount of energy to create sperm. Like the egg, sperm is packed with the incredible amount of biological energy required to create life itself.

His advisors volunteered to travel throughout the kingdom seeking a Nei Kung master that they could bring back with them to the palace to teach the Emperor the ancient Eternal Youth Method.

The Emperor respected their wisdom and granted them permission to search. The three ladies took months visiting all of the leading Taoist temples in China, seeking a Nei Kung master of this special technique.

But, time after time, they were told by the Taoist priests that this special knowledge had been lost thousands of years ago.

Undeterred, they changed tactics and began to visit China's famous 'Noble House Pavilions', where talented women with exceptional expertise in the Art of Pleasure entertained their clients.

When even these exotic masters did not know this special skill, the Imperial Advisors asked if they had ever encountered a very special client who might know about it?

Several of the girls from different pavilions mentioned a physician named Ch'i Po, who had demonstrated extraordinary staying power.

Their story always the same: Ch'i Po would visit the Noble House and make love with many women in the same night, yet show no sign of fatigue the next morning. On the contrary, he was cheerful, full of vigor, and had an excellent appetite.

When the Imperial Advisors finally tracked him down, he proved to be a tall, well-built man that positively radiated energy. They invited him to return to the palace with them to serve the Emperor.

When he had been bathed and dressed in costly robes, he was brought before the Emperor.

Ch'i Po regarded his sovereign with a kindly, intense look. He saw a once-viral man who was now dissipated and running on empty.

The Emperor was skeptical. Ch'i Po looked too ordinary to be the master he had been promised. He insisted on a demonstration of this fabled Eternal Youth Energy.

Ch'i Po acquiesced to his sovereign's request and proceeded to exhaust twelve ladies of the court in an epic all night event! The Emperor and his three advisors watched in awe.

After he finished his incredible feat, the Emperor ordered him a sumptuous breakfast to replenish him. Ch'i Po devoured it all! His eyes were alive with mischief and his spirit was high.

Now the Yellow Emperor was convinced. He listened attentively when Ch'i Po explained that he didn't have to stop making love. He just had to learn how to properly circulate his essence throughout his entire body without releasing it, using it to generate energy, so none was wasted.

Ch'i Po taught the Yellow Emperor his Taoist Eternal Youth Technique. The Yellow Emperor liked him so much, he made Ch'i Po his minister of the bed chamber and asked him to stay in the Palace.
Ch'i Po gratefully accepted this great honor.
The Yellow Emperor learned to enjoy life again with a new zest and lived to 101

years old. He reigned from 2697 to 2598 B.C. His most famous book, "Huang Ti Nei Ching" or The Yellow Emperor's Classic of Internal Medicine is regarded as the bible of ancient Chinese Medicine. He taught his two sons the same Eternal Youth Technique and they both also lived to 101 and 102 years, respectively.

Unfortunately, his sons never taught it to their children, so it looked like this royal line of wisdom would be lost forever.

But fortunately, the Emperor's three lady advisors also learned the Eternal Youth Technique and spread the precious life enhancing and age defying Nei Kung teachings to women all across China.

LI CHING YUAN
-
The 250 Year Old Man

The last person known to practice the Nei Kung Eternal Youth Technique, prior to Grandmaster Sin Kwang The´, was Li Ching Yuan, a famous Kung Fu master and expert herbalist. He is purported to have been the oldest living man in the world at the time of his death.

Born in Sichuan Province in China, Ki Ching Yuan has been variously reported as being born in 1677 or 1736. Astonishingly, he died in 1933, which would make him an astonishing 256 or 197 years old.

Documented in the Imperial files, Tao Kwang Ti, the Qing Emperor of China, sent him a congratulatory message on his 150th birthday and another on his 200th birthday.

Throughout his life, Li Ching Yuan traveled extensively through Kansu, Shansi, Tibet, Vietnam, Thailand and Manchuria to collect rare and exotic herbs, wild Ginseng, Goji berry, He Shou Wu, and other Chinese herbs.

He practiced the Internal Arts of Tai Chi and Pakua for hours each day and taught master level Nei Kung, Tai Chi and Kung Fu. In later years, he created the Chiu Lung Pakua Chang or The Nine Dragon Pakua Palm.

He attributed his extraordinary longevity to a life of intense discipline and Nei Kung training, his rigorous daily exercises in Kung Fu, plus his secret herbal supplements and healthy diet.

In 1827, having grown wealthy and influential, Li celebrated his 150th birthday in his home town in Sichuan Province, attended by many Chinese dignitaries and celebrities.

At the age of 159 years old, Li Ching Yuan moved to a new town and posed as a wealthy 49 year old! He ended up marrying a 19-year old virgin from an affluent family, as his 14th wife.

One day a visitor came to town and recognized him. Imagine the surprise of his in-laws to learn that their daughter had married the famous Li Ching Yuan - a 159 year old man!

What they did not expect is that Li would out live their daughter and live on to marry another 10 times before he died at a purported age of 256 years old.

When Li Ching Yuan died on May 6th, 1933, the New York Times ran a feature article on him. He had outlived 23 wives and was survived by his 24th wife, a 60-year old woman. He had 180 descendants, over eleven generations!

Grandmaster E turned to Sin, "I was still in China then and was amazed by his longevity. I count my blessings that my venerable teacher, Grandmaster Su Kong Tai Gin, entrusted me with these secret technique of the art of longevity. Now I want to pass this sacred art on to you. Remember Son, you may not live as long as Li Ching Yuan, but strive to live a meaningful and productive life of at least 120 years."

With that admonishment, Grandmaster E began teaching Sin the fabled Eternal Youth Nei Kung technique.

This great honor helped to cheer Sin up and he happily set about to absorb the new teachings. He considered this rare knowledge as an extraordinary farewell gift from Grandmaster E to him.

It was literally the Gift of Life.

After their last lesson, Grandmaster E asked Sin what his plans were, now that the future was shaky for the Chinese in Indonesia.

"I am thinking of going to university in the United States to study Nuclear Physics."

Grandmaster E was pleased to hear this. "I brought Shaolin Arts from China to Indonesia many years ago. Now, it's your turn to take Shaolin Arts from Indonesia to the United States of America."

His eyes grew sorrowful as his thoughts ranged back over his life and the devastation that the new Indonesian restrictions on Chinese culture would wreak on his life.

"As you know, Sin, the Indonesian Government has just banned all Chinese culture, including Kung Fu. All I have left now are broken dreams."

Sin began to tear up. He felt so deeply for Grandmaster E. Martial arts were his mentor's entire life – he practically ate, drank and slept Kung Fu. It was so unfair that petty politics and capricious governments could just take his life's blood away from him.

He tried to rein in his emotions. "I'm so sorry, Grandmaster E. I know Shaolin is your life. No one should have the right to take that away from you. You have given me the honor to be your student and it has changed my entire life. In your honor, I promise to dedicate my life to preserving the Shaolin Arts in America."

Grandmaster E was deeply moved. "You have done well, my Son. I have taught you almost everything I know. It is time for a new beginning."

Grandmaster E straightened his shoulders and faced Sin, a strange look of resolve on his worn face. Slowly, he removed the Red Belt that marked his status as a Grandmaster from around his waist. He held it gently, reverently, in his hands for a moment, like a precious, living thing, then held it out to Sin.

Sin's eyes flew wide with shock. What was happening here?

"I have been wearing this belt for too long," Grandmaster E murmured, clearing his throat, thick with emotion. "According to Shaolin tradition, only one person can wear the Red Belt at a time and that person is The Grandmaster."

He beamed at Sin, "Today we have a New Grandmaster: "Grandmaster Sin Kwang Thé´." He bowed low to Sin, who stared back, speechless. Reluctantly, he took the belt and hugged Grandmaster E.

Tears welled from Sin's eyes as he replied, "Grandmaster E, you have been like a father to me and I won't let you down. With this belt comes great responsibility. I will take Shaolin to the new land and spread it across the entire continent, I promise!"

Grandmaster E nodded gravely, his eyes shining with pride. He was too choked up to speak so he wordlessly hugged Sin farewell for the last time.

Newly-minted Grandmaster Sin reluctantly took his leave, looking fondly back at the man and house that had shaped and dominated his entire life. He couldn't remember a time when he hadn't trained and labored and learned at this man's side... All that he knew of the mysteries and miracles of life and the rigors of true martial arts discipline, he had learned at this man's knee.

Since he could never repay him for the honors bestowed on him, he would need to pay it forward. He would take up his mantle and carry it with honor and integrity. He would make the old man proud.

As he waved goodbye to his closest friend and mentor, Sin knew in his heart of hearts that he would never see his venerable master again.

It broke his heart.

After Sin had left, his old master, now looking old beyond his years, stood gazing after him for the longest time. Tears slid down his wrinkled cheeks, unashamedly.

"Good bye, my Son," he whispered softly. "The world is yours now for the taking..."

ACKNOWLEDGEMENT

I was trained in movie script writing rather than novel writing. I was fortunate to have the opportunity to take lesson from two of the World's Best Script Writing teachers, Robert Mckee and the late Sid Field. I grew close to Sid when he helped me edit my screenplay, "The Grandmaster" during his residence in Beverly Hills.

Sid taught me great writing tools, such as how to write in third person instead of first person while writing my life story. It was Sid's wisdom that gave me confidence to write without self-doubt!

The story you are reading is based on my true life story with me writing it as a Hollywood writer would: a BIOPIC.

Several months ago, I received a beautiful book titled "10,000 Steps. Straight Up" from two of my old students, Dennis and Anita Lunt. The book chronicle my early years of taking students all over remote area of China. I immediately fell in love with all the scroll paintings they put in their chapter headers. When I conveyed my feeling to them, imagine the shocking delight they brought me when they offered to provide me with a swet of scroll paintings for my book. If any of you interested in our early days of traveling through China, I HIGHLY recommend their book.

Another student of mine, Master Katy Moeggenberg, wrote a book about our 49 postures of " I CHIN CHING ', similar to yoga postures; another book I highly recommend.

Last but not least, 24 years ago, Master Jim Halladay and I co-authored a book titled "SHAOLINDO: SECRET TO THE TEMPLE" which contains insightful information about our style, available at Amazon.com.

www.ingramcontent.com/pod-product-compliance
Lightning Source LLC
Chambersburg PA
CBHW060037100426
42742CB00014B/2622